Research Methods for History

RESEARCH METHODS FOR THE ARTS AND HUMANITIES

Published Titles

Research Methods for Creating and Curating Data in the Digital Humanities
Edited by Matt Hayler and Gabriele Griffin

Research Methods for Reading Digital Data in the Digital Humanities
Edited by Gabriele Griffin and Matt Hayler

Research Methods for Memory Studies
Edited by Emily Keightley and Michael Pickering

Research Methods for English Studies (2nd edition)
Edited by Gabriele Griffin

Research Methods in Theatre and Performance
Edited by Baz Kershaw and Helen Nicholson

Research Methods for History (2nd edition)
Edited by Simon Gunn and Lucy Faire

Practice-led Research, Research-led Practice in the Creative Arts
Edited by Hazel Smith and Roger T. Dean

Research Methods for Cultural Studies
Edited by Michael Pickering

Research Methods for Law (2nd edition)
Edited by Mike McConville and Wing Hong Chui

edinburghuniversitypress.com/series/rmah

Research Methods for History
Second Edition

Edited by Simon Gunn and Lucy Faire

EDINBURGH
University Press

Edinburgh University Press is one of the leading university presses in the UK. We publish academic books and journals in our selected subject areas across the humanities and social sciences, combining cutting-edge scholarship with high editorial and production values to produce academic works of lasting importance. For more information visit our website: edinburghuniversitypress.com

Edinburgh University Press Ltd
The Tun – Holyrood Road
12 (2f) Jackson's Entry
Edinburgh EH8 8PJ

First edition published in 2012

Typeset in 11/13 Ehrhardt by
Servis Filmsetting Ltd, Stockport, Cheshire,
and printed and bound in Great Britain by
CPI Group (UK) Ltd, Croydon CR0 4YY

A CIP record for this book is available from the British Library

ISBN 978 1 4744 0873 8 (hardback)
ISBN 978 1 4744 0876 9 (paperback)
ISBN 978 1 4744 0874 5 (webready PDF)
ISBN 978 1 4744 0875 2 (epub)

Contents

PART 3   QUANTITATIVE AND QUALITATIVE ANALYSIS

PART 4   DECIPHERING MEANINGS

PART 5   RETHINKING CATEGORIES

Acknowledgements

This book had its origins in a workshop on research methods in history held under the auspices of the Centre for Urban Culture at the University of Nottingham in June 2008. We remain indebted to the Centre, and to Richard Goddard and Helen Meller in particular, for enabling this project to get off the ground. Many of the chapters were first presented at Nottingham and were shaped by discussions during the event. A number of other contributors came on board later. For this second edition we are grateful in particular to Bob Nicholson for his new chapter on digital histories and to all the contributors for their swift and efficient revisions. On the publishing side we would like to thank our editors at Edinburgh University Press for their continuing support for the volume.

Many of the ideas that inform this book have been forged in postgraduate teaching at the Centre for Urban History at Leicester and we are grateful to the numerous colleagues and students who have helped to shape it, directly and indirectly. Since the publication of the first edition in 2012 we have had feedback in reviews and comments from across the world – thank you to those who have written to say they found the essays stimulating and to offer new ideas and directions. We hope this second volume will be productive for all of us trying to engage in the difficult, exciting and messy process of making histories.

Simon Gunn and Lucy Faire
Leicester, 2016

List of Figures and Tables

FIGURES

TABLES

Preface to the Second Edition

For this second edition the chapters have been revised by their authors. Further reading has been updated and we have taken the opportunity to provide more detailed guidance on the practical steps involved in applying particular methods; readers of the first edition have told us that this is one of the features they found most useful. In addition, we have commissioned an extra chapter on digital methods by Bob Nicholson, responding to the rapid increase of interest in the use of online resources for research since the first edition was published in 2012. We hope this new edition continues to prove helpful to historical researchers, from undergraduate students to seasoned historians. Still more than this, we hope it stimulates a creative debate that will enable historians to speak to other disciplines interested in the past and to encourage the generation of new methods and approaches in the future.

Simon Gunn and Lucy Faire
Leicester, October 2015

CHAPTER I

Introduction:
Why Bother with Method?

Simon Gunn and Lucy Faire

This book is about research methods in history, specifically those branches identified with the humanities: cultural history, political history and elements of other branches such as social history. By 'research methods' we mean here the tools or techniques appropriate to history as a field of study, together with 'methodology' or the larger principles which underpin the tools and techniques, and justify their usage.[1] We take 'methods' in both these senses to be a defining feature of any discipline or field of knowledge; how historians construct and investigate their object of study is one means by which history is distinguished from other disciplines that also have an interest in the past, such as archaeology or English studies.

In planning and writing the book we have been very conscious of the fact that research methods have all but disappeared as a component of historiography and a subject of debate among historians. In fields such as economic and demographic history, quantitative methods continue to be required as a preliminary to scholarly work and are taught as part of postgraduate training. But these have become twilight zones of the larger discipline; indeed, it is precisely the requirement for method as well as numeracy that is often blamed for the waning popularity of economic history at all levels. In large swathes of social, cultural and political history by contrast, dissertations, theses and books are written with barely a nod towards methodology. The influence of cultural history and the ubiquitous reference to 'narrative' and 'identity' are sometimes cited as factors here, though there appears to be no clear reason why they should obviate a consideration of matters of definition, procedure and analytical approach. More generally, the wholesale critique of an earlier social structural history which accompanied the cultural turn of the 1980s and 1990s appeared to sweep away much of the infrastructure that attended it, from data sampling to grand narratives. Histories have become 'stories we tell about ourselves'.[2]

Beyond archival research, historians have conventionally tended to borrow their methods from the social sciences. The retreat we describe among historians is therefore all the more striking given the relative efflorescence of methods, old and new, in disciplines such as sociology, anthropology and gender studies in recent years. Discourse analysis, visual methods, standpoint theory, content analysis, Geographic Information Systems (GIS) – to name but a few – have all taken root widely, yet have had limited impact on historical research and writing. Indeed, what has been significant about the various 'turns' affecting the human sciences over the last three decades – linguistic, spatial, material and so on – has been the extent to which they left the basic procedures of history intact. This situation contrasts with earlier phases of innovation in historical practice. The growth of social history in the 1960s and 1970s, for example, was attended by a number of methodological departures including oral history, 'history from below', cliometrics and new forms of computer-based analysis. Indeed, in retrospect one could argue that the social history of these decades, so often associated with the influence of Marxism and feminism, was perhaps more accurately defined by its relationship to new ways of researching and representing the past.[3]

Complaints about the lack of attention to methodology among cultural and other historians are nothing new, of course. Criticism in recent years has come from a variety of directions, including those sympathetic to the new cultural history. The labour historian Richard Biernacki, for example, has argued that the cultural turn created an over-dependence on linguistic models of culture based on semiotics or sign-systems; instead, research should be organised around the comparative analysis of cultural practices and how they can be seen to work, materially as well as symbolically.[4] A different view comes from the historian of childhood, Paula Fass, who suggests that the problems of much recent historical writing lie in its diffuseness and lack of rigour, resulting in 'inquiries that are literally all over the place . . . [and] a profusion of styles and methods that seem to obey no rules but the unique bypaths of the individual historian's mind'.[5] By contrast with Biernacki, Fass urges a return to some of the methods of social history, including working with large bodies of source data as evidence (rather than with a small number of privileged texts) and careful placing of both historical agents and sources within a social and evidential context.

Paula Fass's argument points in the direction of a renewal of interest in 'big data' – unprecedentedly large information sets made available by digital technology – across the humanities and social sciences. 'In the age of digital data banks', Jo Guldi and David Armitage observe in *The History Manifesto* (2014), 'the basic tools for analysing social change around us are everywhere'. Big data, they propose, offers the opportunity to understand urgent long-term historical transformations, such as climate change. By placing different data sets alongside each other – one relating to environmental data, perhaps, another to demography or energy – big data makes it possible to illuminate hitherto invisible patterns of connection or even causal relationships.[6]

Social sciences such as sociology and economics have actively sought to exploit these opportunities in their own fields. One recent example is the Great British Class Survey, a major web survey of social class instigated by the BBC in 2011 and involving over 325,000 respondents.[7] On the basis of the survey the sociologists Mike Savage and Fiona Devine sought to redraw pre-existing models of the British class structure, arguing on the basis of detailed qualitative and quantitative evidence that a new seven-class model had emerged. Here big data allowed not only for a new interpretation but also a new politics of method to emerge, they asserted, as private individuals and public groups sought to dispute, support and debate the survey and the sociological findings based upon it.[8]

On the whole, historians have not followed suit and taken up the challenge of big data. Jonathan Blaney argues that the techniques involved are alien to most historians.

> We must remember that, in History, the familiarity with corpus-driven content analysis and semantic approaches is minimal. Almost all historians of language use purely qualitative approaches (i.e. manual reading) and are unfamiliar even with basic word-counting and concordance techniques. Indeed, the very idea of 'distant reading' with computers, and categorising ephemeral and context-sensitive political vocabulary and phrases into analytical groups is massively controversial even for a single specific historical moment, let alone diachronically or transnationally over decades or even generations.[9]

Why is this so? Blaney blames the combined effect of a reaction against cliometrics after the 1970s and the influence of post-structuralism which favoured 'close reading' and the micro study of small bodies of texts.

Not all historians have adopted this position, however, as the case of *The History Manifesto* illustrates. It might be assumed that big data is restricted to histories of the twentieth century and especially the period since 1945 when governments and corporations began to assemble large data sets for their own reasons. But this is incorrect. Arguably the largest single historical data set, the *Old Bailey online*, gives digital access to 197,000 trials at London's central criminal court between 1674 and 1913. It offers a window over time not merely on crime and justice but on all forms of social behaviour among types of people usually absent from the historical record.[10] Similarly Dilipad ('Digging into Linked Parliamentary Data'), a new project based at the Institute for Historical Research in London, is using two hundred years of digitised records of the British parliament to analyse the languages of gender and the place of women in the rhetoric of British political culture. Here big data is deployed to intervene in more chronologically and textually limited research on politics and the history of gender.[11]

As the case of big data makes clear, within the social sciences, no less than history, methodology is a matter of contention, not something settled. The sociologist of science John Law, for example, has recently proposed the idea of 'creative mess' as the basis for a kind of anti-method. There is a contradiction, Law argues, between a world which is fluid, complex and messy and research methods which aim to simplify and clarify that world: 'Simple clear descriptions don't work if what they are describing is not itself very coherent. The very attempt to be clear simply increases the mess.'[12] This might seem appealing to historians trying to fathom the complexities of past social worlds on the basis of fragmentary sources and who are sceptical of the validity of applying present-day research methods to those worlds. But it ignores the fact that Law's intervention occurs in a field in which methodological justification is routinely required of researchers and that his intervention is not a rejection of method but the opposite: an attempt to 'imagine what research methods might be if they were adapted to a world that included and knew itself as tide, flux, and general unpredictability'.[13]

Nevertheless, if this is the case one is still forced to ask, why bother with method? The answer is a relatively simple one, and not specific to history. Methods matter because the way we study a phenomenon shapes (or may even determine) the knowledge we derive of it. An understanding of, say, colonial rule or the fashion cycle, is integrally bound up with how we have gone about studying these phenomena. Indeed, one could go so far as to say in quaside-terminist mode that it is methods that produce knowledge, not 'research' in the abstract sense. Method should be understood broadly here to encompass everything from the original framing of the research hypothesis to the design of the study, the selection of the sources and the manner in which they are analysed. In other words, method is not just a matter of technique but 'the way the whole problem is seen', to use E. P. Thompson's phrase, including which body of theory and concepts are brought to bear, what sources are deployed and how.[14] As this implies, there is never only one way of approaching or answering a research question; it could always be done differently. A good exercise with researchers (and with oneself) is thus to ask: how could this research be carried out in another way from the one you have designed and why is your way to be preferred?

Methods, then, represent an essential intermediate process between 'theory' on the one hand and the sources or raw data on the other. They are what tie the various parts of research together and make it justifiable to others. This last point is often how the matter of method raises its head, sometimes in questioning from a colleague or supervisor, perhaps more often nowadays in the pragmatic form of a grant application to be completed, a seminar question to be answered, or a tenure panel to be satisfied. It is here too that the methodological naivety of some historical research may become all too visible, when judged by scholars from other branches of the humanities or social sciences versed in an array of specialist approaches and techniques.

The pressure to make explicit methodological assumptions is sometimes identified with the neo-liberal drive to ever-increasing transparency and accountability, now implanted in the academic audit culture. But it would be mistaken to imagine that this is the sole or even the principal driver for it hides a more fundamental issue that all researchers, historians included, must respond to. This is the question of how we justify our histories as knowledge, or, more precisely, what *kind* of knowledge our history represents. Here the inadequacy of arguing that history is simply a 'story' becomes apparent, for the question is then what kind of story, and how – if at all – it is differentiated from, say, fiction or biography. Novels too represent a form of knowledge but as the philosopher Paul Ricoeur argued, while history and fiction are both species of narrative, to conflate them risks disabling the former: 'As soon as the idea of a debt to the dead, to people of flesh and blood to whom something really happened in the past, stops giving documentary research its highest end, history loses its meaning'.[15]

We should bother with methodology, in other words, because it is intimately linked to epistemology, the grounds of knowledge. If historical research and historiography have no specialised, effective claim to knowledge, then it is unclear on what basis 'history' can claim to be a discipline at all. We are some way from this end game, of course, but it is a reminder of what is at stake. Perhaps more urgently than at any time for the last half-century, we need to identify, clarify and debate what we mean as historians when we say we are 'doing research'.

WHY THIS BOOK?

This book both reflects and intervenes in the larger context of academic history which we have just described. In the first place, it reflects the uncertainty among many historians about what exactly 'methods' mean or amount to in historical research. Some contributors to this book openly prefer the concept of 'approach' as designating a less stringent relationship between analytical process and sources. In general, it is noticeable that the closer they are to social sciences the easier historians find it to talk about methodology; the same applies to quantitative as against qualitative methods. Social and economic historians are well used to discussing data sets and computer-based techniques such as nominal record linkage, for example, and quantitative methods can be applied across social, cultural and political history as the chapter here by R. J. Morris indicates. Eliciting what historians do when they are working in archives – the commonest site of historical research – is much more difficult, however. Obviously, they are searching out and examining documents and other primary sources, but how they actually work on these sources is shrouded in mystery. Historical training routinely includes introduction to archives and sources; for some it may include palaeography or language training in order to be able to decipher primary texts generated in other time-periods and societies. But it is rare to find any explicit discussion of what choices might be made in the archive, what strategies pursued or how different types of sources might be interpreted. It is assumed that these skills will be absorbed by students or historians through a form of immersion, time and practice providing eventual mastery. Despite the burgeoning interest in the history of the archive over the last decade, there has been remarkably little discussion of the actual processes of archival research, or of what the historian and theorist Michel de Certeau termed the 'historiographical operation' by which the 'past', or its documentary traces, are turned into 'history' defined as a specific form of writing.[16]

Surveying research methods in English Gabriele Griffin has observed that for all their 'stunning and paradigm-shifting results', English scholars 'have remained surprisingly in- or possibly non-articulate about what they do to achieve these results'.[17] Much the same observation could be made about many branches of history. It is not for lack of literature in and around the subject. There exist a large number of practical introductions to historical research, often aimed at postgraduate and PhD students, which discuss types of sources and provide guidance on statistical and other approaches as well as valuable tips on how to write a history thesis.[18] Many of the 'how to do' books focus on particular branches of history, such as local history.[19] At the other end of the spectrum there are a good number of general texts on the 'nature' of history as a discipline and theory for historians, which deal more at the level of ideas and schools of thought than practices or methods.[20]

The purpose of this book is rather different from both these genres; it aims to contribute to a wider discussion of methods and methodology in historical research, particularly in areas of humanities history such as cultural and political history. In particular, we wish to foster an increased methodological literacy among historians, including postgraduate students of history, so that it becomes easier to discuss the issue of *how* we undertake research as well as what its results are. As we have already argued, these two dimensions are in practice tightly bound up with one another; what we find out about an aspect of the past is profoundly shaped by the methods we use to investigate it.

HOW THE BOOK IS ORGANISED

In fulfilling the aim of the book we have not attempted to provide a comprehensive review of all the research methods employed in historical studies or relevant to it. Rather, we have sought to bring together discussions of well-established or even taken-for-granted methods, such as archival research, with those that are less frequently used, at least in humanities history, such as GIS. Some of the methods here, such as landscape research and collective biography, have their own traditions and devotees; others, like material culture and language analysis, reflect newer trends in the field. We have likewise interpreted 'method' generously to include techniques like database analysis and oral history, approaches like visual analysis and performance studies, and categories such as ethics and temporality. In this last case, their inclusion is intended to underline our point that method covers a wide range of conceptual and theoretical choices, from how cultural difference is handled in the research process to which model of historical time or periodisation we wish to deploy. Such choices may – we argue will – profoundly affect the research and its outcomes.

The book is divided into five parts. Part 1 is concerned with what we term the 'essentials' of historical research: the archive, visual analysis, material culture and place. In the last two cases Alan Mayne and Jo Guldi encourage us to consider the material remains of the past in the form of artefacts and landscapes, and how they can be integrated into historical analysis. The archive and visual culture by contrast are staple elements of historical research, although as Michelle T. King and Ludmilla Jordanova indicate, much of what we assume about them needs to be critically interrogated in the light of post-colonialism and new ideas about materiality.

Part 2 introduces two methods of researching individuals and groups, collective biography and life story. Again, the approaches discussed go beyond conventional wisdom in linking the individual and the collective. Krista Cowman shows how the 'subjective' dimension of collective biography differentiates the method from prosopography and allows the historian to make the most of fragmentary sources to explore marginal groups and experiences. Alistair Thomson likewise explores the significance of what is 'missing' as well as what is present in life stories as a way of making historical sense of people's lives.

Part 3 opens up computer-based techniques of historical research and reveals their value for studying topics in cultural and political history. Keith Lilley and Catherine Porter demonstrate how GIS can be applied to medieval maps and used to analyse environmental and topographical changes in the landscape over time. R. J. Morris similarly shows how databases can be used to explore topics such as patterns of voting and inheritance to reveal unexpected connections between variables. Finally here, Bob Nicholson introduces the new and burgeoning field of digital history and how historians can make the most of the proliferation of online resources now available for researching the past. In these cases the technical language may initially seem off-putting, but the techniques themselves are relatively simple and can be used to harness and ask questions of large amounts of historical data, as we indicated in the discussion of 'big data' above.

Part 4 shifts attention to methods or approaches through which historians can probe the meanings generated by people and events in the past. Language is the most widespread meaning-making system and Julie-Marie Strange offers us ways of 'reading' language that are historically and contextually sensitive. Social behaviour too provides opportunities for decoding meanings. Simon Gunn draws on the metaphor and methods of performance studies to suggest how they can help us think analytically about how to interpret rituals, violence and everyday behaviour.

The final section, Part 5, widens the scope of methodology by prompting us to think about some of the basic categories that inform historical studies. Ethics have begun to permeate the research environment in recent years and William Gallois gives this a specific historical inflexion by enquiring what is at stake, ethically speaking, when historians study cultures whose values may be at odds with their own. Such questions bring historians into direct relationship with their object of study and Prashant Kidambi's reflection on time and temporality does likewise. All historians engage with time in their work, whether in the guise of change, continuity or periodisation. But there are different ways of representing historical time (cyclical, linear and so on) as well as of dividing it by 'period' (epoch, age, phase). The historian is therefore confronted by important decisions when dealing with the most fundamental categories in their conceptual armoury, like time.

All the chapters in the book follow roughly the same format. In each case they begin with an account of the method or approach concerned, where it derives from and how it has come to inform modern scholarship, whether in history or related disciplines. Following from this, the chapters provide a description of the method itself, its basic characteristics and procedures, together with a discussion of debates about its validity, appropriateness and limitations. Discussion of the latter reminds us that we need to be as critical of methods as we are of sources and interpretations. Thereafter, contributors have been encouraged to demonstrate how their methods operate in practice by providing historical case studies, drawing on their own research as well as that of others for examples. The case studies themselves range across the medieval, early modern and modern periods and across different parts of the world, Africa, Asia and Australia as well as Europe. We have not attempted a strict division of chapters in terms of time period or geographical location.

Undertaking historical research in colonial archives requires critical skills that we felt were important to expose, for reasons which Michelle T. King eloquently outlines, but all sources and methods make particular analytical demands on the researcher. We have also encouraged contributors, where possible, to sketch the methodological steps that researchers need to take in actually implementing a particular approach, whether in the form of prompts or questions to be asked.

In the end, though, the intended purpose of this book is to enhance discussion about methods and historiography, not to present a series of essays in 'how to do history'. This has implications for the way the book is used by readers. Researchers will naturally be keen to read the chapter which relates to the method/s deployed in their dissertation, thesis, article or book, or to the method/s which they are considering to use. Our intention, though, has been to stimulate a wider discussion not about this or that approach, but about methods in general. In reality, few historians use only one method in their work, even if they do not recognise much of what they do as methodological at all. Equally, those training as researchers in history should be expected to know about techniques other than their own, which they will need for fresh studies they may carry out in the future. So we are keen that readers try to sample a number of chapters to get a sense of the variety and richness of approaches that exist for undertaking historical research. After all, if history is 'an unending dialogue between the past and present', as E. H. Carr famously claimed, then we should not be seeking to close down the argument, as some scholars might wish to do. We should be seeking precisely the opposite: to extend the intellectual conversation by opening history up to more imaginative, reflexive and rigorous ways of researching the past.[21]

NOTES

1. The literature on methods and methodology is voluminous but for an excellent and relevant guide see William Outhwaite and Stephen Turner (eds), *The Sage Handbook of Social Science Methodology* (London: Sage, 2007).
2. The phrase has become a cliché of course but for a more than usually informed usage of the notion see Quentin Skinner, 'The place of history in public life', http://www.historyandpolicy.org/policy-papers/papers/ the-place-of-history-in-public-life [accessed 12 January 2016]. The often indirect influence of Hayden White's writings in much of this is also significant; see for example, 'The historical text as literary artefact', *Tropics of Discourse: Essays in Cultural Criticism* (Baltimore, MD: Johns Hopkins University Press, 1978, repr. 1985), pp. 81–100.

3. For a sympathetic, detailed and wide-ranging evaluation of the shift from social to cultural history in the Anglo-American context see William Sewell, *The Logics of History* (Chicago, IL: University of Chicago Press, 2005).
4. Richard Biernacki, 'Method and metaphor after the new cultural history', in Victoria E. Bonnell and Lynn Hunt (eds), *Beyond the Cultural Turn* (Berkeley, CA: University of California Press, 1999), pp. 62–92.
5. Paula Fass, 'Cultural history/social history: some reflections on a continuing dialogue', *Journal of Social History* 37:1 (Fall 2003), p. 41. Such debates can also be followed in journals such as *Rethinking History* and *History and Theory*.
6. Jo Guldi and David Armitage, *The History Manifesto* (Cambridge, 2014), chapters 3 and 4. While this work has come under considerable critical fire from historians for its call to *longue durée* history, its appeal to adopt new methods has disappointingly, if predictably, been overlooked.
7. For the website see https://ssl.bbc.co.uk/labuk/experiments/class [accessed 12 January 2016].
8. Roger Burrows and Mike Savage, 'After the crisis? Big data and the methodological challenges of empirical sociology', *Big Data and Society* (January–May 2014), 1–6.
9. 'The historical aspects of Dilipad: challenges and opportunities', IHR blog, 19 March 2015, http://blog.history.ac.uk/category/big-data/ [accessed 25 October 2015].
10. http://www.oldbaileyonline.org/ [accessed 25 October 2015].
11. Jonathan Blaney http://dilipad.history.ac.uk/ [accessed 12 January 2016]; see also Blaney, 'Historical aspects of Dilipad' for further details. As well as the British parliament Dilipad also includes studies of the digital records of the parliaments in Canada and the Netherlands.
12. John Law, *After Method: Mess in Social Science Research* (Oxford: Routledge, 2004), p. 2.
13. Law, *After Method*, p. 7.
14. E. P. Thompson, *The Making of the English Working Class* (Harmondsworth: Penguin, 1968), p. 13.
15. Paul Ricoeur, *Time and Narrative, Volume 3*, trans. K. Blamey and D. Pellauer (Chicago, IL: University of Chicago Press, 1988), p. 118.
16. Michel de Certeau, *The Writing of History*, trans. T. Conley (New York, NY: Columbia University Press, 1988), p. 57. For the wider discussion of the archive see Tom Osborne, 'The ordinariness of the archive', *History of the Human Sciences* 12:2 (1999), pp. 51–64 and the rest of the contributors to this issue as well as *History of the Human Sciences* 11:4 (1998); Carolyn Steedman, *Dust: the Archive and Cultural History* (Manchester: Manchester University Press, 2001).

17. Gabriele Griffin, *Research Methods for English* (Edinburgh: Edinburgh University Press, 2005), p. 1.

18. See for example Anthony Brundage, *Going to the Sources: a Guide to Historical Research and Writing*, 5th edn (Chichester: Wiley-Blackwell, 2013) W. H. McDowell, *Historical Research: a Guide* (Harlow: Pearson Education, 2002). Martha C. Howell and Walter Prevenier, *From Reliable Sources: an Introduction to Historical Methods* (Ithaca, NY: Cornell University Press, 2001) is more critical and ambitious in its approach but remains largely within the genre.

19. For instance, Kate Tiller, *English Local History: an Introduction*, 2nd edn (Stroud: Sutton, 2002); Philip Riden, *Local History: a Handbook for Beginners*, 2nd edn (Chesterfield: Merton Priory Press, 1998).

20. For example Stefan Berger, Heiko Feldner and Kevin Passmore (eds), *Writing History: Theory and Practice* (London: Hodder, 2003); Peter Burke, *What is Cultural History?* 2nd edn (Cambridge: Polity Press 2008); Anna Green and Kathleen Troup (eds), *The Houses of History* (Manchester: Manchester University Press, 1999); Simon Gunn, *History and Cultural Theory* (Harlow: Longman, 2006); Arthur Marwick, *The New Nature of History* (Basingstoke: Palgrave, 2001); John Tosh, *The Pursuit of History*, 6th edn (Harlow: Longman, 2015).

21. E. H. Carr, *What is History?* (London: Penguin, 1961), p. 30.

The Essentials

CHAPTER 2

Working With/In the Archives

Michelle T. King

A rchival research is for many modern historians the bread and butter of their professional existence, as paradigmatic a disciplinary marker as the laboratory experiment for the physical scientist or fieldwork for the anthropologist. It is often the transformative liminal experience that most distinguishes a student of history from the practicing historian: the act of getting one's own hands dirty (sometimes literally, handling mouldering documents covered in decades' or centuries' worth of dust) is one in a series of steps towards independent historical thinking and writing. The student must prove her mettle by first finding, then wrestling with unruly primary source documents, taming them into some coherent written form for public consumption. Yet modern historians have only recently begun to examine the methodological foundations upon which so much of their work is built.[1]

Given its centrality to disciplinary identity, my goal in this chapter is not to convince researchers of the suitability and appropriateness of archival research as a historical method, but rather to do the opposite. Here I want to pry archival research loose from its privileged position as a taken-for-granted historical method – not in order to minimise its utility or replace it with a particular alternative, but so as to examine it more closely and deploy it more consciously, suggesting both its potential and limitations. While archives may contain all manner of historical documents besides manuscripts and written texts (including drawings, prints, maps, photographs, film, music, material artefacts and digital files), I will focus my remarks here on the paradigmatic textual archives that have informed modern historical practices since the nineteenth century.

What constitutes an archive? How have archives been created and maintained? How do we work within, against or around the imposed order and limits of the archive when conducting our own research? What might a history look like that takes into conscious consideration both the internal logic of the archives and the conventions of documentary evidence? What new histories are made possible, and what old assumptions will require readjustment? While the motivation for posing such questions may derive in part from theoretical challenges to normative historical practice made prominent in the last few decades, my approach here is less epistemological than practical. This chapter aims to provide concrete examples of how some historians have attempted to respond to these questions, in the hopes that researchers may draw inspiration from them for their own projects.

One popular vision of the archetypal historical Archive (distinguished here with a capital 'A') comes from the movie version of Dan Brown's blockbuster thriller, *The Da Vinci Code* (2006). Among its mishmash of references to Christian history and European cultural artefacts, one scene in particular alludes to the work of the historian, in which the assiduous hero and heroine stumble into the hidden archive of a centuries-old underground brotherhood, sworn to protect the secret of the Holy Grail. Each wall of the tidy room is covered with glass-covered bookshelves, on which sit neatly labelled file boxes and bundles of documents, all artistically arranged. Touching a bundle of scrolls, the hero-scholar exclaims, 'This is incredible, look at this . . . These records go back thousands of years . . . Good God, could these really be the Grail documents?!'[2]

Working historians may smile at this Hollywood version, since the primary sources contained in any given archive are rarely so monumental, easy-to-find, well-organised or even dust-free.[3] Yet several ideas dominate this filmic version, which may serve as a useful starting point for the observations to follow. Above all else, this archetypal Archive is a collection of *written* texts, a kind of sacred treasure-house of memory. Moreover, some kind of *authority* – a state, an institution, an organisation, or here, a secret brotherhood – has taken upon itself the task of gathering and organising these written documents that pertain to its own history, as well as controlling access to them. Finally, this Archive embodies both *completeness* and *hiddenness*, and their corollary of secrets unveiled. Everything essential to know is contained in this Archive; the industrious historian need only to sift patiently through all of its documents in order to find all of the answers. That which the Archive preserves and hides, the historian brings to light.

Real historians not cast by Hollywood, however, have through both practical experience and theoretical deliberation challenged these normative notions about the nature of the archives and archival research. Instead of appearing as written, authoritative, complete and hidden, actual archives (distinguished by a lower-case 'a') may upon closer inspection appear far less stable, to the point of being unwritten, subversive, partial and exposed. Moving from a fixed and firm understanding of the archives to something more fluid and flexible, though, probably requires more doing than thinking. It may well be that researchers will need to venture unassisted into the archives first, in order to gain a sense of its site-specific densities and peculiar formations, before the ideas discussed here can be put to best use. This was true at least in my own case: the evolution of my own thinking on archival research began at the National University of Singapore and the National Archives of Singapore, where I spent several months in 2001 looking at original registers of correspondence held there, as well as microfilm copies of correspondence from the Public Record Office, exchanged between colonial officials in the nineteenth-century Straits Settlements and their superiors in London. This chapter is an outgrowth of the seeds planted during that archival experience, after several generations of germination.

THE ORIGINS OF ARCHIVAL RESEARCH

Before we can begin to question paradigms of archival research, it is helpful to consider how they came to be in the first place. Archival research and the historical writing that has generally arisen from it have always been intrinsically bound to the legitimation of state power. The maintenance (and fabrication or destruction) of written historical records is a potent idea that has allowed different groups to lay claim to their own version of the past and consolidate control over the present.[4] In the eighteenth and nineteenth centuries, modern archival institutions filled a critical role in the creation of new historical narratives for emerging nation states. One of the first acts of the French Revolutionary government, for example, was to establish the Archives Nationales in 1790. Modern archives were distinguished from those of *anciens régimes* not by the fact of their existence or their use in historical writing, but in their idealised role as egalitarian institutions, both free and open to the public. Access to the Archives Nationales was guaranteed as an essential right of all French citizens.[5]

In certain ways, centralising state control and physical possession of government documents in the nineteenth century did increase archival accessibility through the compilation of new inventories, catalogues and finding aids, as well as through the publication of selected archival documents.[6] Yet the very promise of openness spawned a contradictory and equally potent desire to limit access, in terms of both seekers and documents sought. In the early years of Great Britain's Public Record Office, for example, first established in 1838, the Keepers limited access to those 'sufficiently qualified by age, knowledge and discretion'. Usage favoured those who were already familiar with archival systems. More significantly, the Home and Foreign Offices, as well as other branches of government, demanded exemption from committing all classes of documents to public inspection, particularly those that would threaten foreign relations or inflame sensitive issues, such as the Irish question.[7]

During this same period, a new class of professional historians emerged to take advantage of these archival riches. Modern historians distinguished themselves from their predecessors by basing their histories on documentary evidence gleaned from archival research, as they strove to present objective analyses of historical events. This 'scientific' trend first developed among German intellectuals in the late eighteenth and nineteenth centuries, such as Leopold von Ranke, whose oft-cited injunction was to show history '*wie es eigentlich gewesen*' ('as it actually happened'). Though Ranke is often credited with championing this approach, he was neither the first nor alone in his efforts. Ranke's ideas were made possible in part by institutional changes in the role of nineteenth-century German universities, as well as the rise of an educationally oriented middle class.[8] Such as it was, what we might call the Rankean vision of historical research and writing soon spread to other European nations and the United States, influencing the establishment of professional and disciplinary norms.[9]

Two core beliefs in particular shaped this new, professionalised mode of historiography. One principle was that the methodology most suited to arriving at a 'scientific' view of history was archival research.[10] Whereas earlier amateur historians had achieved their status on the quality of their writing, this new breed of professionals emphasised the quality of their research, and adapted the stylistic apparatus of the footnote to serve as a locus for evidentiary documentation.[11] The second principle concerned the proper subject of modern history. Modern history was in effect political history, and its central focus was the formation and legitimation of the nation state. The generation of nineteenth-century German historians following Ranke shared an overarching desire for their historical work to make manifest the unity of a nation that superseded its individual states. As Robert Harrison, Aled Jones and Peter Lambert have remarked, the existence of this professional guild of nineteenth-century German historians 'prefigured' the German nation, while 'the history it produced contributed to nation-building'.[12]

The ideal of 'scientific' historical writing on the part of disinterested professionals was never impartial, however, even in the age of its conception. The normative nineteenth-century vision of historical production, as Bonnie Smith has persuasively argued, framed not only the type of history worth writing and determined its research methods, it also elected a chosen few – privileged, elite males – to be its most capable practitioners. Historical research and writing was 'manly' work, and women were dismissed as incapable or uninterested in its pursuit. Moreover, gendered notions were woven into the very fabric of the research process itself, as Ranke and his contemporaries often compared their archival finds to sexual conquests. Ranke's description of documents in archives as 'so many princesses, possibly beautiful, all under a curse and needing to be saved', positioned the historian as a hero, gendering both the practice and the practitioner.[13]

CHALLENGING THE CONFINES OF THE ARCHIVE

The interest in producing economic, social and intellectual histories that did more than reify the progress of the nation state or re-inscribe the domination of elites had already developed prior to World War II, but the truly seismic shift in professional interests away from political history towards social and cultural history has occurred since the post-war period.[14] Prompted in part by the infusion of new voices into the historical profession and driven by intellectual influences from linguistic and cultural studies, scholars have since the 1970s questioned the dominant modes of historical research and writing.[15] By drawing attention to archival principles of collection, selection, arrangement and control, a new generation of historians began to render archivisation and archival research as historical processes, subject to a range of temporal, political and practical concerns, rather than self-evident ideals.

This mode of seeing the historical archive as a locus of power/knowledge has been deeply influenced by the writings of Michel Foucault, most notably two early works, *The Order of Things* (1966) and *The Archaeology of Knowledge* (1969). In the former, Foucault called attention to the 'rules of formation' that shaped disparate seventeenth- and eighteenth-century discourses on natural history, philology and political economy, identifying a general yet never consciously articulated impulse toward classification undergirding each of these scientific enterprises.[16] In the latter, he invoked the concept of the 'archive' to refer not to any specific building or collection of documents, but as 'the law of what can be said', which 'lays down' all 'enunciative possibilities and impossibilities'.[17] Whether or not consciously acknowledged, later historians have absorbed the constellation of his ideas, using them to articulate the unspoken principles governing the function of actual archives. It has since become routine to recognise how acts of producing, organising and classifying archival documents constitute forms of knowledge in and of themselves, while archival collections as a whole constrain the types of histories made possible and impossible through them.

Jacques Derrida's subsequent intervention into the trajectory of archival paradigms, elaborated in a 1994 lecture and later translated into English as *Archive Fever: a Freudian Impression* (1996), both reinforced the Foucauldian notion of the archive as a locus of authority and recalled the psychoanalytic dimensions of archival remembering and forgetting. For the most part, historians have fixed upon the evocative title of the English translation, diagnosing 'archive fever' in myriad ways, while ignoring Derrida's meditations on the psychoanalytic search for origins occupying the bulk of the lecture.[18] Several have borrowed Derrida's etymological reading of the word 'archive', derived from the Greek *arkheion*, the home of the commanding magistrates, where official documents were to be held, which re-inscribed in the term a physical sense of authority, in the form of a person and a place. More creatively, Derrida articulated the 'violence of the archive itself' as the manifestation of the destructive principle of the death drive, whereby the archive is not merely or just a site of memory and preservation, but always also a place of forgetting and destruction. Put more plainly, every act of remembering and preserving is fixed to its shadow of loss and forgetting: ideas and experiences are written down in the first place so that they may be forgotten; documents are selected for inclusion into archives by acts of exclusion; the very preservation of documents in an archive 'exposes [them] to destruction'.[19]

While Foucault and Derrida may have offered incisive observations on the functions and limits of archives in the abstract, historians have arrived at similar conclusions and complementary critiques through the dense textures of their own specific historical subjects. Derrida's insight on the death drive of the archives has been borne out by the destruction of records of state violence by the South African government during the rule of apartheid, vividly described by Helena Pohlandt-McCormick: 'There are many brown manila files in the archives that, while retaining the shape of the documents they must once have held, are now filled only with a small slip of paper upon which are written the ominous words "*Vernietig*/Destroyed".'[20] Feminist historians have argued for the need to broaden the concept of the 'archive' to include alternative sites of historical memory, such as the domestic space of the home or the pages of female-authored historical novels.[21] Oral historians have rejected written archives as the sole source of historical legitimacy, gathering interview material from subjects outside of or excluded from state archives and histories by dint of their race, sexuality or oral traditions.[22] These scholars have attempted to breach the confines of the Archive writ large by storming it from without, using alternative historical sources to point out its erasures, gaps and silences.

Not all historians, however, are ready to abandon the research potential of textual archives and many historical issues that pre-date the twentieth century can still only be investigated there. How, then, to proceed? Another set of tactics takes a different approach, one of burrowing deep into the Archive in order to undermine it from within. Initiated primarily by historians of colonial contexts, these tactics call for close attention to the archival forms and conventions that shape and constrain histories. Already in 1983 Ranajit Guha proposed methods of work designed to circumvent the hegemony of the colonial archive under the banner of the Subaltern Studies collective. Guha sought to recover the consciousness of subalterns in colonial South Asia, who had historically been excluded from the dominant networks of political and cultural power, and who were likewise represented in the archives through the eyes of officials, rather than in their own words. For example, peasant insurgents were only ever described in the archive in negative terms, so Guha first identified the precise operational mechanics of this colonial 'prose of counter-insurgency', which could then be read 'as a writing in reverse' to gain some idea of how insurgents might have understood their own behaviour and belief systems.[23] Pressing Guha's work one step further, Gayatri Chakravorty Spivak subsequently questioned whether such an archival project of historical recovery was ever truly achievable, arguing that the reality of a subaltern figure like the Rani of Sirmur could never be reconstructed outside of her colonial trappings.[24]

Most recently, Ann Laura Stoler has proposed an alternative method for delving into the colonial archive, which works not 'against the grain' to recover subaltern consciousness, but probes 'along the grain' to map the contours of 'colonial common sense', or the 'rubrics of rule' that informed colonial categories and mindsets in the Dutch East Indies. Stoler sees the archives not primarily as a historical source for events that happened, but more as an 'ethnographic space', the investigation of which reveals a whole host of anxieties about possible futures, 'failed projects, delusional imaginings, [and] equivocal explanations', particularly at intersections of race and affect, as in documents regarding the fates of mixed-race children.[25] Nicholas Dirks, another scholar of colonial South Asia, urges a similar attention to the 'history encoded on the surfaces of the very files – the numbering systems, the departmental structures, and classificatory rubrics – as well as in the reports, letters, decisions, and scribbled within that make up the archive'.[26]

Aside from these attempts to undermine the Archive from within and without, historians have begun to describe the human and physical interactions that constitute archival research as more than a purely intellectual exercise.[27] Research agendas are shaped by random events and external constraints, as much as or in spite of our own devising: trips to distant archives require difficult to obtain financial support, archives may be temporarily or permanently closed, working hours may be brief and conditions may be difficult. Success in accessing archival holdings may be influenced by one's scholarly or social status, age, nationality, gender, race, or socio-economic level, or may depend on the scope of one's intended research topic. Durba Ghosh was made aware of her own position as a young, unmarried, high-caste female from an American university time and again while researching the sexual and social relations between British men and South Asian women in the early colonial period. In both British and Indian archives, everyone from archivists and librarians to fellow researchers and clerks had something to say about her subject – and her as subject: 'While I was busy reading the archives, I found the archives were reading me'.[28] Even the researcher's own fear, boredom, inexperience, frustration and loneliness can shape decisions made in the archives, and the resulting contours of research. Nicholas Dirks recalls the moment of panic he had on going in the archives for the first time, having no idea 'how to control the chaos' of documents, 'both endless and banal'.²⁹

CLOSE ENCOUNTERS OF THE ARCHIVAL KIND

The traditional understanding of archival research fetishises the moment of the find: think of the hero and heroine of the *The Da Vinci Code*, stumbling into the secret basement archive to discover a cache of priceless historical documents. Though generally under less dramatic circumstances, most historians have experienced some similar flash of recognition upon discovery of a crucial piece of evidence, the ultimate payoff after hours of earlier tedium and frustration. This was the way I felt when I first read despatch 234 of the Colonial Office file 273/81, under the blinking fluorescent lights of the National University of Singapore library, while researching the local colonial administration of the late nineteenth-century Straits Settlements: I knew I had found something, and yet – this is the important point – I could not at that moment articulate exactly what it was that I had found. This powerful imaginary of uncovering what is hidden, and the tantalising promise of touching what is just outside of reach (the documents known once to have existed, the files under lock and key), obscures an essential truth about archival research. While invigorating and encouraging, finding what is hidden may be of less importance than recognising the significance of what one has found.

What Hollywood gets wrong in its conceptualisation of the historical archive is ultimately the work of the historian in it. We go to the archives not to find answers, but articulate a better set of questions. Answers in the archives – in the form of documents – always abound; the real difficulty lies in figuring out what questions to ask of them. This is the hard work that awaits outside the archive, long after one has returned home. Perhaps this idea is both reassuring and daunting: reassuring because it is literally impossible to 'not find anything' in the archives, and daunting because the task that remains can be even more difficult. Instead of forcing the archives to bend to our will, yielding hidden secrets (or slumbering princesses), perhaps a better attitude would be one of attentive curiosity and humility, fully recognising that our forays into the archives, no matter how meticulous and exhaustive, only ever yield partial understandings. As Carolyn Steedman suggests, 'nothing starts in the Archive, nothing, ever at all, though things certainly end up there. You find nothing in the Archive but stories caught half way through: the middle of things, discontinuities'.³⁰

Consciousness of what we can call the 'archival matrix' – the confines of the archive and the ruling conventions of archival forms – can help a researcher with precisely this most difficult task, that of meaning-making and question-asking. Tony Ballantyne offers an excellent example of how a closer consideration of the archival matrix can change the shape of the histories we write, regardless of the topics we choose to write about. Though he had originally conceived of his study on the construction of race in the British empire as a comparative one between distinct imperial locations, he was forced to reframe his project after contemplating the documents of the late nineteenth-century Polynesian Society. Written as they were to and from multiple sites within the empire, the papers collectively served as a literal manifestation of the intellectual connective tissue binding imperial sites together in ways that could not be adequately described within the normative framework of post-colonial national histories. This essential insight transformed the structure and conclusions of his study, even though the contents of the Polynesian Society archive themselves formed only a tiny portion of his end product.[31]

My own encounter with Colonial Office archival materials regarding the late nineteenth-century Straits Settlements also brought me to this realisation: *how* information was presented within them was at least as important as *what* information was being presented. I did not go into the archives with the intention of writing about them or using them in any way other than as fodder for my project, yet my growing appreciation for the archival matrix opened up a new way of conceptualising my project. I was interested in learning more about the Chinese Protectorate, a local colonial institution established in Singapore in 1877 and staffed by Europeans fluent in one of the five regional dialects of Chinese spoken in the Straits. William Pickering was the first man to head the department, and was charged with the task of 'protecting' Chinese migrant labourers from abuse, ensuring a steady supply of labour for the colony's economic engine. My first foray into the archives began with this key institution and key figure, as had the work of other scholars before me.

Yet any historical narrative framed by the person of Pickering or the institution of the Chinese Protectorate tends to reinforce the rational quality of colonial administration: the tale that emerges is essentially a logical one of creating social order from chaos. Neither is it difficult to understand how such a narrative emerges: political events, institutions or individuals often serve as the foci of histories because their stories are discrete and easy to identify in the archives. The massive quantities of paperwork generated by modern state bureaucracies necessitate the imposition of at least some limits, lest the historian be 'buried under the weight of archival excess' and the digging never end.[32] Out of sheer necessity, we narrow our searches by using topical or other indices, or by selecting a series of chronological files to consult.[33] Documents that mention specific, named entities, such as the 'Chinese Protectorate' or 'William Pickering', give the researcher likely spots to start digging. Moreover, identifying one relevant archival document often leads back to a string of others, embedded as they were into existing bureaucratic paper trails at the moment of their creation.[34] Incoming and outgoing despatches in the Crown colonies, for example, were numbered and filed consecutively, and often refer explicitly to prior correspondence in the opening sentences: 'Responding to your despatch of the 4th October'. A historian need only dust off these documents, polish them up and place them sequentially end to end in order to reconstruct a plausible and tidy account of events.

But by unconsciously adopting the conceptual frameworks employed by archival indices and by following obediently its existing paper trails, the historian preserves the internal logic of the archives as a hidden artefact of her research. Like a barnacle tagging along for the ride, the accretion of too many of these archival 'givens' threatens to upend the historical craft, or at the very least, over determine its direction. I was directly inspired to try a different tactic after reading despatch 234, written on 15 August 1875 by William Drummond Jervois, governor of the Straits Settlements, to his superiors in the Colonial Office in London. In it, Jervois describes both the difficulties of Chinese translation and the multiple potential vectors for its management. He confesses that he has no idea how best to handle the situation: 'The question is one which presents considerable difficulties, and I have not found it easy to arrive at a distinct idea as to the nature of the arrangements which would be most desirable.' He goes on to consider the possibility of a range of different candidates that might fulfil the colony's Chinese translation needs, beginning with European officers. He explains, however, that 'most Europeans find the greatest difficulty in catching and reproducing even the commonest words which they hear spoken by their servants', and surmises that most translation work will have to continue to be performed by 'Chinamen' with some knowledge of English. He frets that even if enough Europeans could be found to serve as interpreters, 'from what class in life are such Europeans to be taken? . . . should an attempt be made to get at a lower stratum of English Society . . .? or again, should an attempt be made to find such persons as are wanted among the better class of the Eurasian community here?'[35]

What exactly was happening in the immediate paragraphs of this despatch? I wanted to preserve the anxiety and confusion that shimmered on its very surface, like a slick of oil on water. Jervois had named a number of potential candidates – Europeans, Chinese and Eurasians of varying classes – to solve the knotty problem of translation in the colony, but his repeated questioning and overt hand-wringing hinted at a constellation of anxieties – racial, moral, physical, not to mention pecuniary – that made it impossible for him to take any definitive steps on his own. Rather than thinking of the Chinese Protectorate and William Pickering as natural solutions for the colonial management of a migrant labour pool, this despatch, with all of its self-imposed constraints and worries, inspired me to consider the construction of translation itself as a colonial problem in the Straits Settlements.[36] In this alternative framework, the date of 1877, the institutional establishment of the Chinese Protectorate, and the heroic role of Pickering lose much of their shine, replaced instead by a series of false hopes and failed projects. Aided by a more conscious approach to the archival matrix, a historian feels compelled to ask: Are there certain types of histories that emerge 'naturally' from the archive? What in the archival forms and functions makes this so? What other types of histories might be obscured by these conventions? What essential insights may not be hidden at all, but lying in plain sight?

THE INTERNET AS ARCHIVE OF THE FUTURE

The greatest change to the methodology of archival research that has dominated the historical profession since its inception in the nineteenth century has occurred only within the last two decades, with the advent of innumerable technological innovations. The increasing availability of text-searchable, digitally scanned archival material on the Internet holds the promise of breaking down barriers of physical access. Google's ambitious project to digitise the world's books, for example, has gained the cooperation of universities and library collections around the world. Yet the project is not without controversy, whether in the form of legal conflicts with authors and publishers over copyright protection, or among scholars concerned with Google's effective monopoly over access to digital copies of the world's books.[37] Whether one finds the movement towards digital library collections enthralling or frightening depends much on how and if access to this new digital 'archive' will eventually be regulated – or priced. As in the nineteenth century, the ideal of archival openness is still embedded within larger relations of power, only this time involving technology and capital, instead of the state alone.

Beyond the promise of increased access to digitised archival holdings, the greater potential of the Internet is to make ordinary individuals into public archivists of their own histories, by allowing them to post texts, images, blogs, videos – historical documents, in other words – of their own making. In the wake of the terrorist attacks of 11 September 2001, for example, the Center for History and New Media at George Mason University and the American Social History Project at the City University of New York Graduate Center collaborated on the creation of a digital archive, which offered a central website (http://911digitalarchive.org) for visitors to post their own contributions. Ultimately the project resulted in a collection of more than 150,000 digital objects, including more than 40,000 personal accounts, more than 40,000 emails, and more than 15,000 digital images, representing the largest digital collection of its kind.[38] The subsequent adoption of the September 11 archive into the Library of Congress as its first major digital acquisition in 2003 ironically suggests that the public continues to require inclusion in an official state archive as the foremost measure of historical legitimacy.

Regardless of ever-expanding efforts on the part of government institutions or corporations such as Google to digitise existing paper documents, or the potential of cyberspace to democratise archival curation, most historians have cause for neither immediate celebration nor lamentation. The ephemeral goal of a complete digital archive will remain elusive for many years to come, in spite of increased digital access to public domain books and commonly sought-after archival documents. The vast majority of paper sources are likely still to remain in their original form alone, due to limits of funding and public interest, surfacing only through the patient sifting of scholars. That path will still lead 'to crowded public rooms where the sunlight gleams on varnished tables, and knowledge is embodied in millions of dusty, crumbling, smelly, irreplaceable documents and books'.[39] Moreover, while the acts of researching and gathering historical data may be made ever easier and open to all, making sense of all that is found – the true métier of the historian – is still a skill in short supply.

It may be most fitting to end this archival story, neither at its confident beginning or its uncertain future, but caught up somewhere in the middle. With his historical imagination captured by the nineteenth century and his personal fate bound by the twentieth, Walter Benjamin inherited the earlier commitment to archival research as a historical method while implicitly rejecting the dominant and destructive history of the nation state through his meticulous and idiosyncratic Arcades Project. For more than a dozen years Benjamin laboured in the reading room of the Bibliothèque Nationale in Paris, carefully combing through books to collect quotations related to all manner of urban phenomena of the city's lost nineteenth century. Organised by subject into lettered files he called 'convolutes' and interspersed with his notes and observations, this massive project was never completed in Benjamin's lifetime. Benjamin committed suicide in 1940, during his flight from Nazi-occupied France, in the belief that he would not be allowed to cross the border from Spain into Portugal. The briefcase carrying his last manuscript vanished, probably destroyed.

The remnants of Benjamin's work are a reminder of both the power and the fragility of archival memory and historical ambition. The Arcades Project was posthumously published as part of Benjamin's collected works, preserved in its voluminous fragments after his death only because he had entrusted his papers to various friends.[40] This 'monumental . . . ruin' overwhelms and astonishes the reader with both the vast range of its interconnected topics – the arcades, photography, Baudelaire, Haussmann, boredom, fashion, the stock exchange, conspiracies, to name only a few – and the intimacy of each treasured selection.[41] Taken together, the fragmentary convolutes of the Arcades

Project create a lost dream-world of the quotidian life of nineteenth-century Paris, part of Benjamin's efforts to 'blast open the continuum of history' by grasping the fleeting 'constellation' formed by the intersection of the present and the past.[42] Today, digital archives merely make manifest what Benjamin had already realised more than half a century ago: that the archive is forever incomplete and yet is itself already history. The historian proceeds in the archive only by recognising the dusty trace left behind by a lost briefcase, containing both the possibilities and impossibilities of what might have been.

NOTES

1. Nicolas B. Dirks suggests that historians need to account for their 'arrival stories' in the archives, much as anthropologists have done for their arrivals in the field. See Dirks, 'Annals of the archive: ethnographic notes on the sources of history', in Brian Keith Axel (ed.), *From the Margins: Historical Anthropology and Its Futures* (Durham, NC: Duke University Press, 2002), p. 48. For a broad survey of recent historical scholarship on the archives, see the following edited collections: *History of the Human Sciences* special issues on the archives 11:4 (November 1998) and 12.2 (May 1999); Carolyn Hamilton *et al.* (eds), *Refiguring the Archive* (Cape Town: David Philip, 2002); Antoinette Burton (ed.), *Archive Stories: Facts, Fictions, and the Writing of History* (Durham, NC: Duke University Press, 2005); Francis X. Blouin and W. G. Rosenberg (eds), *Archives, Documentation, and Institutions of Social Memory: Essays from the Sawyer Seminar* (Ann Arbor, MI: University of Michigan Press, 2006).
2. *The Da Vinci Code*, DVD, directed by Ron Howard. USA: Columbia Pictures, 2006.
3. On the materiality of archival dust, see Carolyn Steedman, *Dust: the Archive and Cultural History* (New Brunswick, NJ: Rutgers University Press, 2002), pp. 17–37.
4. On the uses and abuses of medieval and early modern European archives, see Randolph Starn, 'Truths in the archives', *Common Knowledge* 8:2 (Spring 2002), pp. 387–401.
5. Jennifer Milligan, '"What is an Archive?" in the History of Modern France', in Burton (ed.), *Archive Stories*, pp. 159–83.
6. Milligan, 'Archive'; Philippa Levine, 'The rôle of government', chapter 5 in *The Amateur and the Professional: Antiquarians, Historians and Archaeologists in Victorian England, 1838–1886* (Cambridge: Cambridge University Press, 1986), pp. 101–34.
7. Levine, *Amateur*, pp. 105–8.
8. Robert Harrison, Aled Jones and Peter Lambert, 'The institutionalization

and organization of history', in Peter Lambert and P. Schofield (eds), *Making History: an Introduction to the History and Practices of a Discipline* (London: Routledge, 2004), pp. 11–14.

9. Georg G. Iggers and J. M. Powell (eds), *Leopold von Ranke and the Shaping of the Historical Discipline* (Syracuse, NY: Syracuse University Press, 1990); Peter Novick, *That Noble Dream: the 'Objectivity Question' and the American Historical Profession* (Cambridge: Cambridge University Press, 1988).

10. Bonnie Smith, 'Gender and the practices of scientific history: the seminar and archival research in the nineteenth century', *American Historical Review* 100:4 (October 1995), pp. 1150–76.

11. Harrison *et al.*, 'Institutionalization', p. 28; Anthony Grafton, *The Footnote: a Curious History* (Cambridge, MA: Harvard University Press, 1997).

12. Harrison *et al.*, 'Institutionalization', p. 14.

13. Smith, 'Gender', pp. 1162–7.

14. Lambert and Schofield (eds), *Making History*, chapters 4–7.

15. Novick, *Noble Dream*, chapters 13–16.

16. Michel Foucault, *The Order of Things: an Archaeology of the Human Sciences*, trans. Pantheon Books (New York, NY: Vintage Books, 1994), p. xi.

17. Michel Foucault, *The Archaeology of Knowledge*, trans. A. M. Sheridan Smith (New York, NY: Pantheon Books, 1972), p. 129.

18. Steedman, *Dust*, pp. 1–16.

19. On the etymology of 'archive', see Jacques Derrida, *Archive Fever: a Freudian Impression*, trans. Eric Prenowitz (Chicago, IL: University of Chicago Press, 1996), pp. 1–2; on 'violence', see p. 7; on 'destruction', see pp. 11–12.

20. Helena Pohlandt-McCormick, 'In good hands: researching the 1976 Soweto Uprising in the state archives of South Africa', in Burton (ed.), *Archive Stories*, p. 299. For more on the state of South African archives, see also Hamilton *et al.* (eds), *Refiguring*.

21. On feminist alternatives to state archives, see Antoinette Burton, *Dwelling in the Archive: Women Writing House, Home and History in Late Colonial India* (Oxford: Oxford University Press, 2003); Marilyn Booth, 'Fiction's imaginative archive and the newspaper's local scandals: the case of nineteenth-century Egypt', in Burton (ed.), *Archive Stories*, pp. 274–95.

22. On oral histories as an alternative source of historical legitimacy, see Horacio N. Roque Ramírez, 'A living archive of desire: Teresita la Campesina and the embodiment of queer Latino community histories', and Adele Perry, 'The colonial archive on trial: possession, dispossession and history in *Delgamuukw v. British Columbia*', in Burton (ed.), *Archive Stories*, pp. 111–35, 325–50.

23. Ranajit Guha, 'The prose of counter-insurgency', in Ranajit Guha (ed.), *Subaltern Studies* II (Delhi: Oxford University Press, 1983), pp. 1–40; Guha, *Elementary Aspects of Peasant Insurgency in Colonial India* (Durham, NC: Duke University Press, 1999), p. 333.

24. Gayatri Spivak, 'The Rani of Sirmur: an essay in reading the archives', *History and Theory* 24:3 (October 1985), pp. 247–72.

25. On 'colonial common sense', see Ann Laura Stoler, *Along the Archival Grain: Colonial Cultures and their Affective States* (Princeton, NJ: Princeton University Press, 2009), pp. 3, 9, 35–9; on 'rubrics of rule', see p. 4; on the archive as an 'ethnographic space', see pp. 24, 31–5, 47–53; on 'failed projects', see p. 21. For more on the ethnography of the archive, see Dirks, 'Annals'.

26. Dirks, 'Annals', p. 59.

27. On the need for historians to tell their 'archive stories', see Antoinette Burton, 'Introduction', in Burton (ed.), *Archive Stories*, pp. 1–24.

28. Durba Ghosh, 'National narratives and the politics of miscegenation: Britain and India', in Burton (ed.), *Archive Stories*, p. 30.

29. Dirks, 'Annals', pp. 47–8.

30. Steedman, *Dust*, p. 45.

31. Tony Ballantyne, 'Mr. Peal's archive: mobility and exchange in histories of empire', in Burton (ed.), *Archive Stories*, pp. 87–110. See also Ballantyne, *Orientalism and Race: Aryanism in the British Empire* (Basingstoke: Palgrave, 2002).

32. Dirks, 'Annals', p. 52.

33. Archival disorder can actually be a mixed blessing. Ghosh describes how the disorder of the colonial archives in India forced her to look through all extant documents, since there were no finding guides, which yielded unexpected discoveries. Ghosh, 'National', p. 38.

34. For a similar account of archival paper trails, see Dirks, 'Annals', p. 59.

35. Jervois to Secretary of State, 15 August 1875, PRO, CO 273:81, despatch 234.

36. Michelle King, 'Replicating the colonial expert: the problem of translation in the late nineteenth-century Straits Settlements', *Social History* 34:4 (November 2009), pp. 428–46.

37. Robert Darnton, *The Case for Books: Past, Present and Future* (New York, NY: Public Affairs, 2009).

38. For more on the success of the September 11 digital archive relative to other digital archives, see Sheila Brennan and T. M. Kelly, 'Why collecting history online is Web 1.5'. Center for History and New Media at George Mason University. http://chnm.gmu.edu/essays-on-history-new-media/essays/?essayid=47 [accessed 12 January 2016].

39. Anthony Grafton, 'Future reading: digitization and its discontents',

The New Yorker, 5 November 2007. http://www.newyorker.com/maga-zine/2007/11/05/future-reading [accessed 12 January 2016].
40. Ursula Marx *et al.* (eds), *Walter Benjamin's Archive: Images, Texts, Signs*, trans. Esther Leslie (London: Verso, 2007), p. 1.
41. Howard Eiland and Kevin McLaughlin, 'Translators' foreward', in Walter Benjamin, *The Arcades Project*, trans. Eiland and McLaughlin (Cambridge, MA: Harvard University Press, 2002), p. x.
42. Walter Benjamin, 'Theses on the philosophy of history', in Hannah Arendt (ed.), *Illuminations: Essays and Reflections*, pp. 262–3.

FURTHER READING

Arondekar, Anjali, *For the Record: On Sexuality and the Colonial Archive in India* (Durham, NC: Duke University Press, 2009).

Benjamin, Walter, *The Arcades Project*, trans. Howard Eiland and K. McLaughlin (Cambridge, MA: Harvard University Press, 2002).

Blouin Jr, Francis Xavier, and William Rosenberg G. (eds), *Archives, Documentation, and Institutions of Social Memory: Essays from the Sawyer Seminar* (Ann Arbor, MI: University of Michigan Press, 2007).

Burton, Antoinette (ed.), *Archive Stories: Facts, Fictions, and the Writing of History* (Durham, NC: Duke University Press, 2005).

Derrida, Jacques, *Archive Fever: A Freudian Impression*, trans. Eric Prenowitz (Chicago, IL: University of Chicago Press, 1996).

Dirks, Nicholas B., 'Annals of the archive: ethnographic notes on the sources of history', in Brian Keith Axel (ed.), *From the Margins: Historical Anthropology and Its Futures* (Durham, NC: Duke University Press, 2002), pp. 47–65.

Foucault, Michel, *The Archaeology of Knowledge*, trans. A. M. Sheridan Smith (New York, NY: Pantheon Books, 1972).

Schwartz, Joan M. and Terry Cook (eds), 'Archives, Records and Power,' Special Issues, *Archival Science* 2:1–4 (March and September 2002).

Steedman, Carolyn, *Dust: the Archive and Cultural History* (New Brunswick, NJ: Rutgers University Press, 2002).

Stoler, Ann Laura, *Along the Archival Grain: Colonial Cultures and their Affective States* (Princeton, NJ: Princeton University Press, 2009).

CHAPTER 3

Approaching Visual Materials

Ludmilla Jordanova

The phrase 'visual materials' covers a very great deal; in fact almost any source that a historian uses has visual aspects, including books and documents. We could comment, for example, on shape, colour, texture and, if relevant, inks and paper, but it has been conventional to concentrate on the *content* of texts. The word 'visual', then, is shorthand for assumptions about the look of something being, potentially at least, of special historical interest. Since so many things fall under the capacious umbrella 'visual materials', there are no natural or obvious criteria for what counts as being of visual interest. Hence the approaches outlined in this chapter could be applied to most items that have been made by human hands. It is hardly realistic to speak of a method or methods here, since that implies either a mode of address that is more clear-cut and structured than anything discussed here, or a tight relationship between a certain type of source and particular approaches, which simply does not apply. I will outline ways of paying careful and self-aware attention to the types of artefact often called 'images'; it is through such attention that we can make the most of their historical possibilities.

One way of explaining the concerns of this chapter is to note that it focuses on materials that seem to demand special visual skills and focus, even if the fundamental principles upon which their use is grounded are common to everything a historian undertakes. We always ask basic questions of sources, such as who made them, what do they consist of, where were they produced and when, why did they come into being and how. We may also be concerned with provenance – who owned what, when, the cost and how items changed hands. These questions arise whether we are looking at statues, medals and coins, drawings, prints and paintings, or indeed handling a document, a newspaper or a book. Recognising the need to pose such questions is an important starting point: they generate descriptions that blossom into analysis. The drive to assemble the elements of a description relates to the ethical obligations historians have to all the materials they use: to be reflective, accurate, compassionate and responsible, and to share key information with readers so that they can check for themselves the interpretation on offer. If historical works use visual sources without providing what information is available, they risk not commanding respect. In such cases, any illustrations are likely be functioning more as decoration than as integral parts of historical arguments. All too often portraits are used in this way, as if they unproblematically revealed what people in the past looked like, proffering obvious historical insights in the process (see Figure 3.1).[1] One problem here is that scholars are not articulating precisely how visual materials assist historical understanding and hence the materials themselves remain passive and inert, presented as mere reflections of past states of affairs. It is more productive to treat visual sources as active commentaries by their makers.

THE HISTORY OF APPROACHES TO VISUAL MATERIALS

It is not possible to give any kind of straightforward account of the origins and development of the range of approaches that visual materials invite. For many centuries it has been recognised that images and objects help to generate insights about past times. Perhaps this recognition is as old as history itself, but the work of antiquarians in the seventeenth and eighteenth centuries neatly illustrates the point. They were scholars, collectors and connoisseurs, who used diverse visual materials to study the past, often the distant past, and are the direct intellectual ancestors of archaeologists, art historians and historians.[2] Over the nineteenth century, disciplines as we recognise them today were institutionalised, although there have been considerable variations between countries, with art history, for instance, developing in Germany over that century, but only becoming established in Britain after the Second World War. The relationships between the disciplines of history and art history are not especially close, although some practitioners in each engage seriously with the other. For several generations in the nineteenth and twentieth centuries, historians gave priority to documents and other types of written sources. Yet there were always a select few who were interested, for example, in illuminated manuscripts, architecture, satirical prints or court art. Recently, visual materials have become fashionable, often being used by historians who have apparently forgotten the long history of their use. They are deployed by practitioners from a wide range of periods and sub-fields, to shed light on an equally diverse range of historical problems, and with distinctly variable degrees of skill. Given their current ubiquity, it is vital that readers are able to evaluate how well they have been used, and that researchers are able to approach them with confidence.

Figure 3.1 *Portrait of Sir Isaac Newton* (1642–1727), not dated, line engraving,
35.6 × 22.4 cm. The engraver was Jacobus Houbraken, after a painting by Sir Godfrey
Kneller. Newton was famous in his lifetime, but far more widely renowned after his death.
There were many prints of him because he was so famous, while such images spread his fame
yet further. This example was included in a book, compiled by Thomas Birch, which included
short biographies of 'illustrious persons' as well as portraits of them. Note both that the owner
of the original painting is named on the print – John Conduit was married to Newton's niece –
and that the plate mark, showing where the metal has been pressed onto the paper, is clearly
visible. Author's collection.

We are highly dependent on the words used to describe and interpret visual materials. The implications of this point are worth emphasising: while it is vital to develop skills of looking, which involve paying special kinds of visual attention to objects, and to understand both the technical and conceptual issues images raise, just as important are the skills of writing vividly, accurately and persuasively about what has been seen and conveying in words the historical insights that visual materials are capable of providing.

One theme running through this chapter is the relationships between disciplines, since, in using visual materials, historians enter territories already occupied by specialised fields. Ideally, practitioners of history draw upon the skills, methods and expertise of other scholars, blending them with their own. Disciplines are social groups that police boundaries, develop norms and pass moral as well as intellectual judgements on the work of their members. Judging from comments frequently made in seminars, there remains a sense of threat in the face of perceived blurred boundaries, which produces claims about the necessity of maintaining distinctions between, say, history, art history and archaeology. Since fields have habits of mind, honed by their communities, these sentiments should not cause surprise, and they need to be taken on board by advocates of interdisciplinary research. The very title of this chapter implies interdisciplinarity, and I suggest the value to historians of engaging seriously with those disciplines that have paid the most sustained and critical attention to the nature of visual experience and to the ways it is made integral to scholarship. We do have some precedents of our own upon which to draw. The great Dutch medievalist Johan Huizinga, a pioneer of modern cultural history, is one example; another is Dorothy George, who did important work on satirical prints.[3] So, although it is still common for professional historians to confess that they are wary, even frightened, of using sources that are not texts to be read for their content, in practice some historians in each generation have wanted to think with their eyes, and they have done so in a wide range of ways. They provide rich resources for approaching visual materials. Observing how successful scholars from many backgrounds actually use visual materials is one of the most effective ways of thinking about 'method'.

EXEMPLARY USES OF VISUAL MATERIALS

There is no better example of such an inspirational figure than Michael Baxandall, who initially studied English literature, and is usually described as an art historian. He wrote about a wide range of historical phenomena, seeking to link artefacts with contemporary practices and modes of thought in a rigorous manner. In 1972 he published *Painting and Experience in Fifteenth-Century Italy*, based on lectures given to history students at the

University of London, which 'were meant to show how the *style* of pictures is a proper material of social history'.[4] There has been considerable debate about Baxandall's approaches in this and other publications, which remain exceptionally influential.[5] In *Painting and Experience*, he paid meticulous attention both to forms of historical reasoning and to fifteenth-century pictures. As a result he can be used as a methodological resource. But we should note that his claims were always particular, and never general – in other words, his approaches were custom made for each project, tailored to respond to specific places, times, types of visual and material culture and the intellectual problems he explored.

I am not arguing that Baxandall had *a* method, but that he was unusually attentive to his own practices, meticulous in his historical reasoning and able to write in a clear, accessible manner. Although it was not possible for Baxandall to have *a* method, since he developed a fresh approach each time, his work is methodologically powerful, partly because he was unusually explicit about his moves. What he said about fifteenth-century Italian paintings was based on his understanding of that specific society, its skills and habits, forms of patronage, religious, social and economic life. He connected paintings with activities in their parent culture, such as dancing or preaching, which accustomed viewers to the careful interpretation of visual experiences. Painters used such skills and habits in their works. Historians can always make a point of asking about prevailing visual habits and skills, about forms of funding, belief systems, social organisation and the distribution of wealth. They can also pose an even more fundamental question inspired by the opening sentence of *Painting and Experience*: 'a fifteenth-century painting is the deposit of a social relationship'.[6] They can routinely ask, 'in order to understand these made items, to which relationships do I need to give priority?' To the extent we can generalise about Baxandall's approach, it is designed to illuminate the social relationships out of which works of art arise, through an analysis of the visual habits, skills and assumptions that participants in those relationships possessed. Thus he married careful analysis of visual materials with a vivid sense of the practices out of which they arose. He was profoundly historical in his scholarship, which was wide ranging in terms of the times, places and types of art that he studied. If students read only *Painting and Experience* with care, they would learn a great deal about 'approaching visual materials'. They might also be struck by both the range of written sources he brought to bear on pictures, including contracts, letters, poems, treatises and manuals for preachers, and the forms of contextualisation he explored.

DISCIPLINES AND THEIR RELATIONSHIPS

There is more to be said about the relationships between disciplines, since, in the early twenty-first century, many fields exist that take the act of seeing seriously: film studies and visual culture studies, for instance. I have mentioned art history as arguably the most important example, since it has been giving and refining sustained attention to the ways in which the visual experiences generated by works of art may be analysed, written about, and integrated into historical accounts, for a considerable period of time. Art history is strikingly heterogeneous, using a wide range of ideas, theories and frameworks to explore an equally diverse array of materials including prints, photographs, paintings and sculpture, each of which invites approaches that are apt for it.[7] For example, Eric Fernie's *Art History and its Methods: a Critical Anthology*, included twenty-seven texts from the mid-sixteenth century until 1993. They range from early biographies of artists, to discussions of ways of approaching African art, and include writings that are philosophical, architectural, and shaped by feminism and post-colonialism. The glossary, which defines terms such as discourse analysis, iconography, Marxism, psychoanalysis and semiotics, gives further evidence of the range of methods the discipline encompasses. Associated with the influential work of Michel Foucault, the analysis of discourses generally privileges texts and examines the ways in which they structure power and knowledge. There is little here that is specifically tailored to working on visual materials. By contrast, iconography – 'the study of the meanings of images' in Fernie's definition – has formed a central part of art history since the early twentieth century, and traces the meanings both of specific items, animals and plants for example, and of compositions.[8] Designed for students, this anthology simply provides one sample of what art historical methods might consist of.

A more recent, single-authored volume provides an instructive comparison. Gillian Rose is a geographer and her *Visual Methodologies: an Introduction to the Interpretation of Visual Materials*, is avowedly interdisciplinary.[9] She identifies at least seven distinct methodologies: compositional interpretation, content analysis, semiology, psychoanalysis, discourse analysis, audience studies and anthropology. A number of features of her approach are immediately striking. Rose draws extensively on the social sciences, such as anthropology. She foregrounds recent phenomena – the chapter on audiences is subtitled 'studying how television gets watched'. Media studies has been particularly attentive to audience response, not least because it is possible to examine it directly through questionnaires and interviews. In fact, the problem of audiences, both implied and actual, is a general one, always raised by visual materials. For whom were they made and in what contexts have they been displayed and seen? What were the relationships between viewers and makers? In what ways were assumptions about likely audiences built into the artefact in question? How can we document implied and actual audiences? All these questions are properly asked by historians, although one challenge is generating sufficient evidence to answer them effectively.

Visual Methodologies reinforces the point that interdisciplinarity is the order of the day for those interested in the analysis of visual culture. The existence and rapid development of a relatively new field, visual culture studies, is revealing. Note that 'visual culture' is an inclusive category, which encompasses diverse phenomena, from TV, advertisements and propaganda, to photography, postcards and magazines.[10] For some scholars, 'art', which implies aesthetic judgements, is merely a subset of the broader category 'visual culture'. Note too the emphasis on the recent past and the present. Contemporary historians, like modern historians working on the period since the wide dissemination of photography, that is, from the 1840s onwards, are blessed with a huge amount of visual material. But this situation may be less of a blessing in practice. There are so many photographs, and of so many different kinds, that the possibilities can seem overwhelming. One result is that a few get used over and over again. As a consequence they become hackneyed, their historical significance easily blunted by overexposure. To account for this phenomenon, one could emphasise the technologies of photography, showing how easy it is to reproduce such images, to crop more or less at will, and alter tones, shades, colours, and now even major features. At the same time, historians need to appreciate the myth-making around photography, its alleged capacity to tell the truth.

The example of photography, to which many different approaches have been applied, illustrates some important points for historians interested in approaching visual materials.[11] There are indeed technical or quasi-technical considerations that historians need to grasp in order to use photographs. For example, it helps to know about exactly how a photograph was taken and developed. The length of exposure times in early photography is a vital consideration in interpreting portraits, for instance. Who did the developing, what did the original negative, if extant, look like, and what kind of control did the photographer exercise over their work? As with all types of source, there may be limitations concerning the volume and kind of ancillary evidence available. Basic questions still need to be posed. They can be focused more precisely with specialist knowledge, but historical curiosity about who, what, where, why, when and how, remains the driving force. Technical information is useful and, for most types of visual evidence, not difficult to come by. To use prints, for instance, a grasp of the range of printmaking techniques is indispensable and readily available.[12] Nonetheless, it is striking that in relation to images in general and photography in particular, there is a lot more scholarly engagement with what we could call the creative aspects of the medium than with the technological side – types of camera, for instance. The aesthetic dimensions of photography have commanded most interest, to which the equipment is seen as marginal, although the two approaches can be productively complementary. Status issues are involved: there is a long history in the arts and crafts of concern about the social and cultural respect that any given technique can command, especially when it is new. It follows both that we need to be alert to a wide range of phenomena from the technical to the social when using visual materials, and that cultivating a general and critical vantage point is essential. Research that lays bare past assumptions about hierarchies of artefacts and producers is an excellent example of the latter point.

CONTEXTS

In order to develop such an approach, historians emphasise the importance of context. For example, we want to know how occupational hierarchies, between, say, painters, printmakers, designers and photographers were negotiated, and through which institutions. The centrality of context in historical practice can also be used to point up the ways in which some of the approaches evident in much writing on visual culture, valuable though they are in some respects, are limited. Developing a strong sense of the multiple contexts in which visual materials are made, used and re-used, often over centuries, is central to a critical historical vantage point. By examining the processes involved and the settings in which they occurred, any given image ceases to be taken at face value and can be subjected to careful scrutiny. In each case there are many contexts – biographical, economic, institutional, pertaining to patronage and forms of display – to be explored: they radiate out from any given artefact. Close reading of an image may appear antithetical to these contextualising moves, since the former seems to burrow into it, the latter to step back from it. In fact they are complementary.

Thus, when we examine closely the famous statue of Saint Teresa of Avila (1515–1582), in Santa Maria della Vittoria, Rome, by Gian Lorenzo Bernini (1598–1680), try to describe the look on her face and the figure of the Angel above her, and interpret the work as a whole, we can turn to her own writings, and the passages describing her ecstasy (see Figure 3.2). In what circumstances were they written? How widely disseminated were they? Did Bernini draw upon them, and was he told to do so by Cardinal Federico Cornaro (1579–1653), the patron of the chapel, of which the statue is the centrepiece? This is only to begin an enquiry in which a careful description and analysis of what is sometimes deemed Bernini's masterpiece, is inseparable from an investigation into those who made, paid for, housed and responded to it. It is precisely in thinking about a range of evidence and interconnecting contexts that historians do what is most characteristic of their discipline. Thus, Bernini's work, unveiled in 1652, must be connected with abstract and general phenomena such as the baroque style and the Counter-Reformation. I say 'must' because it is in making such connections that we contextualise, and the contextualisation is all the more effective if historians have a strong grasp of

Figure 3.2 The Cornaro Chapel in Santa Maria della Vittoria, Rome, taken May 2011,
reproduced with the permission of the photographer, Francesco Filangeri.

both the nuts and bolts of making a statue in Rome in the 1640s and '50s, and of the prevailing religious, political and aesthetic currents.[13]

In the example I have just given, historical interpretation arises out of particular visual materials, the properties of which drive the approaches adopted. But there are also overarching theories, psychoanalysis would be a good example, that can, in principle, be applied to just about anything. It might even be said to constitute a method. A lot of work in art history has been shaped by psychoanalytic concerns, yet it may be more productive to think of this *not* as a method, but as a way of thinking about human experience, which requires careful looking and visual analysis, together with ancillary research, just as other approaches to visual materials do. Perhaps it is best used flexibly, in combination with other approaches. This would be an eclectic way of proceeding, one that is characteristic of, although not exclusive to, the discipline of history.

VISUAL TURNS

It is useful for historians to be aware of fields, geography and literature are pre-eminent examples, which have undergone a marked visual turn in recent decades, and displayed openness and flexibility in their approaches. A pioneer in this regard is the literary critic and historian John Barrell, whose book, *The Dark Side of the Landscape: the Rural Poor in English Painting 1730–1840*, first published in 1980, has been immensely influential.[14] Written from a politically engaged perspective, Barrell showed that rural scenes were not ideologically innocent, but rather interventions in complex, contested social relationships between classes. It would be possible to describe Barrell as a Marxist – possible, but not entirely helpful, since above all he looked searchingly at a certain type of image, asked critical questions about it, and sought to place artists, patrons and subjects in a rich historical context. His approach was politically coloured, as every scholar's is; he selected a category of source – paintings of the rural poor – and then subjected it, together with relevant materials, to careful, theoretically informed scrutiny.

KEY TERMS

It is time to step back for a moment, and consider again our key terms.[15] 'Visual', I have suggested, is a loose notion, it applies to almost anything, and has been the object of scholarly analysis for a long time. It is associated with a wide range of methods and approaches, and is not owned by any particular field. For the purposes of this chapter, 'visual materials' refers to the diverse forms that images take. The word 'art' implies some kind of judgement about aesthetic quality. Not all images count as art, and what does varies with time, place and the person making the judgement. Art history, then, pays attention not to any old image, but those that have passed some kind of test – they possess qualities that enable them to be referred to as 'art', even if this is necessarily a perpetually contested concept. For historians there are two potential problems here: first, 'art' is deemed to carry elitist connotations, which limits its historical interest; and second, it is feared that it invites approaches that marginalise rich contextualisation in favour of connoisseurial appreciation of great works. The implication is that art and art history are of limited relevance for historians. However, it can be argued that art touches many if not all social groups, and that art history provides a great deal that historians will find useful, including skilled looking. We should not be afraid to use the word 'art', so long as it is done in full recognition of its complexities, and we certainly should be willing to turn to art history as a discipline with many approaches for inspiration as well as practical guidance on close visual analysis.

I have used the term 'image' – the 'representation of the outward form of a person or thing, or a mental picture' – which warrants brief consideration.[16] There is a field that considers the relationships between words and images, for example, and studies of advertising and media are also concerned with images. But 'image' does not only refer to what is literally seen by the eyes. It has another, figurative use, for which 'idea' or 'impression' does just as well. In others words, 'image' does not necessarily imply a physical entity at all, whereas 'visual materials' can helpfully remind us of their material aspect. This is a complex matter, especially given the relatively new area of material culture studies (see Chapter 4). Ideally, historians explore both visual and material culture, and do so together in an integrated fashion. In practice, distinct specialisms have arisen, which cultivate somewhat different habits of mind. One of the most significant features of the discipline of history is its eclecticism. We can think about material culture, *and* visual culture *and* all the arts, drawing on the diverse fields that study them.

It is always good to take account of the physicality of artefacts, even when they are images. For example, many fans have been covered with images, some of which count as 'art', but historians will, ideally, consider the constituent materials, and above all treat the object as a whole, including its life history. Not all fans contain images, but they remain historically eloquent and aesthetically revealing. It may be their size, colours and materials that provide historians with evidence and insights, as well as their cost, provenance and purpose together with forms of collecting and display.[17] This example reveals the inseparability of visual and material culture.

A dominant feature of most of the items that come under the rubric 'visual materials' is that they were expressly made to be looked at and the skills involved in making them specifically appreciated. Sometimes materials were designed to elicit recognition and admiration. Thus visual *materials* depended upon and assumed visual *skills* in their audiences and were the product of the visual *intelligence* of people in the past, who were, in fact, frequently solving problems presented to them by their clients and customers. One of the most familiar of these was how to make the ruler look as powerful, prestigious, admirable and authoritative as possible. Here careful attention to visual culture reveals a great deal about politics in the past.[18] Historians tend to think about this in terms of the ruler in question – Peter the Great of Russia, Louis XIV of France, Queen Elizabeth I of England – but it was the *artists* whose insights made what can be called propaganda possible.[19] They understood and analysed their audiences and clients, and possessed talents and skills of a specialised kind summed up by 'visual intelligence'.

POSSIBLE RESERVATIONS

In the paragraph you have just read, there is a methodological claim. If we probe all conceivable aspects of a thing made to be seen, it is possible to find special forms of historical commentary, as well as evidence of the prevailing habits and skills of the context in which it was made and used. Acts of making contain assumptions about audiences for the end results. Assumed audiences can be carefully assessed for the historically revealing commentaries artefacts contain. This approach overcomes one of the main charges laid against non-textual sources – that they are unreliable. Claims about reliability imply that sources could in principle give *direct* access to the past. No source, however, does this; all our evidence has passed through human consciousness and is a transformation not a reflection of past states of affairs. Sources never provide windows onto or mirrors of past times. Logically, they cannot be *reflections* but must be *interpretations*. If we can show exactly how this works, we can avoid the trap of a false polarity between 'reliable' and 'unreliable' types of evidence. Thereby we can also deal with another possible objection – that we are inappropriately privileging elite culture. The processes of making, buying and selling, displaying and responding to visual materials occur across whole societies. Many images, those in churches, for instance, were designed to be seen by anyone and everyone. The people who made them were well aware of the fact and were often expressly charged with communicating complex ideas to those who possessed little or no education. Charges of elitism are often facile, only useful when they press historians to think a lot harder about both implied and actual audiences.

The approach just outlined may fruitfully be applied to popular culture, which is, after all, profoundly visual. We know from the work of scholars, such as Robert Scribner on the German Reformation, and from extensive writings on broadsides and ballads, that many images were widely disseminated after the invention of printing.[20] We know too that print shops displayed their wares in windows for anyone in the street to see. The basic approaches outlined here can be applied to anything that was made with skill and designed to elicit visual appreciation – stamps and playing cards, inn signs and trade cards, book illustrations and advertisements, postcards and board-games.

A further possible reservation about the value of visual materials is that, compared to documents and printed matter, they are less weighty and historically significant. They can be deemed trivial. Some certainly were luxuries, pertaining to the pleasures of limited numbers of people, but those facts hardly diminish their forms of historical eloquence, they simply mean that, as is always the case, we have to define clearly what phenomena they can and cannot testify to. Since people have always experienced the world through their eyes and given weight to the resulting experiences, it follows that what is artfully made is especially culturally, socially, politically and economically dense. It is unreasonable to marginalise certain kinds of sources *a priori* without first thinking hard about what they do and not reveal.

AN EXAMPLE

I can illustrate some of the main points of this chapter through a brief example, which draws on portraits as deposits of social relationships. An intriguing instance is an oil painting of one of his dealers by the well-known French impressionist Pierre-Auguste Renoir (1841–1919). The canvas depicts Ambroise Vollard (1867–1939), fondling a figurine by a sculptor – Aristide Maillol (1861–1944) – they both knew and liked. He is totally absorbed by the female figure. Renoir gave Vollard the picture, painted in 1908 when they had known each other for more than a decade, as a gift. I chose this example for a number of reasons. One of them is quite prosaic – it is in the Courtauld Gallery, London, close to where I used to work, so I could see it easily and repeatedly. The Gallery is unusual in allowing visitors to take photographs and to use them in publications without a fee. This overcomes many of the practical problems posed by getting permissions, acquiring images and paying for the right to reproduce them. The fact that this canvas came to Britain in the 1920s as part of the collection of a well-known collector and philanthropist, Samuel Courtauld (1876–1947), who came from a wealthy textile-making family, makes it even more interesting (see Figure 3.3).[21]

We can use this portrait to think about early twentieth-century art markets, the status of both Renoir and Vollard, and the taste and values of the collector, as well as forms of display. It is eloquent on the relationships between

Figure 3.3 Pierre August Renoir, *Portrait of Ambroise Vollard*, 1908, oil on canvas, 81.6 × 65.2 cm, Courtauld Gallery, London. It is shown in its location in May 2011, when this picture was taken by the author.

artists and dealers in general, as well as this particular relationship, and artistic networks, both in France and internationally. It can be seen as a kind of commentary on the pleasures of looking at and handling objects, especially when they are made by those known to the two main protagonists. If we wanted to be more 'art-historical', we could probe the image in more detail and compare it with other work on a similar subject, by the same hand, and by those to whom Renoir was close. If, on the other hand, we wanted to be more 'social' in our concerns, it would be possible to investigate Vollard's biography – he was from a French family but born in the colonies, and became both wealthy and powerful in Parisian culture – those who were close to him, his business activities, the books he wrote and the values he propagated. Since he was associated with many prominent artists, including Pablo Picasso (1881–1973), at a time when the art world was undergoing rapid change, Vollard and the close relationships he had with them, many of whom painted him, can be a way into the nature of cultural change, for example, the rise of modernism. It is clear that the portrait is, at least in part, about gender, with a man sensually caressing a model of the female form. Thus a single picture can lead researchers seamlessly into an array of historical issues and problems, as well as contemporary ones concerning collecting, access and display.

CONCLUSIONS

This example indicates a range of possible approaches rather than specific methods, and has touched on broad themes such as institutions, fashion, markets and commercial relationships. The term 'method' suggests instructions, clear-cut ways of doing things, which can be followed with fairly predictable results. I have explained why this does not apply to the use of visual sources in historical practice, and suggested some other ways of conceptualising research that takes thinking with the eyes seriously. I have seven points to make by way of conclusion, perhaps the closest to methodological precepts it is possible to come.

First, to reiterate, I suggested thinking in terms of approaches rather than methods. The former is open-ended, productively looser and more in keeping with the eclectic, flexible orientation for which I argued than the latter. Second, I insisted that the technical basics must always be the starting point. What these consist of is implied by asking what, when, where, how, how much, who and so on. Once these questions are posed, and descriptions generated, the historian is led into interpretation and context. Getting precise details right, such as the genre and medium, the type of print or paint, the date of execution, provenance, and patronage, is absolutely indispensable. Inevitably, there are occasions when ancillary evidence is patchy or missing, but the forms of reasoning that are implied by these questions remain fundamental. Furthermore, they indicate the value of careful comparison, in order to bring out the similarities and differences between, say, works by the same hand, within the same collection, representations of a theme in different media, or at different times and places. I would argue that all history is based on comparative reasoning and that it is fruitful to bring comparative analysis into explicit focus when using visual evidence.

Third, the device that leads researchers from visual sources to historical analysis is description. Whenever historians want to use such a source, their first task should be to look at it for as long and as closely as possible and compose a full description of it. Ideally this is an iterative process – keep looking, and modifying the account, you notice fresh features each time, and out of the words, research questions and analysis emerge. Fourth, as historians practise these activities, they learn how to develop their visual skills, to consciously refine their attention and focus their engagement. This is to cultivate a historian's form of visual intelligence in order to recognise better its manifestations in the past. Fifth, the model of learning outlined here is more akin to apprenticeship than to something formal and academic: watch others doing it well, spend time with them through their publications, try to understand their craft, and emulate them. Our reading is productively focused on the equivalent of artisans' masterpieces, no matter what period or place they discuss, and I suggested Michael Baxandall as an example of an extraordinarily skilled craftsman. Historians of earlier periods have generally been considerably more effective at using and integrating visual materials. Reading in a range of subjects, times and geographical areas enhances intellectual flexibility and encourages us to pay attention to ways of transposing approaches and insights from one context to another.

Sixth, historians benefit from reading as widely as possible in the fields that specialise in visual analysis. Using visual materials generatively necessitates going beyond the confines of the discipline of history, and engaging with other modes of address, theories, vocabularies and operating assumptions. There are many rich scholarly traditions to draw upon. Approaching visual materials is, ideally, an interdisciplinary enterprise. The end results, however, can still be thoroughly 'historical'. Finally, a worthy goal is an integrative way of approaching the past. We do not study visual materials to become archaeologists or art historians, print specialists or experts on medals, but to become better historians, who integrate such artefacts into ways of understanding earlier times that remain 'historical'. In using inverted commas, I am acknowledging that this is not an easy notion to define, nonetheless, history does differ from many other fields in the weight it gives to contextualisation, the breadth of the phenomena it considers and the multiplicity of connections it seeks to draw between them.

It is plausible to take a self-aware, yet innocent stance: so much evidence survives that counts as 'visual materials', and visual experience has played such a central role in all aspects of the past, that it would be perverse not to use their possibilities. We should do so in a manner that both respects the general code of practice for deploying any source and takes account of specialist knowledge.

NOTES

1. Thomas Birch, *Heads of Illustrious Persons of Great Britain* (London: John and Paul Knapton, 1743–1752, 1756); Patricia Fara, *Newton: the Making of a Genius* (London: Macmillan, 2002); Marcia Pointon, *History of Art: a Student's Handbook*, 5th edn (London: Routledge, 2014); Shearer West, *Portraiture* (Oxford: Oxford University Press, 2004).
2. Rosemary Sweet, *Antiquaries: the Discovery of the Past in Eighteenth-Century Britain* (London: Hambledon, 2004).
3. Johan Huizinga, *The Waning of the Middle Ages: a Study of the Forms of Life, Thought and Art in France and the Netherlands in the XIVth and XVth Centuries* (London: Arnold, 1924); M. D. George, *English Political Caricature: a Study of Opinion and Propaganda*, 2 vols (Oxford: Clarendon Press, 1959).

4. Michael Baxandall, *Painting and Experience in Fifteenth-Century Italy: a Primer in the Social History of Pictorial Style* (Oxford: Oxford University Press, 1972), Preface. A second edition appeared in 1988.
5. Adrian Rifkin (ed.), *About Michael Baxandall* (Oxford: Blackwell, 1999).
6. Baxandall, *Painting and Experience*, p. 1.
7. Michael Hatt and Charlotte Klonk, *Art History: a Critical Introduction to its Methods* (Manchester: Manchester University Press, 2006); Marcia Pointon, *Strategies for Showing: Women, Possession, and Representation in English Visual Culture, 1665–1800* (Oxford: Oxford University Press, 1997).
8. Eric Fernie (ed.), *Art History and its Methods: a Critical Anthology* (London: Phaidon, 1995), p. 345.
9. Gillian Rose, *Visual Methodologies. An Introduction of the Interpretation of Visual Materials*, 2nd edn (London: Sage, 2007). A third edition was published in 2012.
10. Matthew Rampley (ed.), *Exploring Visual Culture: Definitions, Concepts, Contexts* (Edinburgh: Edinburgh University Press, 2005); John Walker and Sarah Chaplin, *Visual Culture: an Introduction* (Manchester: Manchester University Press, 1997).
11. Graham Clarke, *The Photograph* (Oxford: Oxford University Press, 1997).
12. Anthony Griffiths, *Prints and Printmaking: an Introduction to the History and Techniques*, 2nd edn (London: British Museum Publications, 1996).
13. For a broad approach to early modern visual issues see Stuart Clark, *Vanities of the Eye: Vision in Early Modern European Culture* (Oxford: Oxford University Press, 2007).
14. John Barrell, *The Dark Side of the Landscape: the Rural Poor in English Painting 1730–1840* (Cambridge: Cambridge University Press, 1980).
15. Raymond Williams, *Keywords: a Vocabulary of Culture and Society*, revised and expanded edn (London: Fontana, 1983).
16. Jonathan Harris, *Art History: the Key Concepts* (London: Routledge, 2006), p. 158.
17. Jane Roberts, Prudence Sutcliffe and Susan Mayor, *Unfolding Pictures: Fans in the Royal Collection* (London: Royal Collection, 2005).
18. Peter Burke, *Eyewitnessing: the Uses of Images as Historical Evidence* (London: Reaktion Books, 2001); Walter Liedtke, *The Royal Horse and Rider: Painting, Sculpture, and Horsemanship, 1500–1800* (New York, NY: Abaris Books, 1989).
19. Toby Clark, *Art and Propaganda in the Twentieth Century: the Political Image in the Age of Mass Culture* (London: Weidenfeld and Nicolson, 1997).
20. Robert Scribner, *For the Sake of Simple Folk: Popular Propaganda for the German Reformation* (Cambridge, Cambridge University Press, 1981);

Andrew Pettegree, *Reformation and the Culture of Persuasion* (Cambridge: Cambridge University Press, 2005).

21. John House, *Impressionism for England: Samuel Courtauld as Patron and Collector* (London: Courtauld Institute Galleries, 1994).

FURTHER READING

Baxandall, Michael, *Patterns of Intention: On the Historical Explanation of Pictures* (New Haven, CT: Yale University Press, 1985).

Burke, Peter, *The Fabrication of Louis XIV* (New Haven, CT: Yale University Press, 1992).

Crow, Thomas, *Emulation: Making Artists for Revolutionary France* (New Haven, CT: Yale University Press, 1995).

Hall, James, *Dictionary of Subjects and Symbols in Art*, revised edn (London: Murray, 1979).

Haskell, Francis, *Past and Present in Art and Taste: Selected Essays* (New Haven, CT: Yale University Press, 1987).

Haskell, Francis, *History and its Images: Art and the Interpretation of the Past* (New Haven, CT: Yale University Press, 1993).

Jordanova, Ludmilla, 'Image matters', *Historical Journal* 51 (2008), pp. 777–91.

Jordanova, Ludmilla, *The Look of the Past: Visual and Material Evidence in Historical Practice* (Cambridge: Cambridge University Press, 2012).

Mancini, J. M., *Pre-modernism: Art-world Change and American Culture from the Civil War to the Armory Show* (Princeton, NJ: Princeton University Press, 2005).

Prown, Jules, *Art as Evidence: Writings on Art and Material Culture* (New Haven, CT: Yale University Press, 2001).

Rotberg, Robert, and Theodore Rabb (eds), *Art and History: Images and their Meaning* (Cambridge: Cambridge University Press, 1988).

Rublack, Ulinka, *Dressing Up: Cultural Identity in Renaissance Europe* (Oxford: Oxford University Press, 2010).

Silverman, Debora, *Art Nouveau in Fin-de-Siècle France: Politics, Psychology, and Style* (Berkeley, CA: University of California Press, 1989).

The following journals may also be of interest: *Art Bulletin* (1918 on); *Art History* (1978 on); *Early Popular Visual Culture* (2002 on); *Journal of Interdisciplinary History* (1970 on); *Journal of Visual Culture* (2002 on); *Oxford Art Journal* (1978 on); *Visual Culture in Britain* (2000 on); *Word and Image* (1985 on).

CHAPTER 4

Material Culture

Alan Mayne

History's purpose is to open pathways for understanding that other country, the past. The public intellectual Ashis Nandy argues that conventional historical methods tend to lock out much of the past from formal historical understanding. He adds, however, that there exist multiple pathways that enable people to connect idiomatically to other aspects of the past.[1] In this chapter I contend that material culture offers one pathway for unlocking the broader possibilities of historical analysis.

Material culture is idiomatic to all of us because it comprises 'the tangible yield of human conduct'.[2] It is 'ubiquitous in our everyday lives; we are surrounded by it and arguably can do little without it'.[3] Research on material culture is undertaken within and across many disciplines in the humanities and social sciences. Much of this activity is directed at present-day subjects, linked for example to mass consumption, design and architecture.[4] By contrast, I focus here upon material culture that has survived from the past. The chapter thus complements the preceding discussion of visual materials by Ludmilla Jordanova, and Jo Guldi's analysis of landscape and place in Chapter 5.

The constituent elements of material culture have been clearly identified by researchers over the past half-century (although the range of things that is encompassed by the term is wide and varied), and historians now regularly engage with such materials. There is also general agreement, following a long formative period of discussion and conceptual development, about the broad relationships between things, social settings and social processes in the past. However, the opportunities for extending the historical interpretation that material culture analysis provides, and the methods by which these opportunities are best pursued across diverse material forms, are much less clear. I aim here to help resolve these uncertainties.

BEGINNINGS

Material culture analysis has emerged as an explicit and coherent historical method since the 1970s, although interest in relics from the past has much older antecedents. Analysis in the English-speaking world drew in part upon the growing popularity of local history studies after the Second World War. It was also influenced by the broadening scope of sources, and the questions asked of them, that accompanied the developing interest since the 1950s and 1960s in the social history of the modern world. Two overlapping applications of social- and local-history method were particularly important during this formative period. One was the investigation of the urban and industrial landscapes of the eighteenth and nineteenth centuries, pioneered by scholars such as H. J. Dyos, who explored the 'shapes on the ground' that mass urbanisation produced,[5] and by Adrian Forty, who contextualised the new commodified products of industrial society.[6] The other was the historical analysis of rural landscapes, begun in Britain by Maurice Beresford and W. G. Hoskins, and extended to case studies on the periphery of British colonialism by scholars such as the historical geographer D. W. Meinig and the cultural historian Rhys Isaac.

Hoskins' analysis of the English landscape, and the 'cultural humus' of multiple generations upon it, has had a wide and enduring influence, as Jo Guldi indicates in her chapter.[7] So too has Isaac's *The Transformation of Virginia 1740–1790*, which contends that any society 'necessarily leaves marks of use upon the terrain it occupies. These marks are meaningful signs not only of the particular relations of a people to environment but also . . . of social relations in their world'.[8] Meinig's *On the Margins of the Good Earth*, an account of the expansion of farming into the low-rainfall fringes of South Australia's wheat belt during the late nineteenth century, similarly describes why today's cultural landscape – 'sprinkled with the stone ruins of abandoned farmsteads' – represents 'the peculiar impress of South Australia's history upon her land'.[9]

These two strands of urban and rural landscape history, with their shared interest in the material expressions of past lives, have been increasingly brought together since the 1970s by overlapping research into the vernacular history of buildings.[10] This approach is exemplified by Henry Glassie's studies, beginning during the late 1960s, that interweave material culture analysis, folklore and history in order to interpret 'the vast and democratic handmade history book of the landscape'.[11]

Historical analysis of the material culture of the modern world has also been informed by research in cognate disciplines across much longer time frames. Art history and architectural history have drawn attention to cultural forms and practices dating back to the Roman and Hellenic worlds. Archaeology and museum studies have consolidated and extended such public knowledge.

Archaeology, for example, covers not only the material culture analysis of prehistoric peoples and the ancient world, but extends to post-medieval archaeology (a field that has boomed since the 1970s and 1980s) and to the material culture of European colonialism. Archaeology and museum studies are also significant for having eroded the Eurocentric geographical focus of these activities by highlighting the material culture of the Middle East, Asia, the Americas and the Pacific. Rather than fetishising the objects of other cultures, they have rethought some of the epistemological foundations of the European Enlightenment in order to study more revealingly things across cultures and time-periods.[12]

These changing parameters in analysis have been considerably influenced since the 1980s by anthropology (and indirectly, by linguistics and semiotics), which hypothesised that 'things have no meanings apart from those that human transactions, attributions, and motivations endow them with'.[13] Pierre Bourdieu in particular postulated that by studying the 'sign systems', or 'habitus', that material culture represented – which he argued functioned 'below the level of consciousness and language' – it was possible to delve into hitherto unexplored realms of human social belonging and interaction.[14] As Mary Douglas put it, objects 'are the visible part of culture'.[15]

EXPRESSIONS

The rubric of material culture analysis is thus tantalisingly simple: as Glassie says, 'Material culture is culture made material'.[16] Elaborating this point of view, historian Jules Prown explained that

> material culture is just what it says it is – namely, the manifestations
> of culture through material productions. And the study of material
> culture is the study of material to understand culture, to discover the
> beliefs – the values, ideas, attitudes, and assumptions – of a particular
> community or society at a given time.[17]

This approach takes us beyond what Raymond Williams called 'the misleading contrast between "material" and "cultural"' – and indeed between artistic cultural expression and everyday culturally mediated behaviour – towards a fuller appreciation of the dynamics of cultural meaning and social interaction.[18] It is premised upon an understanding of culture similar to that of Clifford Geertz, who, 'believing, with Max Weber, that man is an animal suspended in webs of significance he himself has spun', took 'culture to be those webs, and the analysis of it to be therefore not an experimental science in search of law but an interpretive one in search of meaning'.[19] Geertz's search for cultural meaning through these webs of significance was influenced by Paul Ricoeur's concept of the 'inscription' of meaning, which led Geertz to emphasise the readability of the diverse webs that cultures spin. Those webs could be found in language, ritual and material things. As Geertz pointed out, 'We cannot live other people's lives[;] it is with [their] expressions, representations, objectifications, discourses, performances . . . that we traffic'.[20]

Material culture analysis is part of this traffic. It attempts to understand past societies by studying the things and places that survive from the past, and the behaviours associated with them.

Material culture analysis thus ranges across personal possessions and consumer goods, costume and foodstuffs, tools and utensils, artworks and body decoration, landscapes and buildings. It extends to broader aspects less rooted in the 'obviously material', for example 'the cultural significance of sensory media such as smell, taste and sound, to discursive analyses of text and film'.[21] As historian Leora Auslander explains,

> most people for most of human history have not used written language as their major form of expression. They have created meaning, represented the world, and expressed their emotions through textiles, wood, metal, dance, and music. Material culture is simply another vital source of historical knowledge, supplemental to words for those who have had little access to them.[22]

The archaeologist James Deetz pointed out that by studying these things, 'the people who occupied sites which have little documentary evidence are not lost to history, for they did leave a record, in things rather than words'.[23]

Conceptualising material culture in these ways has four important implications. Firstly, material culture analysis should not be used merely to illustrate prevailing word constructions of the past, because the historical significance of objects transcends that of words. As Auslander points out, 'objects are not just seen, but also felt and touched', and therefore, as the archaeologist Martin Hall contends, '"things" anchored meanings and allowed polyvalent interpretations, extending the meanings of verbal forms of expression'.[24] This does not pose an either/or quandary in historical method, because the tendency in contemporary Western common sense to oppose words and things is largely illusory.[25] In Geertzian terms, both fit within a continuum of cultural expression and social function. Thus, as Auslander says, in historical interpretation 'the interplay of things and words offers crucial insights'.[26] Her emphasis on *interplay* is useful because it makes plain that the potential of material culture analysis is not confined to the sort of *salvage* operation implied above by Deetz, important though this is. Material culture analysis is not only relevant for studying societies long ago and about which there is little written or spoken evidence. Anthropologist Danny Miller, for example, in *The Comfort of Things*, studied a selection of households along a contemporary South London street in order to demonstrate 'how people express themselves through their possessions, and what these tell us about their lives'.[27]

Secondly, if we agree with Bourdieu that objects are embedded in symbol systems, it follows that in historical interpretation the study of material culture must be directed towards explaining the social processes that underpinned and animated those systems. The study of material culture is not an end in itself, for as Isaac cautions, 'society is not primarily a material entity. It is rather to be understood as a dynamic product of the activities of its members'.[28] It is therefore imperative that analysis be open-ended, aimed at exploring the dynamics of 'social relations, enacted and embodied through a material world',[29] rather than constricting interpretive possibilities by thinking that objects 'are . . . static [and] yield only arrested moments' from past lives.[30] To think of material culture only as the shell that survives from completed lives and interactions in the past is to risk misinterpreting material culture as providing only reflections of social life in the past. In their construction and use, things were active elements in shaping past societies, and were embedded in the imaginary spaces with which people ordered their private and public worlds.[31] Material culture should therefore be thought of not so much as the product of the past, but as an element in the making of that past. This approach is embodied in the City of Montréal's Pointe à Callière museum, where the site's archaeological stratigraphy (stretching back to the city's beginnings in the 1640s) is made visible, and is augmented by interpretive displays of objects ranging from the fifteenth to the twentieth century, in order to trace 350 years of urban change.

By looking beyond form to process, the study of material culture expresses a broader shift in the humanities and social sciences 'from a stress on concepts such as structure, equilibrium, function, system to process, indeterminacy, reflexivity – from a "being" to a "becoming" vocabulary'.[32] The anthropologist Igor Kopytoff thus likens material culture analysis to a 'cultural biography of things'.[33] Echoing that thinking, Arjun Appadurai has called for research that probes the social life of things, arguing that it is 'only through the analysis of these trajectories that we can interpret the human transactions and calculations that enliven things'.[34] As recent research by historical archaeologists has demonstrated in relation to the development of capitalism and colonialism, 'the material "world of things" is not just an external manifestation of gender and class relations, but is rather at the heart of the construction of identity'.[35] This is evident, for example, in the lavish villas and the elaborate systems of service and etiquette that sustained them, which were created during the eighteenth and nineteenth centuries by the emergent colonial elites of South Africa, the Americas and Australasia.[36]

Thirdly, the most exciting discoveries in material culture analysis are occurring where the contexts and objects of study appear peripheral to conventional methods of historical analysis and to their hierarchies of historical significance. The currency of material culture analysis comprises mundane things, overlooked places, everyday events and ordinary people. North American historical archaeologists have been especially innovative in tapping into these aspects of the recent past, and none more so than Deetz, who pointed out that

> in the seemingly little and insignificant things that accumulate to create
> a lifetime, the essence of our existence is captured. We must remember
> these bits and pieces, and we must use them in new and imaginative
> ways so that a different appreciation for what life is today, and was in
> the past, can be achieved.[37]

An example of this approach, combining archaeology and history, is Mary Beaudry's *Findings: the Material Culture of Needlework and Sewing*, which shows how 'seemingly simple and commonplace artifacts that everybody readily recognizes and "knows" – pins, needles, thimbles, and scissors – have complex histories and even more complex and varied social meanings than we might at first think they do'.[38]

Fourthly, as Beaudry's analysis exemplifies, paying attention to small things from the past, to non-verbal expressions of social life in the past, and to the ongoing processes of earning a living and of constructing and displaying identity in the past, taken together, provide a way of more fully studying agency and resilience within subaltern lives. Material culture analysis provides not only supplementary data for doing so, but a more nuanced approach for appreciating the strategies employed by marginalised groups who are either underrepresented in documentary sources, or (as is considered further below with reference to John Moloney's cesspit) are disparaged by them or submerged within them. This approach is well illustrated by material culture analyses of African American slave plantations.[39] As Glassie puts it,

> The way to study people is not from the top down or the bottom up,
> but from the inside out, from the place where people are articulate to
> the place where they are not, from the place where they are in control of
> their destinies to the place where they are not,[40]

and the prompts for doing so lie in the material culture evidence of everyday life that historians still too often eschew.

Given the complexities and wide-ranging possibilities of material culture analysis, the subject is best studied across disciplines and specialisations: for example, in collaboration with anthropology, archaeology, art, architectural and planning history, critical theory, cultural studies, design studies, geography, literary studies, museum studies, phenomenology, psychology, semiotics and sociology. A key aspect of the development of material culture studies to date has been that it does not aspire to become an exclusive method; its strength is that it can readily be combined with and flow across other approaches for interpreting the past.

NEW POSSIBILITIES

Material culture analysis has moved far beyond its apprenticeship years, when it was assumed that the new field's significance lay only in embellishing historical themes that had already been constructed using documentary and oral history records or in illustrating known historical events. It has also moved beyond the initially overstated counter-claim, that it counteracted the 'dreary elitist bias' of documentary-based history,[41] and unlocked – as no documentary analysis supposedly could – the hidden histories of lives amongst oppressed and overlooked groups such as women, children, immigrants, wage workers, slaves and indigenous peoples. Analysis has also moved beyond the possibilities that were aired during the follow-up phase as the field began to mature, when it was said that its significance lay in the ancillary role of filling gaps in historical knowledge about past times.

The future significance of material culture studies lies in its potential to generate new questions in historical analysis, and to establish additional emphases and connecting threads in interpretations of the past. As Leora Auslander contends, by embracing the study of material culture scholars can 'change the very nature of the questions we are able to pose and the kind of knowledge we are able to acquire about the past'.[42] Martin Hall's *Archaeology and the Modern World* is a bold illustration of how this might be done. However there still remains a gap between Auslander's prediction for the future and the current methodological consensus about how material culture studies should be undertaken. There are two obstacles in particular that stand in the way of further research innovation within the field.

Firstly, doubt now surrounds what once was the bedrock of methodological thinking: that in order to interpret the social context and symbolic meaning of material culture one aims to 'read' objects as one reads text; that we should 'try to read objects as we read books – to understand the people and times that created them, used them, and discarded them'.[43] The ethnographic historian Greg Dening, for example, whose subtle work transformed understanding of eighteenth- and nineteenth-century exchanges between European mariners and islanders in the Pacific, described material culture as 'texts caught in the forms of material things'. He argued that there are messages to be read from them: they might 'show sex in a colour, status in a type of wood, class in a design'.[44] Likewise, archaeologists often argue that material culture is 'a medium of inscription, of "writing" discourse through and on landscapes, houses, bodies, pots, animals, and written texts'.[45]

However, metaphors of text and inscription, appealing though they may be, threaten to collapse the multiple dimensions of sensory experience that are the essence of things that have been shaped and trafficked through human intervention. As the founding editors of the *Journal of Material Culture* objected in 1996, treating objects as 'quasi-texts is to overlook their most fundamental properties'.[46] Objects have non-textual qualities: for example, they are tactile, they may trigger the imagination, their provenance may well be tied to the social lives of non-literate people. Moreover, reading a text (whether complete or fragmentary) requires that it be clearly delineated, and comprehension occurs in an 'experience-near' situation whereby readers establish coherence and attribute meaning by drawing upon their own knowledge and immediate experience. Material culture evidence likewise had 'experience-near' currency in the past, in the contexts of its production and use, but in the present day its uses and meanings have often faded into the 'experience-distant'.[47] To stroll today through any of the relic landscapes from mining and industrial activities during the nineteenth and early twentieth centuries is quickly to realise this point.[48] In order to assess the significance of such material evidence, we have to grope beyond what is familiar to us, to how others may have thought and acted. The clarity, immediacy and coherence of a text have been lost. Artefacts are the ambiguous residues from an unfamiliar past. It follows that we cannot build our methods for interpreting material culture evidence upon the assumption that the things we study have ingrained within them an immediacy and familiarity for us that transcend the passage of time.

This highlights the second problem that impedes nuanced study of material culture. Much analysis to date rests upon the claim that material evidence has an innate immediacy that connects us to the past; that because it is tangible, uncomplicated and transparent in its meanings it provides a bridge to understanding the past.[49] Anyone who has visited the Taj Mahal – especially at evening on a full moon – or has witnessed evensong framed within the massive pillars of Durham cathedral, will empathise with the bridge analogy. Expert commentary reinforces such responses. Lowenthal remarked upon the 'tangible familiarity' of relics from the past, and emphasised their bridging function in analysis since 'artefacts are at once past and present'.[50] Deetz dramatised these connections between artefacts lost and recovered in *Flowerdew Hundred*, an archaeological study of a sixteenth-century farm in Virginia, which begins with an imaginative account of a servant woman dropping a clay pipe in 1626, and ends with a similar vignette of a woman archaeologist uncovering its fragments from an excavation pit in 1983. Deetz concludes, 'Alicia, meet

Alice. The circle is closed'.[51] Auslander gives this line of argument a powerful emotional twist, arguing that the reuse of personal objects across generations 'provide[s] a sensory experience of continued contact. The rings I never take off that belonged to my dead grandmothers provide a daily connection to them, as if our fingers could still touch'.[52]

The implication of this thinking is that 'experience-near' cognition telescopes time and transcends cultural difference. However, a great deal of material culture evidence – because it is fragmentary and incomplete, or because of its scale and volume, or its imperfect fit with other historical sources – is profoundly opaque and unfamiliar to interpreters in the present day. A good example is the confusing material footprint of accelerating urbanisation and accompanying urban ways of life since the mid nineteenth century. For Ian Hodder, material data 'are often more ambiguous than their verbal counterparts'.[53] This is their value. It is because material culture is not simple and transparent in its meanings that the effort required to comprehend its full complexity and to compare it usefully with other sources translates into open-ended research questions which can extend our understanding of past societies and habitats. Such an approach does not necessarily reject the analogies of text or inscription, but insists upon the need for translation in order to make material culture fully 'readable'.[54]

The key method for doing so is to start from small things and specific contexts and build outwards, generating a hermeneutic spiral of accumulating analysis and supporting data. There are pitfalls here, for example the risk of stalling in a mire of detail, or of asserting rather than demonstrating key linkages between small things and big ideas. The British archaeologist Dan Hicks also cautions that a preoccupation with big interpretive themes such as capitalism and colonialism in modern world history can result in analysis that delves into '"meaningful" material culture' but downplays the inconsistencies, incoherency and 'messiness' of other material culture evidence about the past.[55] These problems can be avoided by applying ethnography to historical method. Applied to historical analysis of material data (as it has been by the cultural historian Robert Darnton in respect to archival data)[56], the ethnography used by Geertz in cultural anthropology 'to see things from the native's point of view'[57] becomes a methodological framework for switching back and forth between particular and broader contexts in the past, and between actions in the past and present-day interpretations of them, in order to mesh together multiple strands of evidence and continually test the inferences that are being drawn from them. The collection of essays on the history of urban inequality that I edited with Tim Murray is a pointer in this direction.[58] There is an 'inescapable circularity' to such interpretation:

in the course of empirical research, existing understanding is refined into ever more discriminating appreciation of the subtle nuances of cultural forms. Through a process of elucidating contexts, structures, and meanings, we can learn to reconstruct something of the participants' worlds as they experienced them.[59]

APPLICATIONS

Puzzlement triggers innovation in historical analysis. The ambiguities of material culture are a case in point. They invite questions, and in attempting to answer them we are drawn into a dialectical process of probing the specific contexts of an object's use while simultaneously testing and adjusting our mediating interpretive frameworks. The effort to contextualise objects carries with it a sensitivity to the 'fundamental material dimensions [of] social relationships' in the past.[60] This opens up exciting new perspectives upon a theme of long-standing interest in the historiography of the modern world: relationships of power, and the intersections between hegemony and subaltern agency.

A good example is the research on colonial Annapolis, Maryland, that has been undertaken over many years by the historical archaeologist Mark Leone.[61] Annapolis was three-quarters poor and one-third African American, and yet tolerated the increasing polarisation of wealth during the seventeenth and eighteenth centuries without violent protest. Leone attributes this to 'capitalism's masking ideologies',[62] the material expressions of which he studied with particular reference to the 1760s formal garden of the merchant-lawyer and American revolutionary leader, William Paca, and the broader baroque design of streets and carefully placed public buildings that defined the hubs of the city's civil and religious power. Leone's approach, which is based on Marx as reinterpreted by Althusser and Habermas, has been widely debated and contested for thirty years.

Leone opened a parallel line of analysis by using material culture to tease out unexpected (and indeed sometimes denied) aspects of an African American 'alternative world' to that of Annapolis's mercantilist elite.[63] Leone's interpretation hinged upon recognising traces of 'spirit bundles', which he first encountered during excavations at the famous Charles Carroll House in 1991. In a tiny cache below the floor of one basement room was found a collection of rock crystals, bone discs, a smooth black pebble, coins, the bottom of a decorated pottery bowl, and pins. Some experts were dismissive of the find, saying that 'the stuff was trash; nothing'. However Leone distrusted these knee-jerk reactions, alert to the likelihood that because the assemblage 'had no obvious meaning in anyone's experience, it was regarded as bits and pieces of virtually no importance'.[64] The materials dated to the late eighteenth and early nineteenth centuries. Similar caches were found in other basement rooms of the Carroll household, and cross-disciplinary analysis identified them as spirit bundles that perpetuated spiritual practices originating in West Africa. The basement rooms were used by Carroll's cook (traces of another bundle were found beneath the kitchen hearth), and Leone speculated that 'she had protected her environment with these ritual bundles, and she may have worshipped through them as well. Thus, while the Jesuits were upstairs saying Mass, she was in an African safe zone beneath'.[65]

By comparing the Carroll House material with evidence from other archaeological sites, and drawing upon folklore research, studies of West Central African spirit traditions and the memories of former slaves (documented by the 1930s Federal Writers' Project), Leone and his collaborators were able to identify overlooked but enduring cultural practices. The purpose of these rituals was to control the spirits of the dead, and their effect was to 'preserve an African identity and a coherent sense of community' beyond the confines of white American culture.[66] The spirit bundles embodied rubrics of protection and equilibrium, and possibly also expressed resistance and aggression. Some of the bundles' contents were identified as having malign purposes aimed at directing spirits to harm or kill others. Leone speculated that seemingly tranquil elite Annapolis households were actually sites of symbolic violence, and that some of the malign intent may have been 'aimed at owners, overseers, employers, masters, mistresses, and those who caused the working conditions in which people of African descent found themselves'.[67] Indirect though such resistance would have been, Leone argues that the very existence of this parallel African American spirit world 'showed that the ideology in the rest of Annapolis was not . . . inevitable'.[68] Conceding that many unknowns still surround the broader implications of spirit bundles, Leone invites further analysis to test and extend his hypotheses: 'Now that we can see that the people at the bottom created an option for themselves, can we know why? Can we know what they saw that made them stay different?'[69]

Similar questions could well be asked in Britain regarding the social rhythms of York's now vanished Hungate district. The neighbourhood attracted notoriety after B. Seebohm Rowntree surveyed it in 1899 and labelled it a 'slum'.[70] That descriptor, with its implications of living spaces 'unfit for human habitation' and social dysfunctionality, led to Hungate's demolition during the 1930s and the relocation of its inhabitants to new public housing. The authorities assumed that they would be grateful, and in many ways they were. But there was sadness too among the former residents, for homes destroyed and a community broken up without first testing local opinion.[71] Oral histories record their nostalgia: 'all them little houses were small', recalled one former resident, but 'some of them were little palaces. Brass fenders, brass spittoons, everything brass'.[72] The material culture of Hungate has been destroyed or dispersed, but through such word pictures it is still open to interpretation.

The interplay of words and things in material culture analysis, and between historical and archaeological methods with the aim of meshing both elements, is especially evident in the reinterpretation of another supposed slum, the 'Little Lon' district in Melbourne, Australia. Little Lon was resumed by the federal government in 1948 and redeveloped, but archaeological and historical research since the late 1980s has revealed unexpected details about nineteenth-century households and neighbourhood social interactions that complicate the 'slum' stereotypes. Little Lon was a mixed neighbourhood, in which shops and factories stood alongside brothels, and Chinese cabinetmakers toiled in workshops beside homes owned or rented by working-class families.[73]

One such household was that of Irish labourer John Moloney who emigrated from County Clare in 1849. In 1855 he bought a new three-roomed wooden cottage in Little Lon. John was soon joined by his elder sister Hannah and younger brother Edward, and later by their younger sister Margaret. Their elder brother Thomas and his family lived nearby. After John's death in 1882 his sisters lived on in the family home. Margaret became its sole proprietor upon Hannah's death in 1886, and built a small brick house. The original wooden cottage was demolished in 1891. Margaret lived in the new home until her own death in 1901, aged 82.

This microhistory of an obscure family is drawn from rate books, post office directories, registrations of births, deaths and marriages, and probate records. They reveal stability and continuity within a supposedly slum-land underworld. The Moloneys regarded themselves, and many of their neighbours, as respectable self-improvers. John and Thomas joined with neighbours in 1880 to petition the police to take 'strict measures' against local prostitutes so 'that the neighbourhood be freed from this disgrace and annoyance'.[74] The Moloneys' family stability, working-class respectability and modest social mobility – replicated across many other families in Little Lon – enriches present-day understanding of social life within a supposed slum. Similar neighbourhood studies, using material culture evidence to energise documentary research, are being undertaken of many other nineteenth- and twentieth-century cities.[75]

None of this analysis of the Moloneys at Little Lon would have been possible had not archaeologists discovered traces of a wood-lined cesspit and asked the question, who lived near here? The Moloney story highlights the synergies that can develop between the study of material culture and broader historical analysis. Without the ambiguities posed by artefacts recovered from a built-over cesspit, on which no human name was inscribed but to which a property identification could be assigned, no-one would have had a reason to search the archives for John Moloney. The cesspit's material culture provides a further interpretive dimension. It comprises over 2,500 items of domestic refuse such as ceramics, glass, bone and personal items. They had been discarded, probably during the 1870s, when the house was sewered and the old cesspit filled with rubbish. The assemblage suggests that the Moloneys had decorated their home with Staffordshire figurines, one commemorating the death of Nelson and one of a shepherdess. The items are mundane, but that is their interest: these material survivals from a poor household, with their overtones of domesticity and respectability, contradict representations of Little Lon as a dangerous and deviant slum.[76]

The Moloney's cesspit contained small things that had accumulated as the family pursued livelihoods, established a home and forged relationships. The Canadian novelist Jane Urquhart encapsulated similar dynamics in *Away*, her story of an Irish couple building new lives in mid nineteenth-century Canada:

> With money [earned from labouring on] the roads, Brian had been able to purchase crocks and sealer jars, cutlery, tools, dishes, farm implements, and finally, for his wife, a wheel and loom. Starting, as they had, with nothing, the two adults were like gods creating a universe. The arrival of a pewter jug or a soup ladle could be an occasion for celebration. Household goods were fondled or stroked like pets, and under such care developed an animate life, a soul.[77]

I noticed a similarly loved household item, a simple wooden rolling pin, much worn from use, on display in Montréal's McCord Museum when I visited in 1998. A display card stated that it dated from the early twentieth century, but without further clues little could be deduced from looking at the rolling pin. However, an explanatory text provided by its owner, Carol Pauzé, elucidated:

> This rolling pin is one of the few objects I have that come from my mother's family. At either end there are grooves, worn by three generations of magic fingers. My grandfather, Omer Bourret (1879–1931), made it for his wife Adéline Larivière-Bourret (1879–1956). My grandmother left it to my mother Lucette Bourret-Pauzé (1917–1974) and I inherited it from her when she died. It reminds me of Sunday afternoons when I was young. We peeled, sliced and ate the fruit to fill the pies, while Mummy briskly rolled out the pastry. It was also a time of confidences, of childhood memories. She told us about the grandparents I had never known and the lively family of sixteen children, of whom she was one of the youngest. The rolling pin is still famous for making the best apple pies ever, according to Lucette's special recipe![78]

The historical value of studying material culture lies in such interweaving of words, things, places and memories, in order more fully to understand lives and habitats in the past, and their points of connection with the present day.

CONCLUSION

In this chapter I have given a short overview of material culture analysis, together with a discussion of its potential as a research method in historical studies. I emphasise the word 'potential' here. I do so in part because of the relatively recent origins of material culture analysis as an explicit historical method. It remains invisible to many academic historians while flourishing as a trigger for community engagement with history, in diverse areas such as quilt-making, railway museums and heavy horse ploughing displays. I also empha-sise potentiality because much of the value that I see in this research method flies in the face of what has conventionally been said about it. The study of material culture is ultimately less about things than the practices, relationships and value systems that produced them (a point of view that intersects with Simon Gunn's concluding comments in Chapter 12 in his discussion of behav-iour as performance). Further, material culture does not, as many maintain, provide a reassuringly solid bridge that connects us easily to the past times that produced it. One of the chief reasons for rigorously studying objects from the past relates to their ambiguity and our resulting puzzlement. Ambiguity and puzzlement have value because they generate new questions and a rethink of our prevailing interpretive emphases and categorisations. They can thereby test and confirm our assumptions, or open up new possibilities for better understanding the past.

What are these possibilities? Material culture can be usefully studied in relation to all places and cultures. In terms of time period, too, the approach has relevance wherever you would like to apply it. Material culture analysis is not limited to the 'pre-history' period before the written word, nor ancient civilisations, nor the medieval world, nor the early-modern intersections between European colonialism and the New World (although all of these times do present fascinating opportunities for its application). It has relevance wher-ever you think material objects provide 'an integral and inseparable aspect' of the social relationships that surrounded them.[79]

In terms of an appropriate taxonomy for the objects that can usefully be studied, the possibilities are likewise wide open. Some have high visibility. I am drawn to the executioner's axe displayed in the Tower of London, whose blade was last used to sever the head of one of my ancestors (seemingly a traitor, but whose behaviour at the block entered the colloquial vocabulary in the expression 'to laugh one's head off'). However, the objects I find most rewarding to study are those that Deetz called 'small things forgotten': the seemingly obscure and insignificant things, embedded in supposedly small places and mundane activities, that can nonetheless be used to open up grand and enthralling lines of inquiry. This is historical ethnography at its best.

My earlier stories about Little Lon and Hungate are pinpoints in the enthnographic spirals of analysis that fashion big historical themes out of seemingly small elements. The former resident of Hungate to whom I referred remembered the brass household ornaments that made 'little palaces' out of the houses that outsiders dismissed as 'slums'. These stories, grounded in the conjunctions between material culture, oral history and archive, resonate with the 'detective work' described in Chapter 7 by Al Thomson in his discussion of life stories as historical method. Our common purpose is to explore traces of the intimate cosmologies and overarching social relationships of people in the past. That objective cannot be achieved by following any one method. To study material culture effectively one needs travelling partners and a willingness to explore unexpected pathways.

NOTES

1. See, for example, Ashis Nandy's Nelson Mandela Lecture, University of South Australia, 21 September 2010, podcast download from http://www.unisa.edu.au/Business-community/Hawke-Centre/Nelson-Mandela-Lecture/2010-UniSA-Nelson-Mandela-Lecture [accessed 12 January 2016].

2. Henry Glassie, *Material Culture* (Bloomington, IN: Indiana University Press, 1999), p. 41.

3. Matthew D. Cochran and Mary C. Beaudry, 'Material culture studies and historical archaeology', in Dan Hicks and Mary C. Beaudry (eds), *The Cambridge Companion to Historical Archaeology* (Cambridge: Cambridge University Press, 2006), p. 191.

4. See, for example, Daniel Miller, *Material Culture and Mass Consumption* (Oxford: Blackwell, [1987] 1991); Daniel Miller, *The Comfort of Things* (Cambridge: Polity Press, 2008).

5. See H. J. Dyos and Michael Wolff (eds), *The Victorian City: Images and Realities*, 2 vols (London: Routledge and Kegan Paul, 1973).

6. Adrian Forty, *Objects of Desire: Design and Society 1750–1980* (London: Thames and Hudson, 1986).

7. W. G. Hoskins, *The Making of the English Landscape* (London: Hodder and Stroughton, 1935), p. 235. See P. S. Barnwell and Marilyn Palmer (eds), *Post-Medieval Landscapes: Landscape History after Hoskins* (Bollington: Windgather Press, 2007).

8. Rhys Isaac, *The Transformation of Virginia 1740–1790* (Chapel Hill, NC: University of North Carolina Press, 1982), p. 19.

9. D. W. Meinig, *On the Margins of the Good Earth: the South Australian Wheat Frontier 1869–1884* (Chicago, IL: Association of American Geographers, 1962), p. 217.

10. See, for example, Peter Ennals and Deryck W. Holdsworth, *Homeplace: the Making of the Canadian Dwelling over Three Centuries* (Toronto: University of Toronto Press, 1998).

11. Henry Glassie, *Passing the Time in Ballymenone* (Bloomington, IN: Indiana University Press, [1982] 1995), p. 603.

12. See Philip Jones, *Ochre and Rust: Artefacts and Encounters on Australian Frontiers* (Kent Town, South Australia: Wakefield Press, 2007).

13. Arjun Appadurai, 'Introduction: commodities and the politics of value', in Arjun Appadurai (ed.), *The Social Life of Things: Commodities in Cultural Perspective* (Cambridge: Cambridge University Press, 1986), p. 5.

14. Pierre Bourdieu, *Distinction: a Social Critique of the Judgement of Taste* (London: Routledge, [1979] 1984), pp. 172, 466. See also Jean Baudrillard, *The System of Objects* (London: Verso, [1968] 1996).

15. Mary Douglas and Baaron Isherwood, *The World of Goods: Towards an Anthropology of Consumption* (London, Allen Lane, [1978] 1979), p. 66.

16. Glassie, *Material Culture*, p. 41.

17. Jules David Prown, 'The truth of material culture: history or fiction', in Steven Lubar and W. David Kingery (eds), *History from Things: Essays on Material Culture* (Washington, DC: Smithsonian Institution Press, 1993), p. 1.

18. Raymond Williams, *Culture* (London: Fontana, 1981), p. 87.

19. Clifford Geertz, *The Interpretation of Cultures* (New York, NY: Basic Books, 1973), p. 5.

20. Clifford Geertz, 'Making experiences, authoring selves', in Victor Turner and Edward Bruner (eds), *The Anthropology of Experience* (Urbana, IL: University of Illinois Press, 1986), p. 373. See Clifford Geertz, *Local Knowledge: Further Essays in Interpretive Anthropology* (New York, NY: Basic Books, 1983), p. 31.

21. Daniel Miller and Christopher Tilley, Editorial, *Journal of Material Culture* 1 (1996), p. 14. Available at http://mcu.sagepub.com/content/1/1/5. citation [accessed 12 January 2016].

22. Leora Auslander, 'Beyond words', *American Historical Review* 110:4 (October 2005), p. 3.

23. James Deetz and Patricia E. Scott, 'Documents, historiography and material culture in historical archaeology', in Mary Ellin D'Agostino, Elizabeth Prine, Eleanor Casella and Margot Winer (eds), *The Written and the Wrought: Complementary Sources in Historical Anthropology. Essays in Honor of James Deetz*, Kroeber Anthropological Society Papers, no. 7 (Berkeley, CA: Kroeber Anthropological Society, 1995), p. 110.

24. Auslander, 'Beyond words', p. 2; Martin Hall, *Archaeology and the Modern World: Colonial Transcripts in South Africa and the Chesapeake* (London: Routledge, 2000), p. 197.

25. See, for example, Appadurai, 'The social life of things', p. 4; Steven Lubar and W. David Kingery, 'Introduction', in Lubar and Kingery, *History from Things*, p. ix.
26. Auslander, 'Beyond words', p. 10.
27. Daniel Miller, *The Comfort of Things* (Cambridge: Polity Press, 2008), p. 1.
28. Isaac, *The Transformation of Virginia*, p. 324.
29. Judy Attfield, *Wild Things: the Material Culture of Everyday Life* (Oxford: Berg, 2000), p. 264.
30. David Lowental, *The Past is a Foreign Country* (Cambridge: Cambridge University Press, 1985), p. 243.
31. See Gaston Bachelard, *The Poetics of Space* (New York, NY: Orion Press, [1958] 1964).
32. Victor Turner, *On the Edge of the Bush: Anthropology as Experience* (Tuscon, AZ: University of Arizona Press, 1985), p. 152.
33. Igor Kopytoff, 'The cultural biography of things: commoditization as process', in Appadurai, *The Social Life of Things*, pp. 64–91.
34. Appadurai, 'Introduction', in *The Social Life of Things*, p. 5.
35. Martin Hall, 'The architecture of patriarchy: houses, women and slaves in the eighteenth-century South African countryside', in D'Agostino *et al.*, *The Written and the Wrought*, p. 68.
36. See, for example, Anne E. Yentsch, *A Chesapeake Family and their Slaves: a Study in Historical Archaeology* (Cambridge: Cambridge University Press, 1994).
37. James Deetz, *In Small Things Forgotten: an Archaeology of Early American Life*, revised edn (New York, NY: Anchor Books, 1996), pp. 259–60.
38. Mary C. Beaudry, *Findings: the Material Culture of Needlework and Sewing* (New Haven, CT: Yale University Press, 2006), p. 137.
39. See, for example, Laurie A. Wilkie and Paul Farnsworth, *Sampling Many Pots: an Archaeology of Memory and Tradition at a Bahamian Plantation* (Gainesville, FL: University Press of Florida, 2005).
40. Glassie, *Passing the Time in Ballymenone*, pp. 86, 603.
41. Ibid. p. 603.
42. Auslander, 'Beyond words', p. 2.
43. Lubar and Kingery, *History from Things*, p. viii.
44. Greg Dening, *The Death of William Gooch: a History's Anthropology* (Carlton South: Melbourne University Press, 1995), p. 14; Greg Dening, *Performances* (Carlton South: Melbourne University Press, 1996), p. 42.
45. Mary Beaudry, 'Introduction: Ethnography in retrospect', in D'Agostino *et al.*, *The Written and the Wrought*, p. 3.
46. Miller and Tilley, Editorial, p. 8.
47. See Geertz, *Local Knowledge*, p. 57.

48. See, for example, Alan Mayne, *Hill End: an Historic Australian Goldfields Landscape* (Carlton South: Melbourne University Press, 2003).
49. See Alan Mayne, 'On the edges of history: reflections on historical archaeology', *American Historical Review* 113:1 (February 2008), pp. 93–118.
50. Lowenthal, *The Past is a Foreign Country*, pp. 246, 248.
51. James Deetz, *Flowerdew Hundred: the Archaeology of a Virginia Plantation, 1619–1864* (Charlottesville, VA: University Press of Virginia, 1993), p. 174.
52. Auslander, 'Beyond words', p. 5.
53. Ian Hodder, *Reading the Past: Current Approaches to Interpretation in Archaeology*, 2nd edn (Cambridge: Cambridge University Press, 1991), p. 126.
54. Geertz, *Local Knowledge*, p. 31.
55. Dan Hicks, '"Places for thinking" from Anapolis to Bristol: situations and symmetries in "World Historical Archaeologies"', *World Archaeology* 37:3 (2005), p. 386.
56. Robert Darnton, *The Great Cat Massacre and Other Episodes in French Cultural History* (New York, NY: Basic Books, 1984).
57. Geertz, *Local Knowledge*, p. 56.
58. Alan Mayne and Tim Murray (eds), *The Archaeology of Urban Landscapes: Explorations in Slumland* (Cambridge: Cambridge University Press, 2001).
59. Isaac, *The Transformation of Virginia*, p. 325.
60. Manuel Castells, *The City and the Grassroots: a Cross-Cultural Theory of Urban Social Movements* (London: Arnold, 1983), p. 311.
61. See Mark P. Leone, *The Archaeology of Liberty in an American Capital: Excavations in Annapolis* (Berkeley, CA: University of California Press, 2005). An extensive literature has been generated by Leone and his colleagues, and in reaction to it. This book and its large bibliography provide a good introduction to this debate.
62. Ibid. p. 260.
63. Ibid. pp. 58–61.
64. Ibid. pp. 200, 201.
65. Ibid. p. 204.
66. Ibid. p. 61.
67. Ibid. p. 232.
68. Ibid. p. 244.
69. Ibid. p. 244.
70. B. S. Rowntree, *Poverty: a Study of Town Life* (London: Macmillan, 1901), pp. 5, 199.
71. See Alan Mayne, 'Beyond metrics: reappraising York's Hungate "slum"', *International Journal of Historical Archaeology* 15:4 (December 2011), pp. 553–62.

72. Van Wilson, *Rich in All but Money: Life in Hungate 1900–1938*, revised edn (York: York Archaeological Trust, 2007), p. 26.

73. The analysis that follows draws upon Alan Mayne, Tim Murray and Susan Lawrence, 'Historic sites: Melbourne's "Little Lon"', *Australian Historical Studies* 31:113 (April 2000), pp. 131–51; Alan Mayne and Susan Lawrence, 'Ethnographies of place: a new urban history research agenda', *Urban History* 26:3 (1999), pp. 325–48.

74. Inward Registered Correspondence to the Chief Commissioner of Police, VPRS 937, Unit 303, Bundle 3, 19 October 1880, Public Record Office Victoria.

75. Mayne and Murray, *The Archaeology of Urban Landscapes*.

76. See Tim Murray and Alan Mayne, '(Re)constructing a lost community: "Little Lon", Melbourne, Australia', *Historical Archaeology* 37:1 (Spring 2003), pp. 87–101.

77. Jane Urquhart, *Away* (New York, NY: Penguin, [1993], 1995), pp. 153–4.

78. Author's fieldnotes from a visit to the McCord Museum, Montréal, September 1998.

79. Miller, *The Comfort of Things*, p. 286.

FURTHER READING

Auslander, Leora, 'Beyond words', *American Historical Review* 110:4 (October 2005).

Beaudry, M. C., L. J. Cook and S. A. Mrozowski, 'Artefacts and active voices: material culture as social discourse', in Randall H. McGuire and Robert Paynter (eds), *The Archaeology of Inequality: Material Culture, Domination and Resistance* (Oxford: Blackwell, 1991), pp. 150–91.

Glassie, Henry, *Material Culture* (Bloomington, IN: Indiana University Press, 1999).

Hall, Martin, and Stephen W. Silliman (eds), *Historical Archaeology* (Oxford: Blackwell, 2006).

Jones, Philip, *Ochre and Rust: Artefacts and Encounters on Australian Frontiers* (Kent Town, South Australia: Wakefield Press, 2007).

Hicks, Dan, and Mary C. Beaudry (eds), *The Oxford Handbook of Material Culture Studies* (Oxford: Oxford University Press, 2010).

MacGregor, Neil, *A History of the World in 100 Objects* (London: Allen Lane, 2010).

Miller, Daniel, *The Comfort of Things* (Cambridge: Polity Press, 2008).

Woodward, Ian, *Understanding Material Culture* (London: Sage, 2007).

CHAPTER 5

Landscape and Place

Jo Guldi

The relationship between landscape, the built environment, and mapping serves as a context within which a range of political entities from body to group to neighbourhood to nation can be reconceived in terms through a radical historical methodology. Such an approach would utilise methods of history traditionally practiced under the separate headings of political, cultural and environmental history. When the historian focuses his lens upon a particular landscape, he has the opportunity to raise questions about the impact of visual and architectural environments on social experience, changing modes of embodied interaction in public spaces, and the constructedness and flexibility of national borders. Historians of landscape have synthesised this range of methodologies into their practice. This combined set of practices, in a large part, constitutes what has been dubbed a 'spatial turn' in historical research.

In history, the spatial turn takes on manifestations so diverse that they confound association, such as the birth of street lighting in Wolfgang Schivelbusch, the ordering of the asylum in David Rothman, the politics of Central Park in Roy Rosenzweig, and to the alignment of borderlands in Pekka Hamalainen.[1] The spatial turn's promise comes when we imagine putting the approaches of such diverse conversations next to each other, synthesising body politics and political boundaries into a new history of the modern.

Over the last twenty years, a series of articles claim to have identified a 'spatial turn' to match the cultural and linguistic ones.[2] Typically, they ascribe the rise of spatial concerns to the introduction of French theory among cultural historians in the 1970s. In this story, a succession of disciplines contributed a variety of approaches to landscape. Geographers like Pierce Lewis stressed the need for first-hand contact with American neighbourhoods in the 1970s. In art history, Ann Bermingham and John Barrell argued that landscape painting idealised the centralisation of land among elites. Another spatial turn appeared in literature at about the same time, pointing to the role of country-house poetry and countryside descriptions in perpetuating regional and nationalist sentiments. In anthropology, researchers excavated how oral traditions were fixed in memory by story telling around particular landmarks. Recently there has been rumoured a 'geographical turn' in economics, which employs geographical theory to draw out the relationship of trade between centres and peripheries.[3] Each of these disciplines has contributed to the range of possible strategies that a researcher might pose to a single view of land, asking how it exists in the ideal view of elites, in nationalist sentiment, in the cultural memory and oral traditions, and as an economic factor in broader networks of exchange.

The application of spatial awareness to radical history stretches back to the beginning of the twentieth century with what might more properly be called a 'landscape turn' than a 'spatial turn'. Early in the twentieth century, English radical historians began to walk the landscape, inspired by the land reform movement in contemporary Ireland and Scotland, to search for the property basis of an alternative political economy. The radical historian Henry Randall and his followers suggested that the reading of cadastral surveys, vernacular dwellings and hedgerows would produce a history of common life in the period preceding and during enclosure, designed to challenge the rights of British elites to the land. Under Randall's influence, a body of radical historians turned to walks through everyday space as the basis for a new methodology. Over the course of the twentieth century, this interest in the politics of landscape would continue to inspire historians of the built environment, social history and textual analysis to synthesise diverse methodologies around the experience of ordinary space. Their common methods underlie the spatial turn of the 1980s and 1990s, whose synthetic eye is even now informed by the political ideals of radical history in the 1920s.

HISTORIANS WHO WALK

By the end of the nineteenth century, questions of property inspired by the land reform movement provided new reasons to walk the land. By the first years of the twentieth century, archaeological findings had begun to suggest that the history of property ownership could be revealed in the patterns of town settlement still visible in the English landscape.[4] From the 1930s to the 1960s, three radical historians – the aforementioned Randall, along with W. G. Hoskins and Maurice Beresford – turned to walking the landscape as a method of historical reinterpretation.

Their interest in land use was strongly influenced by earlier debates about the history of property holding in Britain. In 1861, Sir Henry Maine's *Ancient Law* proposed that written law had corrupted the entire system of modern landholding. Maine emphasised the role of literate elites in disenfranchising the illiterate English free-holder from his land. Around the time of the Norman Conquest, Maine suggested, the law was increasingly handled through documents rather than oral traditions. Basing his findings largely on amateur philology and the testimony of colonial anthropologists in India, Maine suggested that ancient Britain resembled oral societies like those found in Indian villages. He urged historians to search for new sources that would uncover the original, egalitarian ideas of Britain's constitution.[5]

Maine's work was still current as twentieth-century historians like Randall and Hoskins attempted to contextualise the contemporary land reform movement of the early twentieth century. They asserted that the discovery of pre-Norman commons meant that all of modernity had to be viewed as the long history of the working man's disenfranchisement from the land. Each of the three followed Maine's suggestion that working people had traditionally left few written resources, and that a history of proletarian life would necessarily depend on a search for alternative sources. The radicals promoted walking as a new model for writing and pedagogy. They urged the writing and teaching of history in such a way as to encourage mass participation in the work of history, arguing that the buildings and boundaries hidden everywhere in plain view provided ample evidence that individuals barely trained in history could assemble to interpret for themselves the modern threat to ancient British liberties.

Henry Randall, lawyer and amateur historian of Glamorgan in Wales, composed one of the earliest and most influential treatises on researching history by walking.[6] In the 1920s and 1930s, Randall forwarded, in a series of scholarly articles, a suggestion of ways in which radical and amateur history challenged the dogmas of official history. He explained that walking the landscape, studying houses and contemplating hedgerows offered important sources that were accessible to local historians but rarely considered by documentary historians of Acton's school. The articles, collected in Randall's *History in the Open Air* (1936), offered an early methodological text for radical popular history.

Under the influence of Randall and others, the young economist W. G. Hoskins turned to archaeology and local history as the foundation for a study that revealed in greater depth the effect of enclosure on the deracination of the working class.[7] After publishing several studies of enclosure and its effects on the livelihood of working-class people, Hoskins offered his *Making of the English Landscape* (1955), a call for a people's history of Britain. He urged that by studying the landscape, ordinary citizens could discover for themselves how the 'evils' of capitalism, urbanisation and centralisation had threatened the livelihood of working-class people.[8] By the 1960s, a historian of medieval fields, Maurice Beresford, became the tradition's apostle. His *History on the Ground* (1957) depended upon landscape for a history of the villages destroyed by enclosure, while his *Walks Round Red Brick* (1961) encouraged students of the new state universities to profit upon their surroundings far from Oxford and Cambridge by assembling a history of working-class Britons that depended on buildings as sources.

Walking radicals established their critique on the strengths that first-hand experience of the landscape had to offer. 'There is one document that no historian can neglect except at grave peril', wrote Randall, 'and that is the face of the country'. History, wrote Henry Randall, 'can be gained in one way and one way only'. The historian learns 'by tramping the country on his own feet'.

Randall described methods that would place the amateur historian on par with professional researchers. He appealed to fifty years of archaeological research, extrapolating strategies that needed no particular expertise for their application: the tracing of old roads, investigating the national borders of Britain and England, and considering the significance of place names. Given the range of available approaches, Randall reasoned that attention, not expertise, was the necessary virtue for interpreting landscape.[9]

The practical approach to landscape history depended on the researcher's ability to synthesise diverse fields of study. Randall recommended that the historian take up a knowledge of 'stratigraphical geology' as well as knowledge of 'the principles of transport by water and by land'; perhaps some military knowledge of 'strategy and tactics . . . and the conditions that govern the movements of bodies of men'. Some social history was necessary as well: 'He must know where and how men lived at different levels of civilization, the conditions that attracted them and the reasons therefore'.[10] Hoskins likewise recommended that the traveller on foot diversify his practical toolset: 'One needs to be a botanist, a physical geographer, and a naturalist, as well as an historian'. He recommended that travellers profit from archaeological research by learning to distinguish ancient salt ways from Roman roads, Saxon lanes, and the turnpike and 'enclosure' roads of the eighteenth century. He prodded the traveller to ask questions: 'Why is the town just like this, this shape, this plan, this size?' Hoskins also recommended intensive research in local archives. 'Slowly one pieces together', he instructed, 'from the records, from the archaeological finds in the local museum, and from the evidence of one's own eyes, what has happened'.[11]

Beresford described his methods of tacking back and forth between library and 'open air'. 'The traveler, armed with maps, was sometimes seeking what a document suggested he might find, and sometimes coming back to books and documents in order to explain or confirm what he noticed in the landscape'. That work 'examines maps and landscapes when documents themselves are lacking, seeking always to call in one technique to supplement the other'. The researcher would plot a 'triangular' journey from field to archive, archive to library, and back again.[12] The potential of this kind of research was vast, he explained. Beresford pillaged local records and the Ordnance Survey for the material, but the bulk of his findings were simply the close inspection of vernacular architecture. He took the reader past cemeteries and pubs, pointing to ornaments and portraits in stone, terrace housing and pavement. No item in the visible landscape was too mundane to be of possible relevance.

The radical walkers proved extremely influential in historical scholarship. Strains of radical walkerdom shot through discussions of material culture in the 1950s and 1960s. 'The artifact is potentially democratic', wrote anthropologist Henry Glassie, arguing that houses and objects opened themselves to interpretation by those with only practical experience, regardless of their exposure to disciplinary training. In his essays, Glassie assailed disciplinary practices that he argued left 'most people and most artifacts out of consideration'.[13] A flood of historical works documented the changing shape of the country house in the era of enclosure, relying on the built environment as a source for a social history that could cut across the lines of class.[14] Others extended study to the changing pattern of landholding, village arrangement and rural institutions.[15] Working-class historians, driven by the search for visual and spatial sources for a history of the masses, mined the vernacular landscape of informal building and design.[16] Various historians traced the migration of ethnic traditions through the history of housing.[17] Early feminist historians also found a trove of evidence of the undocumented lives of women who left no papers themselves, documented in works such as Dolores Hayden's history of modern kitchens.[18] Material culture had become the major point of entry for studying the story of those who left no other records behind.

Radical historians afoot were on the cusp of a major transition across the humanities that linked the undocumented history of experience to the everyday environment of popular life. Their work inaugurated a hunt for alternative sources that would disclose the experience of the illiterate masses by disclosing sources of material and visual culture found in the everyday environment. Through the twentieth century, their influence was felt as anthropologists and historians turned to everyday objects and houses as sources, while other disciplines would reflect the same impulse into still more specialised methodologies.

LOOKING AT BUILDINGS

By at least the time of Jacob Burkhardt, cultural historians had begun to treat the built environment explicitly as the indicator of cultural tendencies. Burkhardt's student Heinrich Wölfflin formalised the practice of comparing architectural styles in his works on the Renaissance and the baroque, defining the discipline as the study of chronological turning points in the making of the modern built environment. Through the work of Pevsner, Giedion and Banham, twentieth-century historians trained themselves to describe the evolution of particular building types according to social and technological innovations.[19]

By the 1960s, the search for wider sources drew historians towards this trove of methodologies. As scholars like Georges Duby adopted the categories of architectural history, social historians looked to the emergence of public spaces like medieval cathedrals and village fairs as exemplars of changes in popular culture.[20] As Gwendolyn Wright observes of this moment, 'a few historians reframed architectural biographies', the typical essay of architectural connoisseurship, into a broader cultural portrait of space. Historians, 'trained to use archives and attentive to cultural milieus', began to use accounts of buildings as emblems for larger stories of social and political relationships. In continental history, Carl Schorske's *Fin-de-Siècle Vienna* positioned an account of the Ringstrasse and its buildings as the keystone in an account of social and political realignments.[21] American historians began to analyse patterns of colonial village settlement and nineteenth-century suburbia as keys to social organisation.[22]

Gradually, scholars clad this habit of spatial analysis in a theoretical apparatus. By the late 1970s and early 1980s, historians were routinely citing Foucault, Benjamin and Habermas as sources on the organisation of institutional space, public space and private space as symptoms of political culture. Their texts provided the metaphors of 'surveillance', 'public space', 'the prospect' and 'the gaze' as rubrics for deciphering the play of power in spatial relationships. Analogies based in landscape spread across the humanities. Observers in anthropology and geography, for instance, have argued for Foucault as the origin of spatial metaphors like 'boundary' and 'field' that began to permeate social theory in the 1980s.[23] William Sewell traces his interest in the built environment of French factory towns to Bourdieu; Vanessa Schwartz her interest in wax museums to Benjamin; while Simon Gunn, studying reading rooms, libraries and churches, cites Castells.[24] Their analytics contributed to historians making more explicit the role of architecture and urban planning in naming, representing and controlling national space.

The result was a flood of historical works that foregrounded the role of landscape painting, architecture and urban planning in the making of modern nations and subjects. Art and literature historians dedicated themselves to the representation of the nation through images of wilderness and rural life.[25] Another wave was predominantly characterised by studies in particular buildings: the asylum, alehouse and town hall among them.[26] They found examples of panopticons and their variations at work in schools, prisons and reading rooms.[27] Social and political historians capitalised on the techniques of architecture historians to study the making of 'civic identity' and to critique the manipulation of civic identity by landed elites.[28]

Others looked beyond the local institution to how landscape more generally inculcated modern nationalism into the minds of individuals. The work largely covers the role of memorials and cemeteries in establishing national identity, valorising national conflict and suppressing alternative accounts, for instance the ongoing legacy of slavery in the American South.[29] Dana Arnold has explained the translation of monumental forms from country-house architecture to public buildings in the city in the era of the Napoleonic Wars, when commemorative arches and splendid clubhouses began to ornament the polite side of town.[30] Histories of urban planning have described the role of architects in constructing cities to serve consumption, technology and the middle-class family.[31] The rise of historic preservation in North America with artificial colonial villages such as Storrowtown, Williamsburg, the Henry Ford Museum and Disney World have been linked to social engineering programmes like Helen Storrow's arts-and-crafts training of immigrant workers and Ford's Americanisation of labourers' eating habits.[32] Such accounts highlight the degree to which, in the modern period, elites have used landscape as a tool for social engineering. They further demonstrate how, even after the tide of social engineering, the modern landscape continues to structure worlds of consumption and technology, persistently tinting the desires and attitudes of modern subjects.

SEEING THE MAP

Scholarship about the representation of space developed further with the critical reading of historical maps and the application of maps to discovering new patterns about historical information. Maps tended to appear in mid-century histories as markers in the heroic march of scientific knowledge.[33] Only gradually were they taken as tools for revealing invisible watersheds in the genesis of political rule.

The study of historical maps evolved with the cultural turn, foregrounding the symbolism of power in Enlightenment cartography, the application of cartography in modern social engineering projects, and the contestation of expert mapping in the twentieth century. From the 1980s forward, literary scholars and art historians began to inspect the cartouches and texts of Tudor and Enlightenment atlases for cues about the moral characteristics ascribed to each continent and the origins of centralised bureaucracy.[34] These early studies loosely followed a programme of showing evidence that maps, like other texts, could be used to reveal the prejudices of power. The historical geographer J. B. Harley's study of Enlightenment espionage explained that furtive mapping was carried out by most of the militaries of eighteenth-century Europe, establishing a pattern where 'political silences' show up as 'white spaces' on the map.[35]

Historians of cartography gradually coalesced behind a Foucaultian programme of revealing the role of state mapping in rendering information about the colonies knowable, organising territory and people, and assorting information about taxation and disease. Scholars returned to the birth of cadastral survey, the morality and morbidity maps of the nineteenth century, the maps used to chart the progress of cholera, and the poverty maps of Jane Addams and Charles Booth, showing how these maps defined the city as a zone for centralised legislation, and how they named populations that would be targeted by later legislation.[36] Maps became a lever in the making of official knowledge. As Patricia Gilbert explained in her reading of John Snow, the maps of the era 'redefine a space, usually an urban space, by relating a certain human experience – vulnerability to disease – to some hidden or non-obvious feature of the landscape'.[37] Through this work, prejudices about identity and order formerly taken for granted have been shown to have evolved with official knowledge and the making of maps. Mary Burgan has argued that the spatial segregation of London's poor into the East End was accomplished as the result of the mapping of the diseases of the poor and the subsequent evaluation of the area around Victoria Park in guide books.[38] Such historians suggest that cartography was instrumental in manufacturing, not merely documenting, the social order.

At the same time, early users of digital tools began to manipulate the spatial components of data to force new patterns to appear. In the 1990s, historians such as J. A. Yelling applied early Geographical Information Systems (GIS) to geographically encoded datasets of late nineteenth-century records documenting overcrowding by neighbourhood. The resulting maps demonstrated that the slum clearance projects and re-housing projects of the 1930s resulted in further concentrations of poverty.[39] Today, initiatives such as the Stanford Spatial History Project are allowing historians to manipulate even grander datasets, like the tax returns on land for nineteenth-century Rio de Janeiro, studied by Zephyr Frank, which show the gradual displacement of poor craftsmen paralleled by their increasing political marginalisation.[40]

LOOKING BACKWARDS: THE NEAR SPATIAL TURN

At the end of the twentieth century, it became routine to characterise landscape in terms of political movements. Scholars in the spatial turn assert that landscape offered a route for understanding the historical evolution of nation, race, class, gender, sexuality, expert rule and the experience of power.[41] The romanticisation of landscape plays a major role in accounts of enclosure, the clearance of eighteenth-century villages, the promotion of manifest destiny, modern nationalism, and the contestation of those movements.[42] Landscape has proved to be an important medium in the formation of race and class, where the misrepresentation of poverty through medical and crime statistics led to urban clearance and the resultant informal segregation of subalterns into economically isolated neighbourhoods.[43] Historians have located the emergence of modern sexual subculture in the early twentieth-century urban neighbourhoods of Paris, Chicago and New York where slumming elites met working-class men.[44] Landscape lies at the bottom of tensions between metropole and periphery; artificially constructed landscapes structure the separation between expert and local rule, working class and bourgeoisie, and public and domestic spheres.[45] In discussions of the construction of modern gender, race and class, of national boundaries and the dynamics of power, landscape studies has become a uniting methodology among historians, literary critics and sociologists trying to make sense of the modern. Spatial stories offer some of the most persuasive accounts of how identity is structured by institutions, neighbourhoods and networks.

These characterisations have dominated at the cost of other methods of analysis. The deeper history of landscape methods, stretching back to the early twentieth century, shows how an urge to tell the story of illiterate peasants sent scholars to the landscape itself for answers.

Landscape work begins by diversifying the scholar's understanding of where history takes place. Landscape opens the scholar to consider how events may be experienced from the very local to the global scale, from a street corner in Beijing to the Pacific Ocean itself. From the very vast to the very small, the earth itself offers a landscape that unites individuals in common experience, and it is the changes that punctuate that experience that the historian seeks.

As a lens, landscape methods force the scholar to expand their vision of agency. In my own work on the British roads system, I describe how the activities of political lobbyists and civil engineers created a new landscape – the road system – whose social consequences surpassed their capacity to plan. An early location of centrally organised expertise, the roads took watersheds out of the hands of local fishermen and orchards out of the hands of local farmers. They launched networks of travellers – soldiers, Methodists and artisans – who forged political identities and social organisations that rivalled the nation state in scale. A study of particular agents, like the civil engineers, would have never tied their work to the experience of Methodists riding on circuit. Concentrating upon the emergence of a new landscape, however, draws seemingly diverse actors into the same frame. These approaches afford the scholar the opportunity to put social, political and environmental history on the same page, to see how multiple causal factors converge in a variety of realities, intermingling, literally, in a single field. Considering the subject of history as the landscape itself breeds in the scholar the habits of looking at experience as a whole, asking what political, economic, environmental and social causes shade the experience of a particular place.

Finally, landscape works to encourage historians and students alike to remember that history is happening around them in everyday experience, where it may be observed by ordinary individuals as well as trained disciples. From the early twentieth century, radical historians began taking their students on walking tours of villages and everyday environments, even as labour historians of the 1970s took their students on tours of ethnic settlements and workers' housing. Historians like myself travel through decaying factories of the American Rust Belt to meditate on the economic fate of regions, while similar questions take Vanessa Schwartz to the burgeoning airports of the jet-set and Mike Davis to the slums of the global south.

These travels remind us to keep looking. For history is not some jewel locked in a rare archive, only accessible to the funded and privileged few. History is around us all the time, in the ever-present archive of the built environment. It is the purview of any who open their eyes. Ordinary journeys motivate us to ask how the landscape reflects the death and birth of new social forms. They remind us to ask how history takes place on the small scale of space as well as the great, in the alleyway as well as on the Silk Road. In the landscape, we remember to ask how tangled are the experiences of many actors, who interact, work, organise and consume in public spaces, where environment, politics and economics meet. Everyday journeys through ordinary environments inspire historians to draw together diverse methods, for they train the eye to read many stories on the same page.

NOTES

1. David J. Rothman, *The Discovery of the Asylum: Social Order and Disorder in the New Republic* (Boston, MA: Little, Brown and Co., 1971); Wolfgang Schivelbusch, *Disenchanted Night: the Industrialization of Light in the Nineteenth Century* (Berkeley, CA: University of California Press, 1995), [first published in German in 1983, *Lichtblicke, Zur Geschichte der Künstlichen Helligkkeit im 19 Jahrhundert* (Munchen: Carl Hanser Verlag, 1983)]; Roy Rosenzweig and Elizabeth Blackmar, *The Park and the People: a History of Central Park* (New York, NY: Cornell University Press, 1992); Benjamin Johnson and Pekka Hämäläinen, *Major Problems in the History of North American Borderlands*, Major Problems in American History Series (Andover: Cengage Learning, 2011).
2. Simon Gunn, 'The spatial turn: changing histories of space and place,' in Simon Gunn and Robert J. Morris (eds), *Identities in Space* (Burlington, VT: Ashgate, 2001), pp. 1–14; James Epstein, 'Spatial practices/

democratic vistas,' *Social History* 24:3 (1994), pp. 294–310; Diarmid A. Finnegan, 'The spatial turn: geographical approaches in the history of science,' *Journal of the History of Biology* (2008), pp. 369–88.

3. J. Barrell, *The Idea of Landscape and the Sense of Place, 1730–1840: an Approach to the Poetry of John Clare* (Cambridge: Cambridge University Press, 1972); John Barrell, *The Dark Side of the Landscape* (Cambridge: Cambridge University Press, 1980); Ann Bermingham, *Landscape and Ideology* (Berkeley, CA: University of California Press, 1986); J. Turner, *The Politics of Landscape* (Cambridge, MA: Harvard University Press, 1979); M. Andrews, *The Search for the Picturesque* (Palo Alto, CA: Stanford University Press, 1989); Keith Basso, *Wisdom Sits in Places* (Albuquerque, NM: University of New Mexico Press, 1996); Douglas S. Massey, Andrew B. Gross and Kumiko Shibuya, 'Migration, segregation, and the geographic concentration of poverty', *American Sociological Review* 59:3 (June 1994), pp. 425–45.

4. See D. Cosgrove, 'Landscape and Landschaft', *German Historical Institute Bulletin* 35 (2004), p. 64.

5. Henry Sumner Maine, *Ancient Law: its Connection with the Early History of Society, and Its Relation to Modern Ideas* (London: J. Murray, 1861).

6. 'Henry John Randall', *Dictionary of Welsh Biography 1941–1970* (London: Honourable Society of Cymmrodorion, 2001).

7. W. G. Hoskins, 'Review', *The English Historical Review* 72:282 (January 1957), p. 161; Henry John Randall, *The Creative Centuries, a Study in Historical Development* (London: Longmans Green and Co., 1945); Henry John Randall, *Bridgend, the Story of a Market Town* (Newport: R. H. Johns, 1955).

8. W. G. Hoskins, *The Making of the English Landscape* (London: Hodder and Stoughton, 1955).

9. Henry Randall, *History in the Open Air* (London: Allen and Unwin, 1936), pp. 35, 7.

10. Ibid. p. 35.

11. Hoskins, *The Making of the English Landscape*, pp. 210, 230.

12. M. W. Beresford, *History on the Ground: Six Studies in Maps and Landscapes* (London: Lutterworth Press, 1957), p. 19.

13. Henry Glassie, 'Eighteenth-century cultural process in Delaware Valley folk building', *Winterthur Portfolio* 7 (1972), pp. 29–30.

14. M. W. Barley, *The English Farmhouse and Cottage* (London: Routledge and Kegan Paul, 1961); Lawrence Stone, *The Crisis of the Aristocracy, 1558–1641* (Oxford: Clarendon Press, 1965), esp. ch. 10; Malcolm Airs, *The Making of the English Country House, 1500–1640* (London: Architectural Press, 1975); Colin Platt, *The Great Rebuildings of Tudor and Stuart England* (London: UCL Press, 1994).

15. Christopher Taylor, *Fields in the English Landscape* (London: J. M. Dent, 1975); Oliver Rackham, *Trees and Woodland in the British Landscape* (London: J. M. Dent, 1976); Tom Williamson, *Property and Landscape* (London: George Philip, 1987).

16. David P. Handlin, *The American Home* (Boston, MA: Little, Brown and Co., 1979); Kenneth Jackson, *Crabgrass Frontier* (New York, NY: Oxford University Press, 1985).

17. Rhys Isaac, *The Transformation of Virginia, 1740–1790* (Chapel Hill, NC: University of North Carolina Press, 1982); J. M. Vlach, 'The Shotgun House: an African architectural legacy,' *Afro-American Folk Art and Crafts* (1986), 275ff.

18. Gwendolyn Wright, *Moralism and the Model Home: Domestic Architecture and Cultural Conflict in Chicago, 1873–1913* (Chicago, IL: University of Chicago Press, 1980); Meryl Aldridge, 'Only demi-paradise? Women in garden cities and new towns,' *Planning Perspectives* 11:1 (1996), p. 23.

19. David Watkin, *The Rise of Architectural History* (London: Architectural Press, 1980); S. Giedion, *Space, Time and Architecture* (Cambridge, MA: Harvard University Press, 1941).

20. Hannah Arendt, *The Human Condition* (Chicago, IL: University of Chicago Press, 1958), chapter on fairs; Georges Duby, *The Europe of the Cathedrals, 1140–1280* (Geneva: Skira, 1966); Mona Ozouf, *Festivals and the French Revolution* (Cambridge, MA: Harvard University Press, 1988).

21. Gwendolyn Wright, 'Cultural history: Europeans, Americans, and the meanings of space', *Journal of the Society of Architectural Historians* 64:4 (December 2005), p. 437. Richard A. Goldthwaite, *The Building of Renaissance Florence* (Baltimore, MD: Johns Hopkins University Press, 1980); Carl E. Schorske, *Fin-de-Siècle Vienna* (New York, NY, 1980), esp. pp. 24–115; Joseph Rykwert, *The First Moderns* (Cambridge, MA: Harvard University Press, 1980); Lizabeth A. Cohen, 'Embellishing a life of labor: an interpretation of the material culture of American working-class homes, 1885–1915', *The Journal of American Culture* 3:4 (December 1980), pp. 752–75.

22. Sumner Chilton Powell, *Puritan Village* (Middletown, CT: Wesleyan University Press, 1963); James Sterling Young, *The Washington Community, 1800–1823* (New York, NY: Columbia University Press, 1966); Sam B. Warner Jr, *Streetcar Suburbs* (Cambridge, MA: Harvard University Press, 1962).

23. Akhil Gupta and James Ferguson, 'Beyond "culture": space, identity, and the politics of difference', *Cultural Anthropology* 7:1 (February 1992), pp. 6–23; Regenia Gagnier, 'Introduction: boundaries in theory and history', *Victorian Literature and Culture* 32:2 (2004), pp. 397–406;

Barbara Bender, 'Place and landscape', in Christopher Tilley (ed.), *Handbook of Material Culture* (London: Sage, 2006), pp. 303–24.

24. William Sewell, *Logics of History* (Chicago, IL: University of Chicago Press, 2005), p. 364. Simon Gunn, *The Public Culture of the Victorian Middle Class: Ritual and Authority in the English Industrial City, 1840–1914* (Manchester: Manchester University Press, 2000); Simon Gunn, 'Knowledge, power and the city since 1700', *Social History* 27:1 (2002), p. 61.

25. Roger Ebbatson, *An Imaginary England* (Aldershot: Ashgate, 2005); M. Warnke, *Political Landscape* (Cambridge, MA: Harvard University Press, 1995), p. 165; Jonathan Bordo, 'Picture and witness at the site of the wilderness', *Critical Inquiry* 26:2 (2000), p. 224ff.

26. David J. Rothman, *The Discovery of the Asylum* (Boston, MA: Little, Brown and Co., 1971); A. Scull, 'The insanity of place', *History of Psychiatry* 15:4 (2004), pp. 417–36.

27. Patrick Joyce, *The Rule of Freedom* (London: Verso, 2003); Robin Evans, *The Fabrication of Virtue* (Cambridge: Cambridge University Press, 1982); Miles Ogborn, 'Discipline, government and law: separate confinement in the prisons of England and Wales, 1830–1877', *Transactions of the Institute of British Geographers* 20:3 (1995), p. 295ff.

28. Asa Briggs, *Victorian Cities* (Berkeley, CA: University of California Press, 1993); Robert Tittler, *Architecture and Power* (Oxford: Oxford University Press, 1991); James Vernon, *Politics and the People: a Study in English Political Culture, c. 1815–1867* (Cambridge: Cambridge University Press, 1993).

29. Pierre Nora, *Les Lieux De Mémoire* (Paris: Gallimard, 1984); J. Winter, *Sites of Memory, Sites of Mourning* (Cambridge: Cambridge University Press, 1995); Kirk Savage, *Standing Soldiers, Kneeling Slaves* (Princeton, NJ: Princeton University Press, 1997).

30. Dana Arnold, *Re-Presenting the Metropolis* (London: Ashgate Publishing, 2000).

31. Peter Hall, *Cities of Tomorrow* (Oxford: Blackwell, 1988); James Burkhart Gilbert, *Perfect Cities* (Chicago, IL: University of Chicago Press, 1991); David Matless, *Landscape and Englishness* (London: Reaktion Books, 1998).

32. David Gebhard, 'The American Colonial Revival in the 1930s', *Winterthur Portfolio* 22:2 (Summer–Autumn 1987), pp. 109–48; Edward N. Kaufman, 'The architectural museum from world's fair to restoration village,' *Assemblage* 9 (June 1989), pp. 21–39; Stephen Meyer, 'Adapting the immigrant to the line: Americanization in the Ford factory, 1914–1921,' *Journal of Social History* 14:1 (Autumn 1980), pp. 67–82.

33. A. H. Robinson, 'The 1837 maps of Henry Drury Harness', *Geographical*

Journal 121:4 (1955), pp. 440–50; E. W. Gilbert, 'Pioneer maps of health and disease in England', *Geographical Journal* 124:2 (1958), pp. 172–83.

34. Justin Stagl, *A History of Curiosity* (Chur: Harwood Academic Publishers, 1995); Richard Helgerson, 'The land speaks: cartography, chorography, and subversion in Renaissance England', *Representations* 16 (Autumn 1986), pp. 50–85.

35. J. B. Harley, 'Silences and secrecy: the hidden agenda of cartography in early modern Europe', *Imago Mundi* 40:1 (1988), p. 59ff.

36. Matthew H. Edney, *Mapping an Empire* (Chicago, IL: University of Chicago Press, 1997); Josef W. Konvitz, 'The nation-state, Paris and cartography in eighteenth- and nineteenth-century France', *Journal of Historical Geography* 16:1 (January 1990), pp. 3–16; Antoine Picon, 'Nineteenth-century urban cartography and the scientific ideal: the case of Paris', *Osiris* 18, 2nd series (2003), pp. 135–49.

37. Pamela K. Gilbert, *Mapping the Victorian Social Body* (Albany, NY: State University of New York Press, 2004), p. 19.

38. Mary Burgan, 'Mapping contagion in Victorian London: disease in the East End', in Debra N. Mancoff and D. J. Trela (eds), *Victorian Urban Settings: Essays on the Nineteenth-Century City and Its Contexts* (New York, NY: Garland, 1996), pp. 43–56.

39. J. A. Yelling, 'The metropolitan slum: London 1918–51', in S. Martin Gaskell (ed.), *Slums* (Leicester: Leicester University Press, 1990), pp. 186–233.

40. Frank Zephyr, 'Layers, flows and intersections: Jeronymo José de Mello and artisan life in Rio de Janeiro, 1840s–1880s', *Journal of Social History* (Winter 2007), p. 319ff.

41. Mary Ellis Gibson, 'Review: representing the nation: poetics, landscape, and empire in nineteenth-century culture', *Victorian Literature and Culture* 27:1 (1999), pp. 337–52; W. J. T. Mitchell (ed.), *Landscape and Power*, 2nd edn (Chicago, IL: University of Chicago Press, 2002).

42. J. Turner, *The Politics of Landscape* (Cambridge, MA: Harvard University Press, 1979); John Barrell, *The Dark Side of the Landscape* (Cambridge: Cambridge University Press, 1980); Ian Ousby, *The Englishman's England* (Cambridge: Cambridge University Press, 1990); Stephen Daniels, *Fields of Vision* (Cambridge: Polity Press, 1993); Elizabeth K. Helsinger, *Rural Scenes and National Representation* (Princeton, NJ: Princeton University Press, 1997).

43. Sharene Razack, *Race, Space, and the Law* (Toronto: Between the Lines, 2002); Benjamin J. Lammers, 'The birth of the East Ender: neighborhood and local identity in interwar east London', *Journal of Social History* 39:2 (Winter 2005), pp. 331–44.

44. George Chauncey, *Gay New York* (New York, NY: Basic Books, 1994);

Seth Koven, *Slumming* (Princeton, NJ: Princeton University Press, 2004); Chad C. Heap, *Slumming* (Chicago, IL: University of Chicago Press, 2009).

45. Gareth Stedman Jones, 'Working-class culture and working-class politics in London, 1870–1900: notes on the remaking of a working class', *Journal of Social History* 7:4 (Summer 1974), pp. 460–508; Leonore Davidoff and Catherine Hall, *Family Fortunes: Men and Women of the English Middle Class 1780–1850* (New York, NY: Routledge, 2002).

FURTHER READING

Barrell, John, *The Dark Side of the Landscape* (Cambridge: Cambridge University Press, 1980).

Beresford, M. W, *History on the Ground; Six Studies in Maps and Landscapes* (London: Lutterworth Press, 1957).

Bermingham, Ann, *Landscape and Ideology* (Berkeley, CA: University of California Press, 1986).

Giedion, S., *Space, Time and Architecture* (Cambridge, MA: Harvard University Press, 1941).

Gunn, Simon, 'The spatial turn: changing histories of space and place', in Simon Gunn and Robert J. Morris (eds), *Identities in Space* (Burlington, VT: Ashgate, 2001).

Hoskins, W. G., *The Making of the English Landscape* (London: Hodder and Stoughton, 1955).

Jackson, Kenneth, *Crabgrass Frontier* (New York, NY: Oxford University Press, 1985).

Mitchell, W. J. T. (ed.), *Landscape and Power*, 2nd edn (Chicago, IL: University of Chicago Press, 2002).

Nora, Pierre, *Les Lieux De Mémoire*, 2 vols (Paris: Gallimard, 1984). Randall, Henry, *History in the Open Air* (London: Allen and Unwin, 1936).

PART 2

Researching Individuals and Groups

CHAPTER 6

Collective Biography

Krista Cowman

INTRODUCTION: COLLECTIVE BIOGRAPHY, WHAT IT IS AND WHAT IT IS NOT

Biographies, or written accounts of lives constructed by an author other than the biographical subject, were some of the earliest histories. Biography is, at its simplest, the history of an individual's life, generally arranged chronologically from birth to death and set in a wider historical context. Biography is sometimes considered to be a rather poor relation to 'serious' history. Its subjects are condemned for being too trivial (rock stars, models, footballers) or it is criticised for perpetuating an old-fashioned 'great men' approach to history (prime ministers, generals, royalty). Yet its popularity amongst the general reading public remains high with the genre continuing to dominate lists of bestselling books. Biography has also enjoyed something of a rapprochement with history in recent decades. Many historians are rediscovering an interest in individuals and their subjective experiences. This interest has often had political motivations; socialist and feminist historians found that this was one way in which they could restore the marginalised lives of workers, women and children to the historical record.[1] It may also be part of a broader shift away from a focus on nation states or collectivities, parties and systems to consideration of how the individual acts within these or is affected by them. Biographical approaches were also influential in enabling historians to move into new or different fields of inquiry and interrogate more private arenas such as childbirth or fatherhood.[2] Although historians do write biographies of single subjects, many who use biography as a methodology will focus on several lives, producing a collective rather than an individual biography. The methodology of collective biography has an equally long presence in history and has enjoyed something of resurgence in recent decades, particularly in women's history and social history as well as in certain forms of political history. Despite this, very little has been written to date about the method. Rather, there is a large degree of imprecision surrounding the use of the term 'collective biography' by historians. This imprecision has become so pronounced that any attempt to define what the methodology of collective biography might actually be or to suggest how a researcher might go about constructing a collective biography needs to begin by first explaining what it is *not*.

Since the 1970s it has been common for many discussions of historical methods to switch between the two separate terms of 'collective biography' and 'prosopography', interchanging them as if these were one and the same thing. At first this conflation was not necessarily awkward. Although usage of the term 'prosopography' has been traced back to the sixteenth century, its most commonly cited definition amongst historians remains that coined by Laurence Stone in 1971. He defined prosopography as 'the investigation of the common background characteristics of a group of actors in history by means of a collective study of their lives'.[3] Stone's definition did not exclude other levels of enquiry, but he did suggest that the main utility of such an approach lay in the light it shed on the 'roots of political action' as well as in its ability to engage with 'social structure and mobility'.[4] At this point in the 1970s, Stone saw prosopography as having two main applications in historical research. The first of these was in elite studies as practised by Classicists but also being applied to more recent centuries by historians such as Namier and Neale. 'Elite' could also be used in a broader sense to encompass newly emerging power groups such as in Lasswell and Lerner's 1965 examination of revolutionary leaderships.[5] The second field, which was more concerned with social than political history, Stone termed the 'mass school . . . concerned with large numbers, about all . . . of whom . . . nothing very detailed can be known'.[6]

Although there could be some discussion of individual biographical data in each of these fields, in both a focus on the group was paramount, as was an interest in how the group impacted on certain things – systems, organisations, institutions – rather than a more subjective concern about how engagement with these things affected the individuals of whom the group was comprised. Nevertheless, within the studies Stone offers as examples, individuals' lives can be disaggregated without too much difficulty. More recently, prosopographers have been keen to develop a clear distinction between their work and the methodology of biography, collective or otherwise. Technological advances have fed into this: whilst earlier research relied on the painstaking processes of handwritten notes or index cards common to biographers and prosopographers alike, the latter can now draw on a variety of numerous sophisticated computer programs capable of dealing with vast amounts of data. Consequently prosopography now tends towards larger-scale quantitative analyses that 'present[s] evidence about the individual . . . only in order to uncover the collective and the normal'.[7] Its focus lies increasingly 'not on the individual *per se*, but upon the total collection of individuals in aggregate' and prospographical research projects are as likely to produce databases as texts, as in *The Continental Origins of English Landowners*.[8] In the light of this, the historian undertaking a collective biography can no longer 'insist on using . . . [the term prosopography] because she likes it' as one leading prosopographer has pointed out.[9]

Several historians continue to do exactly this, often in texts aimed at introducing undergraduate readers to the terminology of historical studies. Writing on Namier in *The Pursuit of History*, for example, John Tosh described how 'his method was essentially collective biography [for which the technical term is "prosopography"]' whilst Arthur Marwick defined prosopography as 'multiple biography, the building up of an interpretation of the past by detailed biographical study of individuals'.[10] Consequently, few historians engaged in collective biography have paused to consider how their projects might differ from prosopography. One exception is Barbara Caine, a historian who has used biographical techniques in much of her work. She suggests that prosopgraphy should be viewed quite separately from biography as 'its aim is not in any way to create or establish a better understanding of individuals and their motives or their life experiences'.[11] The distinction implied here between the 'subjective', close focus of collective biography and the broader 'objective' represented by prosopography has led some observers to imply a weakness in the former methodology, encapsulated in the assertion that collective biography 'is not based upon rigorously established selection criteria' but lacks precision.[12] This chapter aims to show that collective biography is not a 'watered down' form of prosopography; rather it is a distinct methodology which self-consciously retains a focus on the individual even when it sits within work which aims to use individual lives to explore collective experiences, or within studies of communities (geographically, socially or culturally defined).

Another interpretation of 'collective biography' which does not reflect its use by historians emerges when the term is used to denote work which contains elements of both biography and autobiography. In Britain, Liz Stanley was amongst the first to challenge the artificiality of the distinction between 'biography' and 'autobiography' through the concept of 'auto/biography'. Stanley does 'not . . . deny that there are differences between different forms of life writing' but argues that 'these differences are not generic'.[13] The blurring of the auto/biographical distinction is taken much further in the radical work of German sociologist Frigga Haug, best known to English-speaking readers through the translation of her 1987 work *Female Sexualization*. Haug and her colleagues, concerned with processes of socialisation, were reacting against what they saw as an unbridgeable gap between Marxist theory on the one hand and their own experiences as women on the other. To overcome this they evolved a methodology of 'memory work', a collaborative exercise which placed their own, not necessarily chronological, reconstructed experiences at the centre of their research. Bronwyn Davis, Susanne Gannon and others have developed a research technique now popular in women's studies which operates on similar lines, describing their methodology as 'collective biography'.[14] In their recent work, the actual 'formation of the collective' – usually around seven participants – is the first step of the research.[15] In both of these examples, the biographies considered were those that the researchers themselves constructed of their own lives.

Haug's work has had less influence amongst historians although there are a small number of collective biographies which have attempted to break down the auto/biographical distinction. Carolyn Steedman's *Landscape for a Good Woman* merges her mother's biography with that of her own life to consider broader themes of class and education in the lives of women in post-war Britain. Rather than attempting to stand aside from her biographical subjects, Stanley argued for 'the encapsulating of process in biography', something she practised directly in her co-authored study of the suffragette Emily Wilding Davison.[16] In this text (which is really a collective biography of the women who comprised Emily Davison's friendship network) the narrative is punctured in several places by descriptions of conversations between the co-authors which detail false leads as well as research successes. In her *Autobiography of a Generation: Italy 1968* the Italian historian Luisa Passerini interjected personal narratives even more directly, juxtaposing her interviews with political activists with descriptions of the progress of the psychoanalysis she underwent whilst writing the book as a means of exploring some of the collective historical experience of Italian radicalism.[17] More recently, in a project entitled 'ego histories', Pierre Nora has encouraged historians to construct their own biographies as a way of enhancing understanding of the complex connections between historian and historical subject.[18] Nora's approach has inspired further projects such as *Ngapartji ngapartji/In turn in turn* where European and Indigenous life stories were grouped together to offer new perspectives on both experiences.[19] Generally, however, the collective biographies produced by historians focus on the lives of subjects other than the writer/researcher.

HISTORY AND VARIETIES OF COLLECTIVE BIOGRAPHY

The first collective biographies date back to classical times. Works such as Nepos' *Lives of Eminent Comanders* and Phaenias' *Tyrants of Sicily* were in effect compilations of biographical essays giving overlapping or comparative details about a number of individuals. These earliest collective biographical compilations focused on civic, military or religious leaders. They were joined in the eighteenth century by collections which appeared throughout

Europe, defined by the occupation of their subjects and prompted, according to Keith Thomas, by 'the desire of emerging professional groups to establish a pedigree for themselves'.[20] Collective biographical compilations were originally constructed by men (and frequently included mostly male subjects) and the methodology remains popular in the field of leadership studies today.[21] Nevertheless, by the nineteenth century the practitioners of what Sybil Oldfield has termed an 'often naïve but always influential' form of historical writing were overwhelmingly female as were the subjects of their writing.[22] Compilations of female lives became an international phenomenon with collections such as Fortunée Briquet's *Dictionnarie Historique, Littéraire et Bibliographique des Françaises* (1804), Wanyan Yn Shu's *Precious Record from the Maiden's Chambers* (1831) and Elizabeth Ellet's *Pioneer Women of the West* (1852) spanning the globe in their place of publication as well as in the scope of their content.[23] The growth of an organised feminist movement augmented this process, increased the number of female authors involved in it and expanded the subject base to include more secular and less exceptional subjects. The aim of this work was to transform women's experience into a matter of historical record and thus to legitimise contemporary feminist activity by suggesting precedents. Rohan Maitzen has argued that they offered 'a female tradition' which allowed women to draw on 'the empowering sense of historical inheritance', which was particularly critical 'in an age placing so much importance on history'.[24] Compilations, at their most basic level, functioned by furnishing more examples and thus were more desirable than individual subjects. By the start of the twentieth century other political movements were making pragmatic use of collective biography's ability to furnish a number of historical precedents or examples. Similar work was thus undertaken by socialist parties who offered biographical sketches of national and local leaders in publications such as the *Labour Annual and Reformer's Year Book* and provided the inspiration (and much of the raw material) for a generation of later works such as the *Dictionary of Labour Biography* or the *Dictionnaire Biographique du Mouvement Ouvrier Français*.

Many of the works cited above also served to challenge a further, distinct type of collective biographical compilation, that of the national biographical dictionary. Such works, according to Thomas, had become 'an obligatory accompaniment to the process of European state formation' by the end of the nineteenth century and are still seen as critical to the process of forging a sense of national unity in the present day.[25] In South Africa, for example, although dictionaries of national biography existed under apartheid, a *New Dictionary of South African Biography* was published in the year after its fall. Nelson Mandela contributed a foreword in which he emphasised the importance to a new South Africa of a work which would acknowledge 'the role of the many hitherto unclaimed people whose past work and struggle have contributed to much to the future of our nation'.[26] Essays in national biographies tend towards the commemorative rather than the interpretive; as Thomas noted of the *New Dictionary of National Biography*, 'essentially, it offers narratives of public careers' and not detailed considerations of the inner lives of its subjects.[27] Yet the subjects selected for inclusion in recent national biographical projects do reflect broader social changes since the nineteenth century. Old 'heroes' are displaced; the *Neue Deutsche Biographie* has just over eight pages on Bismarck compared with the 200 given to his entry in an earlier edition whilst the *New Dictionary of South African Biography* shifted from Afrikaner nationalists to prominent members of the African National Congress or participants in the anti-apartheid movement.[28] Another noticeable change has been the increased numbers of women in these works. This represents more than a reflection of the broader opportunities for women in many countries over the past century, which have offered larger numbers of potential female subjects. Thomas explained how whereas in the original *Dictionary of National Biography* 'subjects were children of a father *by* a mother' they were granted 'a father *and* a mother' in the 1950 edition with many of these mothers becoming subjects in their own right in later editions.[29]

Although the intent behind them may differ, biographical compilations all function as sources offering factual data which is intended to underpin further historical research. In the latter part of the twentieth century two further types of collective biography developed, both with a more analytical dimension. These can be described as 'group biographies' where the focus on individuals is joined by an interest in the structures, networks and ideologies which connect them. In some instances their production has been enabled through advances in technology; the 'themes' section of the *Dictionary of National Biography*, for example, currently hosts essays on more than 300 'group essays' on subjects ranging from participants in the fifteenth-century Battle of Agincourt to the members of the inter-war 'Tots and Quots' dining club.[30] Much of the history presented in these themes is concerned with the origins, activities and philosophies of the groups themselves; information on individual members is accessed via a further layer of weblinks which direct readers back to the original dictionary entries. The second type of 'group' collective biography involves a study where the biographical subjects considered are linked or connected in some way through family, métier or politics. This approach has been used in many fields of historical inquiry including social and political history but has been particularly popular within women's history where biography's focus on the intimate, interior and personal life of its subject fitted well with studies of private or domestic life or friendship and personal relations which characterised this field.

A useful attempt to navigate these varying descriptions of collective biography when practised by historians comes from Barbara Caine who suggested that collective biography was best conceived as 'a continuum, extending from individual studies which are grouped together to make up a collective whole. . . to those works in which the primary subject is a group of people, and which focus on the interactions and shared experiences of its members'.[31] Biographical collections, intended to facilitate further research, continue to be produced although these are more likely to be large, joint project such as the *Biographical Dictionary of Scottish Women,* which had four editors and almost 300 contributors. Historians using the methodology to investigate specific questions tend to favour the 'group' forms of collective biography and look to it as a means of investigating connections between individuals as well as considering some of the personal motivations which might underpin collective actions.

WHAT DOES COLLECTIVE BIOGRAPHY BRING TO HISTORY?

The biographer's engagement with sources that shed light on the individuals' experience mirrors that of the historian. Both work with the same raw material – sources which are closely associated with a particular individual (birth and death certificates, census returns, school reports, letters, diaries, personal statements) – in order to reconstruct and interpret their lives. Like historians, biographers too 'try to make a coherent narrative out of missing documents as well as existing ones', contextualising their material and filling in gaps with the help of less personal sources.[32] Often, the biographer's problem is one of too little material, a problem which similarly concerns the historian. When she began the work of constructing a life of the English artist Roger Fry, Virginia Woolf posed a question which all historians would recognise; 'How can one make a life out of six cardboard boxes full of tailors' bills, love letters and old picture postcards?' For many women's historians, an initial reaction could well be one of envy. Six boxes of material is five more than one often has to work with, heightening Woolf's sense of anxiety amongst those trying to reconstruct a life out of much less. Nevertheless, the 'recovery' of forgotten or unknown women as historical subjects was an essential part of the women's history associated with second-wave feminism, which emerged as a distinct academic subject in Britain in the late 1970s. The lives of a number of earlier feminist activists were reconstructed from disparate and sparse archival sources as expanding curricula demanded materials for students eager to learn more about women's history. Although these were mainly single-subject biographies they were marked by certain characteristics which had implications for a collective approach. The first of these was a commitment to interdisciplinarity. In many universities women's history was closely connected with the emergence and growth of women's studies courses, which encouraged the incorporation of theoretical perspectives from disciplines such as literary studies, psychoanalysis and sociology into historical research. Secondly, women's historians often faced a paucity of sources which rendered convenional biographical approaches (replicating real time and offering a life from start to finish) impossible; fragmentary records of women's lives required a different approach.

Both of these had implications for collective biographies with female subjects. Inter-disciplinarity enabled a shifting of the biographical focus from the life of an individual to an approach which viewed aspects of the world through the prism of a particular life. An excellent example of this is Carolyn Steedman's biography of Margaret McMillan, which uses its subject's life as a means of exploring the themes of childhood, culture and class in the late nineteenth and early twentieth centuries. Steedman's biography reflects Angelica Schaser's observation that 'the choice of a female subject' challenges the accepted form of 'standard male biography' and 'turns the traditional form of biography into an innovative affair'.[33] In her text, the conventional chronology of a biographical narrative (birth and childhood, adolescence, young adulthood, maturity, old age) is replaced by a series of thematic engagements with the subject. Strands of nineteenth-century socialist thought, which emphasised the importance of improving the lives of working-class children and arguably paved the way for key elements of the post-war British welfare state, are interrogated through McMillan's own work in this area.

Steedman also had to overcome the second common problem for women's historians, that of a lack of sources. Her biography of McMillan was rendered problematic by the fact that her subject was 'a public woman who lived in a public space' leaving none of the conventional biographical sources such as diaries, letters or expansive personal testimonies from which an interior life could be reconstructed.[34] There were no apparent secrets which could be uncovered, no close relationships where ideas could be seen to be formed or shared. Instead, what McMillan left was a large quantity of public writing; articles for the socialist press, pamphlets and records of her numerous political speeches. Any personal detail about her life which she committed to paper survived only in the peculiar form of a biography that McMillan herself wrote of her sister, Rachel. Steedman's work suggested that McMillan's public life was troublesome to a biographer because women's lives, when they were written, were shaped by 'the dead weight of interiority'.[35] Thus presenting only the public life of a public woman was a radical departure from previous biographies of female subjects which concentrated on their personal lives in a way which arguably upheld gendered notions about the separation of public and private life.

Steedman's decision to compensate for the lack of private sources about her single subject by applying a bibliographical approach to her public writing offered a useful model for collective biographies of female political activists. Although extremely valuable as sources in their own right, some of the earlier biographical projects of women's history had come dangerously close to replicating what Natalie Davis criticised as the 'women worthies' school of historical writing, focusing on leaders of parties or organisations who tended to be the subjects for whom the most information was available. If Margaret McMillan's life could be recovered and interpreted without the help of a significant archive then this opened the possibility for further work considering aspects or parts of lives which were even less well documented. One work that does this is Sandra Holton's *Suffrage Days*, which uses the lives of seven individuals (six women and one man) as a means of exploring the changing preoccupations and priorities of the women's suffrage movement in Britain. Holton's work is an excellent example of a collective biography where the lives are linked by a theme rather than intertwined through deep personal connections. Holton admitted that her subjects 'did not . . . form, in life, a distinct grouping of their own making' and although each of them 'knew at least one of the others personally' some of her subjects were unlikely to have ever met each other.[36]

Holton explained that she chose to use collective biography as she believed that this would enable her 'to escape from the existing frameworks and conceptualisation presently organising' suffrage history at the point that she was writing.[37] Her book emerged at a point when suffrage history (and particularly engagement with militancy) was enjoying renewed popularity, and offers a good example of how the methodology of collective biography might alter conventional views of a subject. Much of the new suffrage history of the 1990s was motivated by a desire to move away from the orthodoxy promulgated by a series of narratives which placed both London and the Pankhurst family (or more accurately the mother and daughter combination of Emmeline and Christabel Pankhurst) at their centre in order to explore how the campaign may have had different forms elsewhere. Holton's text was not shaped by the traditional chronology of the suffrage movement which revolved around the formation and splitting of particular organisations or the rise and fall of governments. Instead it is arranged around the activities and concerns of a group of individuals whose engagement with suffrage extended its chronology back to the early 1860s. Focusing on this particular group also broadened the focus of the campaign's concerns through exploring how the individuals selected had negotiated the boundaries of class and sexuality in their own lives. Although many of Holton's subjects offered more in the way of public than private sources she did not follow Steedman's approach in attempting to move away from their interior lives entirely. Rather she emphasised the ways in which 'the entwining of formal politics and the politics of personal life;

of gendered identities, concepts of citizenship and the passions of love and friendship' illuminated the political movement which is the book's main focus.

The two examples above draw implicitly on literary theories of biography, but historical collective biography has also been particularly influenced by methodological trends in the social sciences. Here, a 'biographical turn' (with significant involvement by practitioners of oral history) has displayed a renewed interest in personal and individual experiences whilst at the same time encouraging the study of 'linked lives' rather than single exhaustive reproductions. Searching for the antecedents of more recent biographical approaches, Chamberlayne, Bornat and Wengraf have noted engagement with personal sources such as diaries, letters or autobiographies in both history and sociology throughout the twentieth century but concur that the 'more decisive shift to embrace personal accounts' came in social science and history in the 1960s.[38] In history, approaches associated with social history or history from below took up this approach as one way of reinstating marginalised groups within the historical record, most obviously in the field of women's history as discussed above. Personal testimony – in the form of oral history where possible, or in other forms such as court testimonies or similar for the less recent past – replaced more traditional documentary sources to create histories of the family, childhood, crime and industrialisation which all placed a value on subjective experience. The main force behind the move from single to plural studies by social scientists has been to counter accusations of atypicality or unrepresentativeness. For historians who are less likely to create their own data (unless using oral history) collective studies have suggested some useful ways in which sparse sources can be spread. Prue Chamberlayne and Antonella Spanò, researchers on a large project concerned with exploring social change in modern European society, explained what they felt was its particular utility:

> While it is often feared that working from individual case studies will lead to false generalisations, in our experience the particularity of case studies has enriched our appreciation of complexity and differentiation and alerted us to the interpenetration of contrasting social forms. In fact the 'single case' is not single, since it is relativised by other cases in the study, and by the wide knowledge of the researchers which is brought to bear in the interpretation.[39]

COLLECTIVE BIOGRAPHY

Many historical collective biographies have selected their subjects in line with the concept of generations as used by social scientists. Historical generational studies have sought to answer how 'people who have been born . . . in the same period of time come to a common understanding of their experience'.[40] This concept underpins much recent work on the internal mechanisms of the Nazi regime in Germany where historians have combined an emphasis on the history of the ordinary, everyday life viewed from below encompassed in *Alltagsgeschichte* with material emerging from newly available archives from eastern Europe. Michael Wildt, who studied the workings of the Reich Security Head Office (RSHO) from 1939, noted that the majority of its leadership 'was from a specific generation' born just after 1900 who were old enough to remember the First World War but not to have served in it.[41] Wildt argued that the experiences this generation shared at the same age moulded their consciousness and shaped their responses. However, although he is keen to use a collective biographical approach to understand what motivated the RSHO leaders to commit certain acts, Wildt remains cautious about relying on this alone, arguing that 'the question about the motivation . . . must also take into consideration an analysis of the society, the structures of the power apparatus' in which individuals were situated.[42] Historians of eastern Europe have similarly used cohorts as a means of framing collective biographical studies. Robert Miller, Robin Humphrey and Elena Zdravomyslova have argued that 'when genuinely important historical transitions happen to coincide with one's entry into young adulthood, personal and historical significance interact and intensify'.[43]

Other historians take a broader view of what comprises a generation. A good example of a historical collective biography which draws on this approach but applies it in a more flexible manner is that of Brian Harrison's 1987 work *Prudent Revolutionaries: Portraits of British Feminists Between the Wars*, one of the first studies of the British feminist movement in the interwar years. Harrison opted for collective biography as he believed that this was an excellent way of conveying the range of feminism at this time as well as the importance of 'the interaction between its leading personalities'.[44] He arranged his material in ten chapters which focused on between one and three individuals, fifteen biographical subjects in total. He defined this as 'group-biography' although it is better described as 'collective biography' as the subjects did not belong to an identifiable group beyond that of a large and broadly defined feminist movement. Harrison used the term 'generation' when discussing his subjects but differed from social science approaches in his assertion that 'Group-biography cuts across chronology'.[45] His subjects did not experience the key external events of his study at the same age; although he refers to them as the 'first generation of enfranchised women' the youngest, Ellen Wilkinson, was born in 1891, putting her in the anomalous position of being too young to vote when she first stood as a parliamentary candidate in 1923 whilst Millicent Fawcett and Emmeline Pankhurst were in their seventies.[46] Thus, for Harrison, what united his selected subjects into a generation was shared (and often collective) feminist activism, the 'organizational context' of their lives and the networks they forged through several women's organisations which were enhanced or challenged by their differing priorities.[47] Philippa Levine applied a similar approach to her study of an earlier period of feminist politics, *Feminist Lives in Victorian England*, which takes a heavily biographical approach. Levine looked at four generations of women active in the feminist movement.[48] As in Harrison's work, for Levine it is the overlap and connections between individuals rather than their birth age which determined their political outlook.

Levine's work points us to a further important strand of work, that which adopts a biographical approach but does not organise its narrative around individual biographical studies. June Hannam and Karen Hunt followed this approach in *Socialist Women: Britain, 1880s to 1920s*, using biographies 'to reflect on what the key issues were for women who were socialists' rather than to attempt to identify a homogenous group.[49] Biographical detail permeates the narrative of *Socialist Women* but is not separated out in the text. *Women of the Right Spirit*, my own study of the paid organisers employed by the militant suffrage organisation the Women's Social and Political Union uses a similar biographical approach for three reasons. Firstly, as the paid organisers represented a tier of official leadership largely missing from existing accounts of the WSPU, examining the organisation's work from their perspective (including consideration of their relationship with both their members and their political employers) offered an obvious means of testing statements regarding the extent of the WSPU's autocracy. Secondly, I had no wish to write a conventional political history of the WSPU which would concentrate on its organisational development, policies or interaction with other contemporary political bodies. My concern was to investigate the effect that embarking on political activism had on an individual rather than on considering how a group of individuals shaped a political organisation. Finally, in common with most other historians working on women and politics, I also wished to explore personal links and friendship networks in more detail which again lent itself to a biographical approach. Unlike Hannam and Hunt's work, however, there is some separation of biographical material in the form of an appendix which provides short biographical sketches for over 100 organisers.

CONSTRUCTING A COLLECTIVE BIOGRAPHY

How, then, might a researcher begin to use collective biography in historical research?

1. First, consider whether the project concerned is one which could be enhanced by a biographical approach. As noted above, many historians

have used this methodology in research which has attempted to incorporate personal perspectives on the past. Hermione Lee's study of the varied forms of literary biography noted a shift in the twentieth century towards less censorious, more revelatory approaches which drew readers to 'moments of intimacy, revelation or particular inwardness' in their subject's lives.[50] This trend has been helpful to historians researching themes such as sexuality or the history of the body. Personal perspectives have also been sought in an attempt to answer a range of questions from those concerned with individual motivations and experiences to the complex nature of broader social movements.

2. The next step is to identify the biographical subjects. Collective biographies do not have to contain vast numbers of subjects in order to add weight to their layers of evidence; some have as few as two. Assuming that the project is not one of large-scale biographical compilation there are a number of models which can be drawn on, as we have seen. An important guiding principle here is that the researcher should remain aware of the need to offer a sound rationale for the subjects chosen. It is important to avoid creating what Hannam and Hunt termed 'a patchwork of individual stories' which can lead to a lack of coherence, leaving the reader in some doubt as to why these particular lives have been combined.[51] Do not presume that the most obvious or apparently closest connections will lead to the strongest coherence. Barbara Caine's biography of the nine Potter sisters, *Destined to be Wives*, concluded that although 'the similarities in the general situation far outweigh any of the differences' in the experiences of her subjects' early years, the twenty years that separated the birth of the oldest daughter Lallie from that of her youngest sister Rosie ensured that some of the sisters experience 'whole historical epochs which were outside the knowledge of the others'.[52] On the other hand, studies which take more arbitrary connections, such as membership of political movements, have demonstrated how the genealogy of such movements can develop commonalities in individuals with no familial ties.

3. Once the subjects have been identified, biographical data must be assembled. Some subjects may have left significant archives but for others the researcher may have to undertake genealogical research to locate data on birth, education, marriage and death. Historians of nineteenth- and twentieth-century Britain have begun to make productive use of new online packages aimed primarily at family historians. These tools are particularly useful in collective biography as they enable rapid searches of census and similar data.

4. Once the data is assembled there are questions of how to handle different quantities of material. To retain a sense of balance, a collective biography must avoid falling into the trap of allowing the better-represented sources

to dominate its narrative as this will compromise the collective nature of the work. *Suffrage Days* dealt with subjects who had left very varied amounts of archival material; some wrote autobiographies supplemented by large numbers of papers whilst others were approached almost entirely through secondary sources such as obituaries or reported speech. Holton merged a chronological and thematic approach to prevent individual subjects from attaining too much prominence. The chapter on Jessie Craigen, the least well-documented of her biographical subjects, is used to explore the suffrage history of the 1880s, a period about which very little had previously been written. An imbalance between source material can also be smoothed over by exercising a degree of selectivity in examples to ensure that different voices are equally represented in the resulting narrative, quietening the dominant voices to enable all of the subjects to have their say.

CONCLUSION

This chapter has outlined some of the ways in which historians have used the methodological approach of collective biography in their work. An important part of this has been to distinguish between the varied uses and misuses of the term, drawing a distinction between prosopography and collective biography as practised by historians and outlining the various distinctions between collected biographies, group biographies and biographies of groups.

Historians have tended to use biographical methods in projects which aim to uncover individuals' experiences and foreground these in the analysis. This foregrounding of personal experience has led to one of the most common criticisms of biographical approaches to history; that they tend towards an uncritical acceptance of their material, overlooking the fact that biography is as much of a construction as other narrative forms. Yet many historians who use biographical approaches are aware of this danger. The best examples of collective biography do not seek to privilege personal experience over other forms of knowledge about the past, or to suggest that a biographical approach provides evidence which is inherently more trustworthy than other historical sources. Liz Stanley acknowledged this in her rejection of the metaphor of a microscope to describe her joint biography of Hannah Culwick and Arthur Munby. Instead, she suggested that biography was better considered as a '"kaleidoscope": each time you look you see something rather different, composed certainly of the same elements but in a new configuration'.[53] Good collective biography does not attempt to divorce individuals' own views of their experience from the social and political contexts in which these experiences were situated. As Ian Kershaw has noted, any individual actions 'can only be understood within the framework of the structures which conditioned them . . . Restricting analysis to one or the other offers a seriously diminished explanation'.[54]

Collective biographies are not unique to any particular field of historical enquiry but are more common in research which simultaneously attempts to uncover the lives of those considered marginal to the historical mainstream, hence their popularity in social history and amongst feminist historians. Collective biography has drawn heavily on literary studies in considering how to interpret and present lives, as well as observing the need to consider any individual life in the context of the other lives which overlapped with and shaped it.[55] More recently historians have also been influenced by methodologies from the social sciences. These have drawn attention to questions such as the number of lives required for a robust research project which might avoid accusations of atypicality. Social science methodology has also encouraged historians engaged in collective biographical research to consider different ways of thinking about what connects their multiple subjects, offering concepts such as that of the cohort or the generation.

The use of collective biography in history does not necessarily involve large numbers of subjects. Some of the more successful examples, as we have seen, involve no more than two lives, but pay constant attention to the connections and overlapping between them as well as the points at which they may have diverged. Collective biographies involving several subjects can often be much more fragmentary than standard biographies, sometimes only considering a few years in an individual's life but juxtaposing this with material from lives which linked in to these to offer a chronologically coherent narrative. In all instances the methodology remains an invaluable way of attempting to recover past experience as well as of suggesting ways in which this was shaped by the broader structures in which it was situated.

NOTES

1. Much of this is inspired by the work of E. P. Thompson who observed that the 'aspirations' of the English working class 'were valid in terms of their own experience'. E. P. Thompson, *The Making of the English Working Class* (London: Gollancz, 1963), p. 13. For histories which take this approach to consider the experiences of children or women, see for example Anna Davin, *Growing Up Poor: Home, School and Street in London, 1870–1914* (London: Rivers Oram Press, 1997); Ellen Ross, *Love and Toil: Motherhood in Outcast London 1870–1918* (Oxford: Oxford University Press, 1994).

2. For example, in John Tosh, *A Man's Place: Masculinity and the Middle-Class Home in Victorian England* (London: Yale University Press, 2007).

3. Laurence Stone, 'Prosopography', in Felix Gilbert and Stephen R. Graubard (eds), *Historical Studies Today* (New York, NY: W. W. Norton, [1971] 1972), p. 107. For origins of the term, see Timothy D. Barnes,'Prosopography modern and ancient', in Katharine S. B. Keats-Rohan (ed.), *Prosopography Approaches and Applications: a Handbook* (Oxford: Linacre College Unit for Prosoprography Research, 2007), pp. 71–82.

4. Stone, 'Prosopography', p. 107.

5. Harold D. Lasswell and David Lerner, *World Revolutionary Elites: Studies in Coercive Ideological Movements* (Cambridge, MA: MIT Press, 1965).

6. Stone, 'Prosopography', p. 109.

7. K. S. B. Keats-Rohan, 'Biography, identity and names: the pursuit of the individual in prosopography', in Keats-Rohan ed., *Prosopography Approaches*(Oxford: Unit for Prosopographical Research, 2007), pp. 139–81.

8. Dion Smythe, 'Putting technology to work: the CD ROM version of the prosopography of the Byzantine empire 1 (641–867)', *History and Computing* 12:1 (2000), pp. 85–98, cited in Keats-Rohan, 'Biography, identity and names', p. 140. The COEL project produced three books and a database which indexes tens of thousands of names occurring in immediate post-conquest administrative records. For more details see www.coelweb.co.uk [accessed 12 January 2016].

9. Keats-Rohan, 'Biography, identity and names', p. 145.

10. John Tosh, *The Pursuit of History*, 4th edn (London: Longman, 2006), p. 122; Arthur Marwick, *The New Nature of History: Knowledge, Evidence, Language* (Basingstoke: Palgrave Macmillan, 2001), p. 289.

11. Barbara Caine, *Biography and History* (Basingstoke: Palgrave Macmillan, 2010), p. 58.

12. Keats-Rohan, 'Biography, identity and names', p. 144.

13. Liz Stanley, *The Auto/Biographical I: the Theory and Practice of Feminist Auto/Biography* (Manchester: Manchester University Press, 1992), p. 3.

14. Bronwyn Davies and Susanne Gannon (eds), *Doing Collective Biography*. (Milton Keynes: Open University Press, 2006), p. 3.

15. M. Gonick and S. Gannon (eds), *Becoming Girl: Collective Biography and the Production of Girlhood* (Toronto: Women's Press, 2014).

16. Stanley, *The Auto/Biographical I*, p. 178.

17. Luisa Passerini, *Autobiography of a Generation: Italy, 1968* (Middletown, CT: Wesleyan University Press, 1996).

18. Pierre Nora and Alexander Geppert (eds), 'European ego-histories: historiography and the self, 1970–2000', *Historein* 3 (2003).

19. Vanessa Castejon, Anna Cole, Oliver Haag and Karen Hughes (eds), *Ngapartji Ngapartji/In turn in turn: Ego-histoire, Europe and Indigenous Australia* (Canberra: ANU Press, 2014).

20. Keith Thomas, *Changing Conceptions of National Biography: the Oxford DNB in Historical Perspective* (Cambridge: Cambridge University Press, 2005), p. 3.

21. See, for example, R. A. W. Rhodes and P. 't Hart (eds), *The Oxford Handbook of Political Leadership* (Oxford: Oxford University Press, 2014), pp. 318–24.

22. Sybil Oldfield, *Collective Biography of Women in England, 1550–1900: a Select, Annotated Bibliography* (London: Mansell, 1999).

23. Bonnie Smith, 'Gendering historiography in the global age: a US perspective', in Angelika Epple and Angelika Schaser (eds), *Gendering Historiography: Beyond National Canons* (Frankfurt: Campus Verlag, 2009), p. 35; Bonnie Smith, *The Gender of History: Men, Women and Historical Practice* (Cambridge, MA: Harvard University Press, 1998), p. 52.

24. Rohan Maitzen, '"This feminine preserve": historical biographies by Victorian women', *Victorian Studies* 38:3 (1995), pp. 371–93, p. 382.

25. Thomas, *Changing Conceptions*, pp. 14, 15.

26. Cited in Caine, *Biography and History*, p. 54.

27. Thomas, *Changing Conceptions*, p. 51.

28. Ibid. p. 44; Caine, *Biography and History*, p. 54.

29. Thomas, *Changing Conceptions*, p. 45.

30. See http://www.oxforddnb.com/themes [accessed 12 January 2016].

31. Caine, *Biography and History*, p. 48.

32. Hermione Lee, *Victoria Woolf's Nose: Essays on Biography* (Princeton, NJ: Princeton University Press, 2008), pp. 7–8.

33. Angelica Schaser, 'Women's biography–men's history?', in Volker R. Berghahn and Simone Lässing (eds), *Biography: Between Structure and Agency: Central European Lives in International Historiography* (New York and Oxford: Berghahn Books, 2007), pp. 72–84.

34. Carolyn Steedman, 'Forms of history, histories of form', in C. Steedman, *Past Tenses: Essays on Writing, Autobiography and History* (London: Rivers Oram Press, 1992), p. 164.

35. Steedman, 'Forms of history', p. 166.

36. Sandra Holton, *Suffrage Days: Stories from the Women's Suffrage Movement* (London: Routledge, 1987), p. 4.

37. Sandra Holton, 'Response to review of *Suffrage Days*', http://www.history.ac.uk/reviews/review/35/response [accessed 12 January 2016].

38. Prue Chamberlayne, Joanna Bornat and Tom Wengraf, 'Introduction', in P. Chamberlayne, J. Bornat and T. Wengraf (eds), *The Turn to Biographical Methods in Social Science: Comparative Issues and Examples* (London: Routledge, 2000), p. 3.

39. Prue Chamberlayne and Antonella Spanò, 'Modernisation as lived

experience: contrasting case studies from the SOSTRIS project', in Chamberlayne, Bornat and Wengraf (eds), *The Turn to Biographical Methods*, p. 334.

40. Michael Corsten, 'The time of generations', *Time and Society* 8:2–3 (1999), p. 280.

41. Michael Wildt, 'Generational experience and genocide, a biographical approach', in Berghahn and Lässig, *Biography: Between Structure and Agency*, p. 148.

42. Ibid. p. 199.

43. Robert Miller, Robin Humphrey and Elena Zdravomyslova, 'Introduction: biographical research and historical watersheds', in R. Miller, R. Humphrey and E. Zdravomyslova (eds), *Biographical Research in Eastern Europe: Altered Lives and Broken Biographies* (Aldershot: Ashgate, 2003), pp. 1–26.

44. Brian Harrison, *Prudent Revolutionaries, Portraits of British Feminists Between the Wars* (Oxford: Clarendon Press, 1987), p. 2.

45. Ibid. p. 3.

46. Ibid. p. 301.

47. Ibid. p. 8.

48. Philippa Levine, *Feminist Lives in Victorian England: Public Roles and Private Committment* (Oxford: Blackwell, 1990).

49. June Hannam and Karen Hunt, *Socialist Women, Britain, 1890s–1920s* (London: Routledge, 2002), p. 12.

50. Lee, *Virginia Woolf's Nose*, p. 2.

51. Hannam and Hunt, *Socialist Women*, p. 12.

52. Barbara Caine, *Destined to be Wives: the Sisters of Beatrice Webb* (Oxford: Clarendon Press, 1987), p. 8.

53. Stanley, *The Autobiographical I*, p. 6.

54. Ian Kershaw, 'Biography and the historian: opportunities and constraints', in Berghahn and Lässing, *Biography: Between Structure and Agency*, pp. 27–39.

55. See Stanley, *The Autobiographical I*, p. 9.

FURTHER READING

Booth, Alison, *How to Make it as a Woman: Collective Biographical History from Victoria to the Present* (Chicago, IL: University of Chicago Press, 2004).

Caine, Barbara, *Destined to be Wives: the Sisters of Beatrice Web* (Oxford: Clarendon Press, 1986).

Cowman, Krista, *Women of the Right Spirit! Paid Organizers in the Women's*

Social and Political Union, 1904–18 (Manchester: Manchester University Press, 2007).

Harrison, Brian, *Prudent Revolutionaries: Portraits of British Feminists Between the Wars* (Oxford: Clarendon Press, 1987).

Holton, Sandra Stanley, *Suffrage Days: Stories from the Women's Suffrage Movement* (London: Routledge, 1987).

Levine, Philippa, *Feminist Lives in Victorian England* (Oxford: Blackwell, 1990).

Stanley, Liz, *The Life and Death of Emily Wilding Davison* (London: The Women's Press, 1987).

Steedman, Carolyn, *Landscape for a Good Woman* (London: Virago, 1986).

Wildt, Michael, 'Generational experience and genocide: a biographical approach', in Volker R. Berghahn and Simone Lässig, *Biography: Between Structure and Agency: Central European Lives in International Historiography* (New York and Oxford: Berghahn Books, 2008), pp. 143–61.

CHAPTER 7

Life Stories and Historical Analysis

Alistair Thomson

History is the story we make of the stories we find. Our first duty as historians is to hear those found stories and understand what they meant in their own time.[1]

This chapter concerns methodological approaches to the life-story sources that people create in diaries, letters, memoirs and oral history. I won't consider approaches to finding such sources within archives or private collections, or indeed to creating them as oral historians do (see the list of Further Reading). I focus here on what methods historians use to make best sense of life-story sources.

Life stories offer rich and beguiling historical evidence, which historians have perceived and used in very different ways. At one extreme personal testimony is criticised as a flawed and unreliable historical source because of bias, self-justification or forgetfulness. Robert Rhodes James, for example, dismissed such sources as 'useful in conveying atmosphere . . . but on specifics . . . highly unreliable'. Memoirs and oral histories which are narrated with hindsight are regarded with the most suspicion. For military history, Richard Holmes argued that 'if you look at what veterans were writing just ten years after the end of the war, it's quite different from what they were writing at the time'. At the other extreme, enthusiasts and especially popular historians respond that personal narratives illuminate the lived experience and meanings of historical events, and the lives of groups of people – so-called 'ordinary' men and women – who are unlikely to be documented in the archives of the governing classes. Another war historian, Samuel Hynes, argues that 'if we would understand what war is like, and how it *feels*, we must . . . seek the reality in the personal witness of the men who were there'.[2]

Historians sometimes use different types of life stories interchangeably and uncritically, as if each variety of personal testimony offers the same type of evidence about the course of events and the participant's motivations, thoughts and feelings. Yet historians are now more likely to be influenced by the 'narrative turn' in the humanities and social sciences. We recognise that no historical source – whether first person account, parliamentary debate or statistical record – provides a direct, unmediated and uncomplicated access to the past. Every source is a constructed and selective representation of experience, and part of the historian's task is to consider the factors that shape the source and their relevance for our analysis.

Historians have no excuse for uncritical usage of autobiographical sources. Conventional methodological skills – background research to situate an account in its historical context, triangulation with other evidence, checking for internal and external consistency – are readily applied to personal testimony. And over the past two decades an extensive, multidisciplinary literature has developed a range of approaches for research using life-story sources. Literary studies,[3] narrative studies[4] and socio-linguistics offer ways of analysing language and story-telling. Anthropologists[5] illuminate the ethnographic contexts of narration, sociologists[6] show how to make connections between individual lives and wider social patterns, and social psychologists explain the relationships between life stories and personal identity.[7] Feminist researchers are particularly insightful about the gendered features of personal narratives and the power relations within which they are created and used, including their use by researchers.[8] Oral historians have helped us to understand the distinctive qualities of recorded memory.[9] This chapter draws on these different approaches and focuses on key features of personal testimony: the autobiographical impulse which motivates some people, in certain circumstances, to write or talk about their lives; the narrative relationship within which the story is recounted; the time of the telling; and the genre in which a life story is narrated.

For illustration I'll use a treasure trove of life stories by one British migrant to Australia. In 1960, Joan Pickett was a 26-year-old Manchester medical secretary when she took up a government-assisted passage and travelled to Australia. Joan spent eight years working her way around Australia and the islands of the Pacific, and might have settled 'down-under' had not her father's death brought her home to Manchester in 1968. Joan's personal archive for this period includes a journal of the voyage to Australia, hundreds of letters to her family, a short written memoir and oral history interviews I conducted in 2000 and 2006.[10]

My different uses of Joan's life stories demonstrate some of the ways in which historians can approach such sources. In *Ten Pound Poms*, Jim Hammerton and I used several hundred interviews with British migrants, along with letters, diaries and autobiographical writing, to write a life history of British post-war migration. Government statistics answered questions about how many and when; our life-story evidence answered more qualitative how and why questions and illuminated patterns, themes and meanings in the lived experience of migration. For example, to explain why people emigrated to Australia we listened closely to several hundred migrant oral histories and identified recurring factors such as economic and family circumstances in Britain, hopes and dreams for an Australian future, personal crises of identity or, most prosaically, the weather. We had enough stories to very approximately quantify the relative significance of such factors. Most important, a close reading of individual stories illuminated the complicated relationship between different factors in any one life story and for British migrants in general. This latter approach was developed more fully in *Moving Stories*, which used in-depth case studies with Joan Pickett and three other women migrants (a collective biography – see Krista Cowman's chapter) to explore the intimate history and subjectivity of women's post-war lives, as expressed in their letters and memories. What were the family dynamics and emotions of migration and how did these change over time? How do these women look back on migration and make sense of their own lives and of migrant women's history? Both thematic history and collective biography required a critical and reflective approach to my life-story sources.[11]

MAKING SENSE, MAKING STORY

The life story is, of course, never a perfect replay of events; it is created through language and is partial, selective and purposeful. As we first experience an event we struggle to articulate that experience, to give it shape and meaning. An initial blaze of short-term memory connections – sensual as much as cognitive – make multiple, fleeting records of experience. Memory theorists explain that within a short space of time we necessarily forget most of what happens – and lose most of those connections – and that a minority of personal experience is preserved in long-term memory through a process of cognitive articulation that creates meaningful neural connections within the brain. Every time we revisit or *re-member* events – and create a new life story – we reconnect to the recorded memory in new ways and make new sense of the past.[12] In Alessandro Portelli's influential formulation, 'memory is not a passive depository of facts, but an active process of creation of meanings'.[13]

Two features of life-story making are important here. First, episodes which have personal significance and impact – such as the migrant's day of departure or arrival – are more likely to become long-term memories. Second, the creation of a story about an experience is one of the key factors in the formation of durable memories. An event becomes a remembered and meaningful *experience* through narrative. Just as the historian emplots the collective past as history, individual lives gain shape and meaning through the life stories we create about ourselves. For example, on a train from Manchester, bound for London and the ship to Australia, Joan Pickett started a journal and began to articulate a life-changing event into a first draft of memory.

Life stories have a cultural overlay and a psychological underlay.[14] Even the most intimate account necessarily draws upon cultural resources of language and meaning (from the stories of our peers and from the wider culture) to provide story-lines and shape and bind first thoughts into a more fixed and coherent, though inevitably selective and partial, state. For example, Joan Pickett's journal uses the commonplace language of youthful adventure to make sense of her emigration. Our life stories also usually seek to create a relatively coherent and comfortable sense of our experience. Social psychologists explain that life stories involve a 'narrative creation of coherence'; historians sometimes use the notion of 'composure'.[15] We create stories that help make sense of our lives and deal with the troubling, jagged edges of experience, and we hope to gain recognition and affirmation from the audience for our life-story telling. In her journal Joan Pickett struggles with ambivalent feelings about leaving home, but emphasises excitement and will-power. In her letters home she is both 'self-fashioning and self-covering'[16] as she persuades herself, and her parents, that she is having a great time. Forty years later her written memoir has none of these mixed feelings and instead represents emigration as a dare that spiralled into a successful, life-changing adventure.

THE AUTOBIOGRAPHICAL IMPULSE

The reasons people record their life stories – including the universal desire to make sense of a life – have a significant impact upon what they choose to write or say. By extension, the factors which motivate some people, but not others, to record life experiences, determine what types of accounts are produced and preserved for the use of historians. This autobiographical impulse is therefore one of the categories which must concern researchers working with life stories.

Some historical experiences are more likely to generate life writing. Few working-class men in the early years of the twentieth century kept journals, but when they went to war they were often moved to write by a heightened sense of their mortality and by their role in an epochal event. Most stopped writing journals or letters when they came home; sources about return are therefore comparatively scarce. Record-keeping and memorialising aims influence both the form and content of a journal. Unlike some diarists, Joan Pickett was not given to introspection in her writing, perhaps because she was practical by nature, perhaps because she thought such intimacies were inappropriate for her future book.

Different types of letters serve different aims. Personal letters are usually spurred by separation and the need to sustain and develop relationships breached by distance. Yet letter-writing is also motivated by a powerful desire to describe and explain the new life to distant families and friends, to make sense of novelty and change, and to create a record about a momentous experience. Joan Pickett stopped writing her journal midway to Australia because she was too busy, but she wanted to write to her family in England and decided that letters could double-up as a personal communication and a record for posterity and publication. On Joan's request her father dutifully numbered and stored each letter in a 'Drawer of Memories' in her Manchester bedroom. Letter-writing involves a creative tension between careful concealment and descriptive detail, between the priority of the relationship or the record, between writing for self and writing for others, and the historian needs to read letters with these intentions in mind.

Written memoirs often have a clear motivation: to create a family legacy for the next generation, set the record straight (about the events of politics or war, for example), or review the life in a way that makes positive sense as it draws to an end. Joan Pickett's two-page typed memoir, 'I was only kidding! (Memories of a £10 Pommie)', which she sent to our research project in 2000, crystallised, in carefully crafted summary form, the life story that matters to Joan and that she wanted to tell. It is a life story of strange tales in exotic places, of coming of age and independence through travel and adventure, and in old age it provides Joan with 'a lifetime of memories to see me through present dark winter nights!'

Oral history recordings, by contrast, are typically initiated not by the narrator but by a researcher. Yet the decision to participate is motivated by factors which will influence the interview. In the early 2000s British migrants in Australia wanted to record their story, which they felt had been neglected in favour of the more exotic and influential history of non-English speaking immigrants. Conversely, some people may decline to be interviewed – because they think their life is none of your business, they do not want to talk about painful or humiliating events, or the project topic has no interest or significance for them – and their experiences and attitudes are thus less likely to be on record. In each case the decision to be interviewed, and the stories which are sought and told, are influenced by the connection between the researcher's aims and interests and the interviewee's feelings about their life and its significance. Whether a researcher is using their own interviews or an oral history archive, he or she needs to consider the aims of both the project and its participants, as well as the significance of non-participation.

LIFE STORY RELATIONSHIPS

Every life story is told in a relationship that influences the account. Even the most confidential diarist usually writes for a real or imagined reader, perhaps a future child or one's older self. Joan Pickett hoped to publish her migration journal – 'English girl travels with a typewriter' – and she wrote a travelogue with an audience in mind. Letters are more obviously shaped by the writing relationship; the addressee is explicit and the account is fashioned for his or her reading. Indeed, sustaining and developing a relationship is a primary motivation for letter-writing. Letters enact important emotional work, they reconfigure personal relationships 'rendered vulnerable by long-distance, long-term separation'[17] and offer 'a token of solidarity and an instrument of reassurance'.[18] Joan Pickett wrote to her beloved father in more detail and depth than they had ever shared in face-to-face conversation, because, she recalls, 'in letters you can always say more, and explain yourself more . . . things that you'd never mentioned before'.

Whom a letter is addressed to affects what is written, but the audience may not be the same as the addressee. Joan Pickett, for example, addressed all her letters to 'Mum and Dad', but 'Mum' was in fact Joan's step-mother and Joan was much closer to her father, who was also her most loyal and regular correspondent. Joan knew that Mum would read her letters, but she recalls that 'I *thought* I was writing to my Dad, I never actually thought about Mum, 'cause there was a closer relationship, obviously, with my father. So I wrote the letters as though I was talking directly to Dad.'

Letters can also be collective affairs. The writer sometimes expects a wide and sociable readership, especially but not only in communities where the literate few act as readers and writers for other people's letters. Joan Pickett recalls her delight when her brother Harry wrote that their father showed Joan's letters to everyone who came to the house. This collective audience almost certainly reduces the likelihood of intimate confidences, yet there can be significant variations in the letters written to different people, both in tone (each letter-writer seeks a familiar conversational style that suits a particular relationship) and content. To her brother, with whom she was very close, Joan Pickett could joke easily about their father's unnecessary protectiveness ('no doubt you will have heard from a staggered Father, I'm moving on again') and about the uncertainty of a new relationship ('I can't work out whether he regards me as a past employee, a present girl friend or a future secretary . . . maybe I will get my answer next Saturday night, Hogmanay!').[19]

Letters also involve concealment and invention. Joan Pickett's letters sheltered her parents from unnecessary worry. There are no references to the anxiety she felt about leaving home; instead she regaled the family with stories about exotic ports and social life on a ship that is 'like a floating Butlins'.[20] By comparison with face-to-face conversation, the separation in time and space between letter-writer and recipient enabled what letter-writing theorists describe as an 'epistolatory masquerade'.[21] As far as we can tell, Joan Pickett rarely lied about her life in Australia; with the regular movement of people and correspondence it was too easy to be found out. But migrant letters to their families are replete with part-truths and concealment, as they negotiated family relationships on their own terms and censored the stories they wrote about their lives.

Just as letters are shaped by an epistolary relationship, autobiographical writings are influenced by an imagined reader. When Joan Pickett and other British migrants typed up their migration stories for our university research project their writing was affected by who and what they were writing for. We had asked respondents to produce a 'personal account of your migration experience', and to 'write as much as you choose, in as much detail and depth as possible. It is your story and we would like to hear what *you* recall as most significant'. We also offered a set of bullet points with 'ideas about the kind of things you might cover' (such as family background; reasons for emigration; initial impressions of Australia and Australians, and so on), but stressed that 'you should feel free to write about what *you* think is important' (this approach to collecting life writing can generate rich evidence and is much easier and cheaper than oral history). Though few respondents used the bullet points to arrange their writing, they did respond to our interest in background, motivation and impact, as we had hoped. But on some topics, such as the intimate family dynamics of migration, they were often careful or reserved; they did not imagine that such personal aspects of their lives were historically significant. Joan Pickett wrote about 'being swept along by events' in 1960, but not about her anxious feelings at the time or about her father's death as a factor for return in 1968.

In our interview, by contrast, Joan's story was very different. Oral historians debate the extent to which interviewers should intervene in the process of remembering. On the one hand, careful, probing questions can uncover experiences and feelings that might have been unspoken. On the other hand, the interviewer should not interrupt the particular ways – meaningful in themselves – in which people tell their life stories. Either way, recent writings about oral history emphasise how the interview relationship always impacts upon the story that is remembered and told.[22]

Storytelling is a performance, animated by a desire to tell a good story and captivate an audience. This is true in all life stories, though in oral history the audience is present and the interaction immediate. In an interview the performance will vary according to the temperament of the narrator, her expectations for the occasion and the relationship between story-teller and audience. Most obviously, the interviewer directs the narrative with questions and responses,

and by establishing an agenda for the interview. Less obviously, each participant perceives and imagines the other in certain terms, and these expectations
can affect both questions and answers. My women interviewees, for example,
may have seen me as a younger man, as an Australian, as an academic historian
or as a fellow migrant, and their perceptions influenced how they responded to
me and my questions. At another, deeper level of projection and transference,
each participant brings to the interview emotional baggage from prior experience and from other, similar relationships, and this affects how we feel and
what we say in the recording.[23] There are also imagined audiences outside the
recording room whose presence at the back of the narrator's mind affects the
story. Joan Pickett, for example, was careful not to speak on the record in ways
that might upset or embarrass her travel companion Jean, who had a more difficult time in Australia and who remains a close friend.

In the process of remembering, and across the span of an interview, stories
usually evolve as the narrator becomes more confident, as each memory triggers another, and as the questions prompt reflection or reconsideration. This
interactive dialogue is very different from autobiographical writing. The
narrator has less control, or rather there is a 'shared authority' in the development of the story, as control of the narrative shifts back and forwards between
interviewer and interviewee.[24] Life writing – such as the accounts by Joan and
others for my migration project – often composes a comfortable life story.
In an interview that story may be prompted and stretched beyond its usual
boundaries. At best, this can be a positive occasion as the narrator responds
to a supportive listener. She may breach a lifelong silence or make new sense
of experience, and perhaps find recognition or even catharsis through stories
that have never been easily told. At worst, if the dialogue opens wounds that
are still raw and offers no way to make new, affirming meaning, it risks a 'dis-
composure' of safe stories and settled identities.[25]

We can hear this conversational dance, and the evolution of the story, in
the section of my first interview with Joan Pickett when I ask why she went to
Australia in 1960. Joan starts by repeating in almost exactly the same words an
anecdote she had already written for our project, about going to the cinema in
Manchester with her workmate Jean 'one dark winter's afternoon', watching
a newsreel about a royal tour to sunny Australia, and joking about taking up
an assisted passage. 'And within six months, the letter came through the post,
you know, "A passage has been arranged." (laughs)' I then ask some follow-
up questions about the response from Joan's parents and about whether or
not she had the 'adventurous streak' noted by her father ('she'll have to get
it out of her system'). At this point Joan begins to provide more contextual
explanation for the 'accidental' decision on that dark winter afternoon. She
was 'brought up on a train' by her engine-driver father and had 'always
enjoyed travel' with a free rail pass in England and Europe. As Joan talks, and

thinks aloud, the story expands and deepens into a more complicated narrative, in which she explains that she was 'getting in a bit of a rut' as most of her friends got married and she felt 'left behind in some way'. Joan says that she 'never tried to analyse it', but between us, haltingly in the interview and then through correspondence and writing, we reach an explanation that, in 1960, the assisted passage offered perhaps the only way apart from marriage that an unmarried working-class woman in her mid-twenties could leave the family home and create an independent life. At the time this was not an easy decision, and Joan was conflicted by loyalty to her family and guilt about leaving home. With the death of her father at the back of her mind, Joan still finds it difficult to describe leaving as her own decisive intention. But the interview dialogue stretches memory and expands her migration story. In our first interview, and indeed our first meeting, this new analysis is not easy and Joan's usual confident flow is broken by hesitation and uncertainty. But over the next decade, as we talk more and Joan responds to my writing about her life with interest and agreement, she makes this historical explanation part of her own story. Given time and space for reflection, and through the shared authority of oral history, the interviewee sometimes develops new ways to understand her life.

THE TIME OF THE TELLING

The stories we tell about our lives vary over time, as changed personal circumstances and understandings suggest new scripts with different emphases and silences. The researcher thus needs to consider how a life story is shaped by the dynamic interaction between 'the time of the event' and the 'time of the telling', as the following example attests.[26]

On the night train from Manchester to London, Joan Pickett commenced her short-lived migration journal:

> 6.9.60 Left Manchester, London Road, on the midnight (11.35 p.m.) train to St. Pancras, after a nightmare last day at home . . . So we waited for the train to move off – the minutes dragged by – could we still turn back – no, there goes the whistle, the light is green and slowly we pull away, waving furiously out of the window until the platform disappears in puffs of steam and we enter the dark night outside. We're off!

Here is the same moment, recalled in our interview forty years later.

> And we got onto this night train, and I always remember, those clouds of steam, it was something like *Brief Encounter*. It was quite late at

night. My father was standing there with his raincoat and his trilby on, you know, and he sort of kissed us and he said, 'Well, come back if you can, but if – don't worry about us, you do what you want to do.' And my mother was crying of course. And we were crying. (laughs) And the train pulled away, and my father sort of disappeared into this cloud of smoke, and I never saw him again.

These two accounts narrate the same moment in markedly different ways. Most obviously, in the journal Joan and her friend Jean are the central characters, but in the interview Joan's father takes centre-stage. In 1960, writing within a few hours of departure, Joan expresses her anxiety about leaving, but also the start of an exciting adventure into the 'dark night' of the unknown. Through the journal Joan represents – and creates – herself as the hero of her own adventure story. In our interview, with the hindsight that migration was a success truncated by the death of her father, the railway scene is now framed by the loss of a beloved parent and by the grief and guilt of an absent daughter, powerfully expressed through the increasing pace and emotion of her voice as she tells the story. And, if the journal of 1960 was written in the contemporary genre of women's travel writing, the memory of 2000 recalls the popular British film *Brief Encounter*, with its clash between romantic adventure and family duty, and the resonance of emotional railway partings in the age of steam. At each point of time Joan Pickett is actively creating a meaningful story about the event, and as the time of the telling changes so too does the meaning and significance of the story. Life stories provide rich evidence about past lives, but also about the continuing and changing significance of the remembered past in people's lives.

At a practical level, detective work is often required to establish the precise provenance of a piece of autobiographical writing. I was lucky to be able to ask Joan about the timing of her journal, which started within hours of leaving home but was retyped and reworked several weeks later. In an archive, correspondence with donors and other evidence in provenance files offers invaluable clues about the time of the telling. The physical evidence of the diary, such as changes in writing materials or handwriting (soldiers' writing is usually much more ragged under fire!) may also be revealing. Textual features, such as anachronistic references to subsequent events or the later insertion of missing details, are clues to provenance; so too are changes in tense (tense can also be misleading, as some diarists write retrospective accounts in the present tense to add a sense of authenticity and immediacy). At war, a confirmed date of death for a diarist provides stark and definitive evidence about the last possible date of writing.

GENRE

Every historical source – a legal transcript, a probate record or a life story – is shaped by narrative conventions. Historians must therefore ask how the narrator perceived and worked within, or perhaps against, the story-telling conventions of a particular genre of life story within a particular time and place. How was a woman expected to write about her life in a letter during the 1960s? How do we narrate our lives in oral history interviews? The study of genre and narrative form opens up more specific consideration of the story-telling types (also labelled, by some theorists, as 'genre') that we adopt and adapt for our own life stories – such as the romance, adventure or conversion story – and indeed of each person's idiosyncratic forms of story-telling.

The 'diary' is perhaps the most heterogeneous type of life story, and the variety of its usage is reflected in a diversity of physical forms. A diary might be a few words about the weather scratched into the half-inch daily space of a pocket book, a detailed account hand-written onto a double page at the end of the day, or perhaps a review of the week typed on the weekend or an online blog comprising text, images, sound and video. Each type of diary comes with implicit expectations about the form and its use. The researcher should consider how the diary format prescribes and constrains usage, but also how diarists often stretch the limitations of the form, such as the soldiers who scrawl onto every space and in every direction of their pocket book in their determination to record a momentous day.

Letters also take many different forms, and the historian should reflect on the relationship between form and content. The business letter, letter of condolence or family Christmas letter all have different conventions, which vary over time and between cultures. The aerogrammes mostly used by Joan Pickett were a short-lived twentieth-century phenomenon (many post offices no long stock them), a cheap and convenient way to send a page and a half of news. Joan's weekly aerogramme presented an update on her life and travels, with a careful selection of descriptive anecdotes squeezed into a limited space that left little room for more extensive personal reflection. Just occasionally, Joan threw off the shackles of the aerogramme; on her first trip to central Australia she sprawled enthusiastically across five hand-written pages. 'For once in my life, I'm just speechless at the beauty and fascination of this area.'[27]

The logistics of correspondence also influence letter-writing and need to be considered. The speed and regularity of postal services in the mid-twentieth century contrasts markedly with both nineteenth- and twenty-first-century correspondence. Nineteenth-century migrant writers might wait many months or even years for a reply, and could not be certain that letters would reach their destination. With such a gap it was harder to sustain a dialogue, and a letter was more likely to comprise an autobiographical review about the events of recent months or years (twenty-first-century emails often record the very moment and demand immediate response). In the mid-twentieth century, letters that took less than a week between Britain and Australia allowed for a more immediate and detailed recounting of daily life in the past week, and a responsive dialogue about questions and concerns. Yet correspondents in both centuries had to deal with separation in time and space. Separation could be painful and frustrating, but it also offered the letter-writer an opportunity to compose their words without the beckoning gaze or interruptions of direct conversation.[28]

There are many different types of autobiographical writing, from the political memoir to the family legacy, and the conventions of autobiography vary markedly across time and culture, for example in the extent to which the story includes intimate revelations. In her response to our request for written accounts of post-war migration, Joan Pickett wanted to produce a 'good story' which was informative and pleasing to read. While shaping and embellishing the story in her own distinctive style, she also responded to familiar generic expectations: the account should be chronological; it should be sustained by tension about character or outcome; it should be fashioned for aesthetic effect and to evoke particular meanings and significance. 'What an experience' – Joan wrote about 'my strangest job so far' on Ocean Island – 'working in an office overlooking the sea and watching the ships load phosphate, not to mention the social opportunities for 8 single girls on the island with 200 Europeans.' Joan distilled the essence of her migration story in two densely typed pages, and a string of anecdotes like this conformed to the genre of women's writing in which an innocent abroad learns the ways of the world and discovers herself through travel and adventure. When using autobiographical writing as a historical source, consider the impact of genre upon content and how that affects your analysis and use of the source.

With television exposure the oral history interview has become a familiar genre and both interviewers and interviewees usually have an expectation about how they should record the story; indeed the fact of recording encourages story-telling about events of 'historic' significance. Alessandro Portelli argues that the oral history interview is a 'composite genre' comprising a 'cluster of genres'.[29] Twice-told tales are recreated in a novel format. The narrator draws upon everyday story-telling conventions and popular cultural forms (like Joan Pickett and *Brief Encounter*) but is also directed by the structure and priorities of the interviewer and anticipation of the wider audience for recorded history. Though speech – like writing – may be artfully constructed and concealing, in the interactive dialogue of an interview the narrator is stimulated to 'think aloud' and the story-telling can take unexpected paths.

Aurality is one of the defining features of oral testimony. When historians use spoken stories as evidence they must ask how each narrator deploys the rich textures of sound to add layers of meaning to their words. In speech we empha-sise significant words and phrases with increased volume, an insistent tone or a well-timed pause. We speed up with excitement or emotion, or slow down for a difficult, unrehearsed story. A long pause or awkward stumbling may indicate pain or embarrassment, and the struggle to recall or relate a memory that has no easy story. Our voice can suggest warmth and pleasure, anger and disap-pointment, sarcasm or disapproval. Laughter can be joyous, anxious or ironic. One of the reasons oral historians are wary of the written transcript of an inter-view is that text is only an approximation for speech and cannot translate many of these aural clues. When we read the transcript of Joan Pickett's interview we miss the meanings in her voice, which gathers pace and catches with emotion as she rushes to escape the conclusion to her story – 'and I never saw him again' – about the family farewell at the Manchester railway station in 1960.

If the sound of speech conveys much of the meaning of oral testimony, then the rhythms and patterns of the spoken word are also different to those of autobiographical writing. Speech is 'ragged at the edges; it twists and turns, gnaws away at meaning and coils itself up'.[30] A spoken account – like Joan's explanation of why she went to Australia – zig-zags from one topic to another, as each memory triggers a connected story or feeling. At different points she adds context and explanation, or detours away from the main narrative; she restarts a sentence when she loses track, she corrects herself and berates her faulty recollection. Her memories are sensory word pictures ('I always remember those clouds of steam'). The spoken word of Joan's interview is less structured and more spontaneous than her more crafted literary account; it has not been edited, or rather, the editorial revisions have not been deleted. Poetic approaches to transcription – which avoid blocks of prose with the punctua-tion and rules of writing, and instead use stanzas broken up and punctuated to show the patterns of speech – can help researchers to see and hear the mean-ings of oral history. Just as reading text requires skill in textual analysis, the oral historian must learn to 'listen in stereo', or with 'a third ear', for the mean-ings of sound and the sounds of silence, and then find ways to reproduce those aural meanings in writing or other types of historical production.[31]

SUMMARY OF LIFE HISTORY METHODS

Find and create life story sources

- Identify which method is appropriate for your research: a sample of life stories (within which you might identify significant historical patterns) or a single narrative (which might illuminate interconnections between the dif-ferent factors affecting a life in historical context).

- You will find life writings in private and public archives, and might create your own oral histories or use other people's archived interviews. You can also generate rich evidence by inviting historical witnesses to write life stories related to the themes of your research.

Apply conventional history research skills

- Conventional methodological skills – background research to situate an account in its historical context, triangulation with other evidence, checking for internal and external consistency – are readily applied to personal testimony.

Assess factors that shape a life story

- Consider the reasons why someone narrates their life, and how that auto-biographical impulse affects what they do or don't say.
- Ask what were the relationships within which a life story (or indeed any historical source) was created, and how did they shape the story?
- Look out for the ways in which narrators draw upon the language and meanings of their culture to articulate experience, and consider the complex interaction between personal meaning and public sense, and between individual and society in historical context.
- Consider how a life story is influenced by the dynamic interaction between 'the time of the event' and the 'time of the telling', and what you can learn about the meanings of the past at the time and as they change over time. Seek to identify patterns of remembrance across a sample of life stories.
- Ask how has a narrator perceived and worked within, or perhaps against, the story-telling conventions of a particular genre of life story, within a particular time and place.

Analyse clues, patterns and meanings

- Listen carefully for the aural meanings of audio interviews (and look for visual clues in video interviews). Poetic transcription may help you to analyse an oral history.
- Listen and read for silences, and identify their role and meaning in the story.
- If you are lucky enough to have a sample of life stories – such as a set of interviews – read and listen to them with care to identify patterns and themes related to your research subject.
- You may even be able to quantify the relative significance of different

factors by checking their recurrence and impact across your sample – but you will need to ask who and what does your sample represent (and who is missing) and qualify your findings accordingly.

- Use new digital tools that enable you to search within and across digitized sets of life writing or oral history.
- If you are writing history from a single narrative, treat it as a 'telling case' which illuminates lived experience in a particular historical context and suggests questions or hypotheses for future research.
- Whether you have a large sample or a single narrative, always ask how each narrator constructs their identity through life story, and consider what you can learn about subjectivity and the meanings and emotions of historical experience.

Consider archival presence and absence

- Remember that beneath the tip of the iceberg of life story sources are those that never make it to the archive and into your historical research. If history is the story we make of the stories we find, then you need to consider those missing stories and the significance of their absence.

NOTES

1. This epigram comes from a fellow member of our Melbourne life writing group, the late Rhys Isaac, to whom I dedicate this chapter.
2. Robert Rhodes James, 'The terrible "ifs"', *Times Literary Supplement*, 13 May 1994, p. 4; Richard Holmes, 'Profile', *Guardian*, 18 May 2004; Samuel Hynes, *The Soldier's Tale: Bearing Witness to Modern Warfare* (London: Pimlico, 1998), pp. xii, 30.
3. Sidonie Smith and Julia Watson, *Reading Autobiography: a Guide for Interpreting Life Narratives* (Minneapolis, MN: University of Minnesota Press, 2001); Barbara Caine, *Biography and History* (Basingstoke and New York, NY: Palgrave Macmillan, 2010).
4. Amia Lieblich, Rivka Tuval-Mashiach and Tamar Zilber (eds), *Narrative Research: Reading, Analysis and Interpretation* (Thousand Oaks, CA: Sage, 1998); Mary Chamberlain and Paul Thompson (eds), *Narrative and Genre: Contexts and Types of Communication* (New Brunswick, NJ: Transaction Publishers, 2004).
5. Judith Okely and Helen Callaway (eds), *Anthropology and Autobiography* (London and New York, NY: Routledge, 1992); J. C. Climo and M. G. Cattell (eds), *Social Memory and History: Anthropological Perspectives* (Walnut Creek, CA: Altamira, 2002).

6. Ken Plummer, *Documents of Life 2: an Invitation to Critical Humanism* (London: Sage, 2001).

7. George C. Rosenwald and Richard L. Ochberg (eds), *Storied Lives: the Cultural Politics of Self-Understanding* (New Haven, CT: Yale University Press, 1992); Charlotte Linde, *The Creation of Coherence* (Oxford: Oxford University Press, 2003).

8. Tess Cosslett, Ceila Lurie and Penny Summerfield (eds), *Feminism and Autobiography: Texts, Theories, Methods* (London: Routledge, 2000).

9. Robert Perks and Alistair Thomson (eds), *The Oral History Reader* (London: Routledge, 3rd edition, 2015); Lynn Abrams, *Oral History Theory* (London: Routledge, 2010).

10. Copies of Joan Pickett's journal and letters, together with the interviews we conducted in Manchester in 2000 and 2006 and her unpublished 2000 memoir, '"I was only kidding" (Memories of a £10 Pommie)', are archived with the British Australian Migration Research Project in the Mass-Observation Archive at the University of Sussex Library, Brighton, England. Joan has given permission for her material to be used for historical research and has corrected and approved drafts of my writing about her emigrant experiences. In quotes from Joan's accounts I use three unbracketed ellipses (. . .) to indicate that I have deleted a section from the original, and three dashes (---) to indicate a pause in speech.

11. James Hammerton and Alistair Thomson, *Ten Pound Poms: Australia's Invisible Migrants* (Manchester: Manchester University Press, 2005); Alistair Thomson, *Moving Stories: an Intimate History of Four Women Across Two Countries* (Manchester: Manchester University Press, 2011).

12. See Alistair Thomson, 'Memory and remembering in Oral History', in Donald A. Ritchie (ed.), *The Oxford Handbook to Oral History* (New York, NY: Oxford University Press, 2011).

13. Alessandro Portelli, 'What makes oral history different', in A. Portelli, *The Death of Luigi Trastulli: Form and Meaning in Oral History* (Albany, NY: State University of New York Press, 1991), p. 52.

14. Michael Roper, 'Re-remembering the soldier heroes: the psychic and social construction of memory in personal narratives of the Great War', *History Workshop Journal* 50 (Autumn 2000), pp. 181–204.

15. Charlotte Linde, *Life Stories: the Creation of Coherence* (New York, NY: Oxford University Press, 1993); on 'composure' see Graham Dawson, *Soldier Heroes: British Adventure, Empire and the Imagining of Masculinities* (London: Routledge, 1994), pp. 34–44; Alistair Thomson, *Anzac Memories: Living with the Legend* (Melbourne: Oxford University Press, 1994), pp. 8–11.

16. Rosemarie Bodenheimer, *The Real Life of Mary Ann Evans. George Eliot,*

her Letters and Fiction (Ithaca and London: Cornell University Press, 1994), p. 3.

17. David Gerber, 'Epistolary masquerades: acts of deceiving and withholding in immigrant letters', in Bruce S. Elliott, David A. Gerber and Suzanne M. Sinke (eds), *Letters Across Borders: the Epistolary Practice of International Migrants* (New York, NY: Palgrave Macmillan, 2006), p. 143.

18. David Fitzpatrick, *Oceans of Consolation: Personal Accounts of Irish Migration to Australia* (Cork: Cork University Press, 1994), p. 20.

19. Pickett, letters to Harry Pickett, 24 August 1961 and 26 December 1961.

20. Butlins was a popular British chain of seaside holiday resorts.

21. Gerber, 'Epistolary masquerades', p. 146.

22. Valerie Yow, '"Do I like them too much?" Effects of the oral history interview on the interviewer and vice-versa', *Oral History Review* 24:1 (1997), pp. 55–79.

23. Michael Roper, 'Analysing the analysed: transference and counter-transference in the oral history encounter', *Oral History* 31:2 (2003), pp. 20–32.

24. Michael Frisch, *A Shared Authority: Essays on the Craft and Meaning of Oral and Public History* (Albany, NY: State University of New York Press, 1990); Alistair Thomson, 'Moving Stories, Women's Lives: Sharing Authority in Oral History', *Oral History* 39: 2 (2011), pp 73–82.

25. Penny Summerfield, 'Culture and composure: creating narratives of the gendered self in oral history interviews', *Cultural and Social History* 1:1 (2004), pp. 65–93.

26. Alessandro Portelli, *The Battle of Valle Giulia: Oral History and the Art of Dialogue* (Madison, WI: University of Wisconsin Press, 1997).

27. Pickett, letters to Mum and Dad, 15 May 1961 and 25 May 1961.

28. For the impact of temporal and spatial separation, see Liz Stanley, 'The epistolarium: on theorizing letters and correspondences', *Auto / Biography* 12 (2004), pp. 201–35.

29. Alessandro Portelli, 'Oral history as genre', in Mary Chamberlain and Paul Thompson (eds), *Narrative and Genre* (London: Routledge, 1998), pp. 23–45.

30. Raphael Samuel, 'Perils of the transcript', in Perks and Thomson, *The Oral History Reader*, p. 391.

31. On poetic transcription see Krista Woodley, 'Let the data sing: representing discourse in poetic form', *Oral History* 32:1 (2004), pp. 49–58. On 'listening in stereo', see Kathryn Anderson and Dana C. Jack, 'Learning to listen: interview techniques and analyses', in Perks and Thomson, *The Oral History Reader*, 2nd edn, pp. 129–42.

FURTHER READING

Abrams, L., *Oral History Theory*, 2nd edn (Abingdon: Routledge, 2016).
Armitage, S. H., P. Hart and K. Weathermon (eds), *Women's Oral History: the Frontiers Reader* (Lincoln, NE: University of Nebraska Press, 2002).
Boyd, D. A., and Larson, M. A., *Oral History and the Digital Humanities: Voice, Access, and Engagement* (New York, NY: Palgrave Macmillan, 2014).
Chamberlain, M., and P. Thompson (eds), *Narrative and Genre* (London: Routledge, 1998).
Jolly, M. (ed.), *The Encyclopedia of Life Writing* (London: Fitzroy Dearborn, 2001).
Perks, R., and A. Thomson (eds), *The Oral History Reader*, 3rd edn (London: Routledge, [1998, 2006] 2015).
Plummer, K., *Documents of Life 2: an Invitation to Critical Humanism* (London: Sage, 2001).
Smith, A., and J. Watson, *Reading Autobiography: a Guide for Interpreting Life Narratives* (Minneapolis, MN: University of Minnesota Press, 2001).
Thompson, P., *The Voice of the Past: Oral History*, 3rd edn (Oxford: Oxford University Press, 2000).
Thomson, A., *Moving Stories: an Intimate History of Four Women Across Two Countries* (Manchester: Manchester University Press, 2011).
Yow, V. R., *Recording Oral History. A Guide for the Humanities and Social Sciences* 3rd edn (Lanham, MD: Rowman & Littlefield Publishers, 2014).

PART 3

Quantitative and Qualitative Analysis

CHAPTER 8

GIS, Spatial Technologies and Digital Mapping

Keith Lilley and Catherine Porter

E ven just a decade ago having a chapter dedicated to Geographical Information Systems (GIS) in a book on methods in history would have been seen as unusual, but such is the development of digital mapping and spatial technologies over recent years that historians cannot now afford to be without them. This chapter provides an introduction to GIS and its application and potential for historical study. Given the scope of the chapter it can only be reasonably cursory and aims to show what can be done with GIS in historical research (and teaching), with some pointers for historians on how they might employ GIS and spatial technologies in their own work. It should become clear that GIS is no longer a highly specialised and technical approach to handling spatial and temporal information but an increasingly user-friendly and accessible basis for integrating, analysing and visualising historical and geographical data of a wide variety, both qualitative and quantitative in nature. With this in mind, the chapter sets out: first, what GIS is and how it works; second, why historians might wish to use GIS; thirdly, how GIS is useful for providing insights into the past; and lastly, what the future might be in using GIS for historical research, particularly its problems and challenges. The chapter also provides some directions for further study, including the locations of a growing number of digital online resources that use GIS to disseminate historical material.

WHAT GIS IS AND HOW IT WORKS

GIS is data-management software that allows users to locate information spatially. Put simply, it is a spatial database. There are two key ingredients to GIS that combine to provide users with a means of storing and retrieving information, and digitising and visualising it: first, data are spatially referenced, most often by using latitude and longitude coordinates, or national mapping coordinate systems such as the Ordnance Survey National Grid for Great Britain; secondly, the software also readily imports and visualises scanned maps, in the form of raster images, as well as digital vector data, such as digitised cartography. The real advantage to GIS though is its ability to link together these two forms of geographical information, thus allowing users to plot out spatially various data sets, as well as to create new spatial data derived from maps and plans. Not surprisingly in this context, GIS has traditionally featured in the fields of applied geography, urban planning, civil engineering and environmental management, but latterly it also has seen use and adoption in other cognate fields where similarly 'geography matters', including disciplines that are concerned with the past such as archaeology, historical geography and history.[1] Here we shall look at some of the basics of GIS, and the generic procedures required to use it, which means dealing with some of its terminology and its technical content. For those who want to know more, there are numerous textbooks on GIS, though many of these are aimed at traditional, more applied users of GIS, rather than historians.[2] First, some consideration will be given to the format of GIS data sets, and then secondly, focus will shift to the methods of digitising in GIS software.

GIS software is either 'open access' or 'proprietary'. The latter, including the widely used ESRI product ArcGIS, are quite expensive to operate, while the former, such as GRASS, QGIS and MapWindow, are by definition available freely, typically via the Internet. This gives rise to a bewildering range of GIS software 'brands', but across all of them certain basic principles apply, as well as common and compatible data formats. A GIS data set contains two types of data: *attribute data*, which is the conventional data usually found in tabular form, and *spatial data*, usually a point, line, polygon or pixel that contains and/or shows where the attribute data is located. This data structure is often called a *layer*, and the shapefile format used in various GIS software is the common way of representing a layer.[3] Databases of all kinds can be used in conjunction with a GIS. The information that they contain may also be either quantitative or qualitative in content, depending on the object of study. So historical data derived from censuses or taxation records, often numeric in nature, can be just as easily accommodated as attribute data as can qualitative, non-numeric information, such as people's names, locales and place names, descriptions, and labels on sources and web links.[4] For a given line in a database, though, the spatial coordinates for each need to be provided, in a form that is recognised by the GIS software. Databases can also be linked through common joins, for which locational coordinates (such as grid references or latitude/longitude) are ideal, as indeed are place names, though here different place-name spellings, or places sharing the same name, can give cause for confusion. When it comes to the 'spatial data', that the 'attribute data' are linked to, a different process of data acquisition is required, using the capability within the GIS of creating shapefiles. One of the great advantages of GIS is its ability to import image files, such as maps and plans, of any scale or size, and allow these to be 'stitched together' and digitised to create layers. Scanning images creates rasters which represent a surface using a matrix of pixels.

The alternative approach to digitising GIS data involves the use of tools within the GIS software to trace off selected features from the raster image, such as streets or rivers, parish boundaries or settlement locations. The technique is called 'heads-up' digitising, and is done within the 'map window' on screen.[5] Through this process, each digitised feature is given a unique identification number, its ID code, as well as additional descriptive information, if required (such as a name or source). The digitising of these map features converts the raster image into digital vector data, and these vectors take three geometrical forms: points, lines and polygons. *Points* might typically be used to digitise locations, such as settlements or find-spots, while *lines* might be used more for linear features, such as roads, railways or coastlines, and *polygons* for delimiting areas, be they administrative units, buildings or fields, for instance. Moreover, the same individual geographical feature, say a settlement, can be digitised in different ways, such as a point or as a polygon, depending on the purpose of the digitising. These points, lines and polygons are spatial data that transform qualitative mapped information into quantifiable numerical data. From this, the GIS tools will allow users to establish easily, for example, the length of a given line, the distances between points, or calculate area within polygons. But to do so requires the source map to be 'georectified', that is, linked to terrestrial geographic or projected coordinate systems.

Georectification is another very useful feature of GIS software where selected features on the raster image(s) are given positional coordinates, for example using national grid references of particular features shown by the map (derived from either survey data or from secondary map data – see below).[6] Generally, such positional points ('ground control points' – GCPs) are based upon points such as buildings, settlements or triangulation stations shown on the map. GCPs at peripheral locations on the scanned map are best used for this, and often the more points used to georectify a map the better. Of course, early historic maps, including those not drawn to a consistent scale, will not rectify well to modern geographical coordinates, although this in itself can provide some interesting insights into the variations of map distortion, and does not preclude the use of historic maps in a GIS.[7] Instead, the GIS measuring tool is used to make measurements of the original scanned map, rather than at the terrestrial scale of the geographical features it represents.

Once a map is scanned and digitised, the resulting shapefiles provide a useful basis for analysis. For some areas of historical research, however, the shapefiles may already exist, ready to use. This might include already digitised administrative units, carried out by another GIS project (a national historical GIS, for example, such as 'The Great Britain Historical GIS'), or spatial data deriving from digital cartography supplied by government mapping agencies such as the Ordnance Survey (in Great Britain and the Republic of Ireland), or Institut national de l'information géographique et forestière (in France) or the United States Geological Survey (USA and Canada).[8] The latter can be expensive to acquire, but in some cases digitised historic mapping may also be available, for example through Edina in the case of early Ordnance Survey maps and plans of Great Britain.[9] Spatial data may also be in ready-to-use digital format from archaeological surveys, either of entire landscapes or of particular features within a landscape, and some of these are available through research organisations and academic institutions.[10] For those with the necessary surveying equipment, using Global Navigation Satellite Systems (GNSS) technologies (GPS), and/or total stations (TS), and who have used this to create their own field-survey data, then GIS can readily be used to import the acquired data to show the locations of individual sites or find-spots for example, or to use such data as GCPs to help in georectifying historic maps.[11]

GIS can cope with spatial data from different sources, therefore, whether digitised by the user from their own rasters or imported from secondary data sets (with permission, of course!). Indeed, this interoperability of different data sources allows a range of vector data to be built up, for example representing different time-periods, combining vectorised map features of different origins, as well as modern, contemporary map and aerial imagery, and historic spatial data from archaeological work and surveys. The end result is a spatial database that has a high degree of 'functionality', allowing users to switch between vectors of different time periods, sources or functions. This is because the shapefiles represent 'layers' of information relating to particular spatial and geographical objects. For example, a topographic map once scanned and georectified can be digitised as a series of shapefiles to separate out its constituent cartographic features, such as roads, fields, buildings, rivers, and so forth. Within the GIS software is a 'window' where these features will appear as layers in a column, and within the software it is very easy to turn layers on or off at will, allowing the user to focus on different or individual features (see Figure 8.1). If maps of different periods have been digitised it is possible to overlay map features from different dates to see how they relate to one another, both spatially and temporally. This will reveal, for example, the realignment of historic landscape features such as roads or railways, or the development of built-up areas.

Through digitisation then, GIS provides a medium for visualising changes through time and space. A further visualisation tool within the GIS can be used to map out 'attribute data' as well as link it to the shapefiles. To map out an entry from attribute data requires having locational information, such

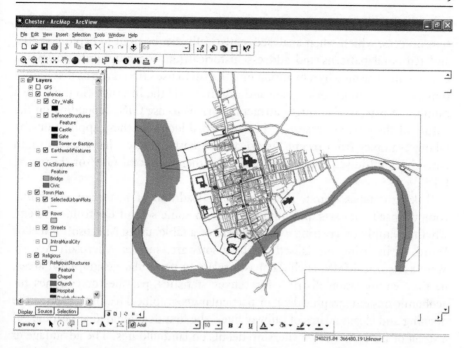

Figure 8.1 A screen shot showing an ArcGIS map window and index (layers) used for mapping the medieval urban landscape of Chester.

as a grid reference, to locate it spatially in the GIS window. Better still, is to connect attribute data to vector data, the shapefiles, and for doing this a common ID number is used and the two are joined within the GIS. This linkage between spatial data and attribute data means it is possible to use the layers as 'containers' for mapping out statistical information from the attribute data, giving information about their character, such as population level, land uses, period of usage, and so forth.[12] This can be done for points, lines or polygons, using a different symbology within the GIS tools to depict different types of information, just as with paper maps and their 'conventional signs'. Moreover, the information in the GIS map window can easily be exported as a high-resolution image file from the GIS (rather than as a 'screen-dump').

WHY HISTORIANS MIGHT WANT TO USE GIS

Already it will have become clear that GIS offers a range of potential uses in historical research. At a basic but practical level, GIS can simply be used as a database for holding historical data, including spatial information. Of more benefit is the facility to digitise rasters, and this includes any digital image, not just maps and plans. Then there are the data sets resulting from the digitisation process, which when analysed statistically can be used to explore spatial and temporal patterns and address historical (and geographical) questions. One further reason why a historian might wish to use GIS concerns dissemination and access to historical data and resources via the Internet. So there are a number of reasons that might attract historians to use GIS, depending on the nature of their area of research. Here we shall look into these applications by taking examples from recent historical GIS-based studies that are part of an emerging multidisciplinary field labelled either 'temporal GIS' or 'historical GIS'.[13]

Taking databases first, there is a long tradition of historians compiling computerised data sets and holding these in some sort of electronic system, whether simply by creating a spreadsheet or a table, using Microsoft Excel or Word, or by using specialised database software, such as Microsoft Access. With a historical GIS, such databases relate to particular geographical areas, be they enumeration districts for census statistics, parishes or counties for economic or demographic data, or particular geographical features, such as the opening and closing dates of railway lines, the first documented appearance of a street or institution, or ownership details on landholdings. The advantage of a spatial (GIS-based) database lies in the ability to use the map window of the software to interrogate, or query, the database through the spatial data (vector) on screen, which using the toolbar will open up a window with information brought up from the attribute data (see Figure 8.2). Alternatively, within the attribute data highlighting certain entries, again querying the data set, will highlight selected features in the map window. This geographically based querying of data sets is useful on a practical level, in making observations about spatial relationships for example, but is rather more powerful as a tool if the data set is used as a basis for creating historical maps that show, for instance, distribution patterns in levels of employment, or types of landholding at key dates. Such applications rely on the capability of GIS software to link a single layer of spatial data (e.g. the polygons of administrative units) to attribute data relating to a given theme or topic, such as population. This approach has proved very popular in the making of GIS-based 'historical atlases', covering in some cases entire countries, or in other cases smaller regions or individual settlements. A case in point is the Great Britain Historical GIS.[14] Here, the boundaries of Registration Districts were digitised, and attribute data acquired from the Registrar General's Decennial Supplements, and by relating the two together, the GIS can be used to generate a choropleth map of mortality rates, for example deaths from lung disease amongst middle-aged men between 1861 and 1871. Such thematic mapping at a national (or state) scale produces distribution patterns that are then useful for understanding historical geographies of whole countries for particular time periods, but the same approach is equally

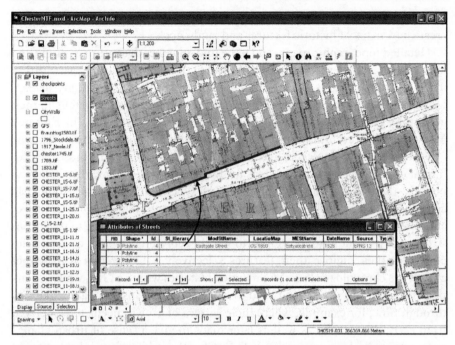

Figure 8.2 A screen shot showing an ArcGIS attribute box with tabulated information relating to a vector feature, in this case a street in Chester.

applicable to smaller geographical areas, such as parishes and counties, where polygons are likewise used as output areas for the attribute data. In so doing, certain patterns emerge from the historical data sets that are not immediately apparent until they are mapped out, a point to which we shall return later.

A wide variety of historic maps and plans are available for historians. They are a rich source of evidence themselves, and through using GIS they can be put to a variety of purposes. At a basic level, maps of the same type, but of different revision dates, can be individually digitised, and their features separated out into 'layers' within the GIS (such as rivers, roads, fields, and so forth; see Figure 8.1). It is also straightforward to begin to compare source maps on screen, either using the transparency tool to overlay the raster images and allow earlier map features to show through on top of later ones, or to select certain vectorised map features from different survey dates, that is, say, a digitised road network, and see how these relate to each other over time according to when the source maps originated. Of course, all this comparative work requires that the scanned maps are georectified (see above), and it helps if they are maps of the same type, scale or projection. Apart from these runs of historic maps, often spanning long time-periods, there are other types of maps that can be used, showing certain areas or features in more detail or for different dates, for example. This is particularly advantageous if attempting to create new maps of historic features and landscapes.

Detailed topographic maps tend to be mid-nineteenth century in origin and later, so to deal with more distant historical periods it is necessary to use earlier maps of diverse origins, such as estate maps, town plans, and county maps.[15] However, these maps are generally less forthcoming and rather patchy in their geographical coverage, especially before the sixteenth century (in Europe). Moreover, they are drawn at a wide variety of scales, or sometimes have no consistent scale at all. Nevertheless, for historians interested in landscape evolution, or in extracting output areas for features representing earlier historical periods, these maps are still useful sources. Once scanned, georectifying can again be carried out (for example using the coordinate system(s) of later maps), and where georectification overly distorts an earlier map (because of the inconsistency of its scale) the solution is to locally georeference parts of the earlier map, and then digitise their features selectively.[16] Doing this will further extend the chronological range of mapped histories within a GIS, which is particularly useful if GIS is being used to map out the expansion of a town or city through time, for example, where their pattern of growth needs to be derived from early cartography as well as later maps to give a sense of urban change over potentially long time-periods.[17] But for those historians whose interest lies with 'pre-modern' periods then contemporary maps are all the rarer, for example during the Middle Ages, or sometimes, for some periods and cultures they are not extant at all.[18] For such instances, GIS has another useful advantage in historical (and archaeological) research, for just as it is possible to scan, georectify and digitise historic maps and plans, the same process can also be applied to site excavation plans or archaeological surveys.[19] In doing this it is then possible to build up a series of temporal 'slices' of landscape evolution across longer time-periods than is represented by historic cartography alone, or to map for a particular period. On this basis it is thus possible to visualise the 'lost' landscapes of historic cities, as has been done for Kyoto, for instance, as well as studies reconstructing imperial Rome, or the urban landscapes of European medieval towns and cities.[20] Of course the same approach equally applies to rural landscapes, settlements and environments, as well as to individual buildings and monuments, such as churches and castles.[21]

Such visualisations of historical change provide viewers with a sense not only of the appearance and character of particular locales and landscapes of the past, but also gives some measure of how places are shaped over time. A further indication and measure of such historical change (or alternatively, temporal continuity) comes from using spatial data – that is, the vectors – resulting from the digitisation of map features within the GIS. These provide a basis for quantifying such changes over both time as well as space. This process is one whereby qualitative geographical information from the map raster is converted to quantitative spatial data. By using tools provided by GIS software, the dimensions and spatial configuration of the digitised vectors are easily exported and analysed, thus giving the historian a numerical measure of, for example, the rate of urban expansion, the extension of transport and communication routes, or the relative area of fields or forests through time. This function alone allows historians to create new sources of quantifiable historical data, relatively straightforwardly, about places, regions or networks, which may then either be analysed in their own right, or integrated with other data sets acquired from written sources, such as official statistics.[22] The spatial analyses involved can be undertaken in standard computer-based statistical software, such as IBM's SPSS or Microsoft Excel, and the results used to explore, and quantify, hitherto under-explored spatial and temporal relationships, as in the case, for example, of the development of property markets in medieval towns, as illustrated by recent work carried out on Leiden, or patterns of urban immigration such as those that occurred in New York during the twentieth century.[23] As Gregory and others have pointed out, though, quantifying *time* in connection with *spatial* data is not easy.[24] One approach they have outlined and used involves designating temporal information to vector data, which can be done using the attribute tables. This lends itself particularly to ascribing to individual shapefiles a 'life-span', a particular date range, to indicate a feature's presence or absence over time.[25] Alternatively, the vectors may be coded, again using the attribute table, according to their temporal characteristics. This then provides a basis for more sophisticated temporal as well as spatial analyses of map-derived features, for example by using bivariate or multivariate statistics.[26] All in all, such spatial analyses open up new areas for historical research, allowing old issues to be readdressed, for example in social and economic history where quantitative methods are fairly widely used, as well as in those aspects of study where traditionally qualitative approaches are more often applied, for example in art and literary history.[27]

In the developing area of digital humanities research digitisation not of maps (in a conventional sense) but visual and textual sources of various kinds can equally be used to create quantifiable data within a GIS.[28] The geospatial representation of images, including photographs, has become increasingly popular as a means of storing, easily retrieving, and analysing views from the past, for example through placing historic images in their geographical context by attaching them to modern coordinate systems, as with 'Enchanting the Desert' created by Stanford University. Other projects have made use of user-generated imagery, from websites such as Flickr, to relate contemporary photographs to historic literary works within a GIS framework. The wealth of information held in textual sources is a new focus in HGIS, academics exploring new ways to investigate spatial narrative. A technique called Geographical Text Analysis (GTA) is a recent development within digital humanities, more specifically, the spatial humanities.[29] The methodology allows for digital corpora to be investigated geographically by combining tools and analytical methods from corpus linguistics and GIS. GTA essentially works by geoparsing place-names in the corpus, assigning them with coordinates using a gazetteer, and incorporating the results within the text using XML tags.[30] The outputs may then be mapped and analysed using GIS. Examples of GTA in practice include, mapping the narrative of disease in the nineteenth century Registrar-General's decennial supplements, mining nineteenth-century newspapers, and investigating the use of language from a geographical perspective in literary texts by Thomas Gray's (1769) and Samuel Taylor Colderidge's (1802) tours of the Lake District.[31]

One final reason why historians might wish to turn to GIS in their work concerns the scope that it offers in broadening dissemination of their research, and also in opening up greater public access to historical sources and data. Electronic publication of historical research is now an accepted and increasingly desirable form of scholarly output, and in this context GIS offers a particularly useful means of developing online resources, especially where there is a spatial as well as a temporal focus. However, while online resources for historians are increasing in number, often with some mapping content, GIS is still relatively underutilised, perhaps because it is somewhat over-engineered for certain applications in distributing resources via the Web. So for those historians familiar with such resources as British History Online, with its Ordnance Survey historic maps available, albeit in low resolution formats, the full potential of serving this material using GIS is not realised. This is the case with many such resources currently, though the tide is turning somewhat, with a growing number of GIS-based digital resources, especially for those with a strong spatial or geographical component to them, as with the 'Vision of Britain Through Time', which allows users to navigate the site geographically, by place, as well as serving information online via a GIS-enabled database.[32] Other similar uses of 'distributed GIS', as it is called, include national and local historical atlases.[33] Such resources not only distribute data via GIS but also often provide users with access to the GIS data themselves, for further such study and analysis. Sharing historical (and geographical) data via the Internet is one of the great advantages of distributed GIS, therefore, as well as opening up – 'democratising' – historical research to broader audiences both specialists and non-specialists alike.[34] Increasingly, research funding bodies like to see such attempts by researchers at providing greater public and commercial access to their work and their data, though as always with the Internet, and electronic media generally, there is a doubtful longevity in such resources, as well as obsolescence of the software used to support them.

Overall, then, GIS offers much to historians, even if maps and map-making are not themselves of primary interest. The addition of spatial data to historical databases can further their potential to address different and new research agendas and questions, while GIS is itself a useful tool from which to derive new sources of historical data from familiar sources. There remains, however, some reticence among historians on the uses of GIS, especially fears over inputting often patchy or unrelated data and deriving from it spurious or anachronistic outputs and results – so for the following section some recent applications of GIS are outlined, partly to showcase how GIS is useful in understanding the past, and partly to try to allay such fears that GIS is too much of a blunt tool in the historians' kit bag of methods and techniques.[35]

HOW GIS IS USEFUL IN UNDERSTANDING THE PAST

On the whole, those historians and historical geographers who have made most use of GIS in their work have tended to be interested in the more recent past, the nineteenth and twentieth centuries especially. In part this is due to the greater availability of both map and written sources for this period, and the way that many of these sources lend themselves more readily to manipulation in a GIS, especially where cartography is drawn to standard and consistent scale, and where written sources, such as official statistics and records, can be relatively easily quantified.[36] With the more distant past, such sources and their availability become more patchy, with gaps or breaks in runs of data, or different kinds of data sources, some qualitative, some quantitative.[37] Nevertheless, these are by no means barriers to using GIS in historical research on more remote periods. To exemplify this, and help promote the idea that GIS has a broad application for historians, the following case studies present how GIS is useful for understanding earlier times, for example in mapping out how medieval landscapes were designed and planned, and also in analysing qualitative sources, such as maps, in quantitative ways. With both, what GIS does is provide otherwise 'hidden' evidence about the activities of surveyors in the Middle Ages, individuals who are often invisible in conventional contemporary written records. GIS thus gives new insights into past cultural processes and agents.

Reconstructing past landscapes, and visualising them cartographically, requires integrating into a GIS various historical, archaeological and cartographic sources, and using these selectively to create new maps that show, to modern cartographic standards and conventions, what landscapes were like at some point in the past or across a range of dates. This approach was the basis for research carried out on a group of medieval 'new towns' in England and Wales founded by King Edward I at the end of the thirteenth century, which although reasonably well-studied by historians are still poorly understood in terms of the mechanisms that created and shaped them on the ground.[38] By adapting the morphological approach of M. R. G. Conzen, whereby historic town plans are used as a basis for analysing historic urban forms and mapping them, GIS provides a suitable medium for selecting features shown on modern historic maps, using these as a basis for attempting to reconstruct the layouts of towns at the time of their formation.[39] As an 'analogue' approach this is a tried and tested method, but somewhat constrained by the materials used – paper maps and tracing overlays – whereas within a GIS with its georectifying, transparency and digitising tools, selecting medieval urban features from historic maps means it is possible, relatively quickly, to undertake a 'digital' plan analysis, and use this as a basis to begin to create new maps of medieval urban landscapes (see Figure 8.3). Of course, as already noted, historic maps are more widely available for later periods, and so following Conzen, the principal source maps used for this exercise are Ordnance Survey 1:2500 (25 inches to one mile) First Edition plans of the mid to late nineteenth century. These georectify very well to modern geographical coordinates and form a sound basis from which to georectify earlier historic maps, such as town plans of the seventeenth and eighteenth centuries. While often not as accurately drawn as Ordnance Survey maps, earlier cartography does show 'lost' townscape features that can be digitised selectively and incorporated as a layer within the GIS, and suitably annotated using the attribute table.[40] This allows the urban historian, for example, to reinstate earlier street patterns, plots and buildings, as well as map relict townscape features, such as defences, gates, churches and chapels.[41] The end result is a map that is a composite made of different historical sources – but to what extent is it a reliable historical representation?

Creating new maps is really the only option open to historians interested in mapping the physical structure and layout of towns and cities of the Middle Ages as so few were depicted cartographically at the time of their formation. However, basing such a map on later – 'modern' – maps, is of course a risky exercise, so within the GIS layers it is also important to add in spatially and temporally located urban features deriving from contemporary – 'medieval' – historical sources, such as written accounts that describe properties, buildings and streets, as well as information about the medieval townscape derived from local archaeological work, particularly excavations that have exposed and mapped lost structures and topographical features, such as ditches, walls, buildings and streets. Locating such information is relatively straightforward within the GIS, either by annotating vectors with historical data on period and function (in the case of churches, for example), or by adding in new vectors, especially from archaeological site plans, which are easily georeferenced within the modern coordinate system of the GIS.[42] By observing the spatial relationships between these vectors, from archaeology and cartography, greater confidence can be given to the medieval provenance of those urban features

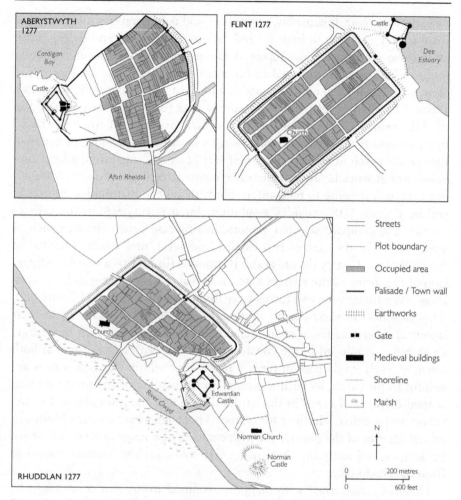

Figure 8.3 Completed GIS-based maps showing three medieval towns drawn to scale, all foundations in Wales belonging to the reign of King Edward I.

digitised from modern cartography. Furthermore, the combination of historical, archaeological and cartographic data allows some estimate of the location and configuration of disappeared medieval townscape features, such as the line of urban defences or the sites of town gates.

The end result – derived from the selective uses of spatial data within the GIS – is a map depicting a medieval urban landscape, representing it for a given period or range of periods. How, then, do we go from visual representations of a medieval urban landscape to understanding those processes that shaped them on the ground? The answer to this lies in the vector data from which these maps are composed, for these can be analysed quantitatively, by exporting their dimensions, geometries and configurations into statistical software for analysis, to look for indications of planning and design, such as the use of right angles, repeated measurements and use of particular ratios. This has been undertaken for medieval Winchelsea, for example, a 'new town' refounded on a new site due to coastal flooding in the 1270s and 1280s.[43] Combining map and field-survey data (derived from GPS) within the GIS provides indications that the original layout of the town was based upon ground measurements made using a local perch measure rather than the statute perch of sixteen and a half feet (5.03 m), suggesting a local surveyor was at work laying out the town's new streets and plots.[44] However, not everyone is going to be comfortable with such a quantitative approach, and here again GIS provides a solution, for it is easy within the GIS to overlay and compare selected vectors, in this case urban features such as street plans. In the case of two English medieval 'new towns' founded in North Wales – Conwy (in 1283) and Beaumaris (in 1296) – a simple comparison of the forms of their street systems reveals a very close match between them, even though the two towns were founded ten years apart (Figure 8.4). This closeness in their design suggests a common plan was used in their layout, and here the finger of suspicion points to Master James of St George, an architect employed in the construction of the castles established at both towns.[45] Such similarities in form – made clear within the GIS – thus are helpful in providing us with a greater understanding of the processes that shaped urban landscapes in the Middle Ages, and the roles played by surveyors and architects in their formation. These agents are so often hidden in official sources of the period, yet with creating new maps of medieval urban landscapes, and analysing these using GIS tools, such individuals come out from the shadows.

Historians concerned with mapping medieval towns and cities might be few, of course, but these examples simply illustrate that GIS as a method in history is flexible enough to be used to address a wide range of issues and topics of interest to historians, including medievalists, and not just those subjects to which it has been applied conventionally, such as demographic, economic and land-use histories.[46] Latterly, too, GIS is seeing use in areas of qualitative history, including the study of literary and artistic sources, as well as historic cartography, and here again the insights it yields can often be surprising.[47] With such potential GIS ought to be at least considered by all historians – whatever their period or subject – as a useful and resourceful approach to historical study, even if it is simply used as a way of storing historical data, though as we have seen here, its value for historians for understanding the past goes well beyond its function as a database.

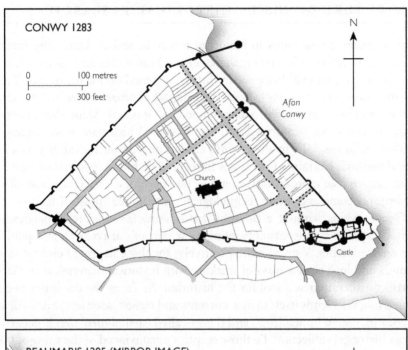

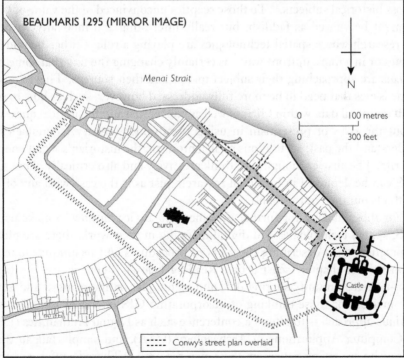

Figure 8.4 A comparison of medieval urban forms based upon GIS-derived map features for two towns founded by King Edward I in North Wales, Conwy and Beaumaris.

THE FUTURE OF GIS IN HISTORICAL RESEARCH

With so many applications in historical research, and an increasing interest in the use of information technologies in the humanities and social sciences, it would seem that GIS has a secure future as a method for historians. There remain, however, those for whom such digital approaches are at best tolerated but not used, and at worse condemned and ignored. Many times have we heard otherwise well-informed and highly skilled historians pass judgement on those who use GIS in their work, calling into doubt its validity as a historical method. Certainly GIS is not for everyone, but as its software becomes more easy to use, more intuitive, and as our everyday lives (and those of our students) become ever more technologically orientated (most of us now turn to Google Maps without a thought, for example), spatial technologies and digital mapping are increasingly going to be part of our research and publication environments. Viewed more positively, for those happy to embrace such changes and look at new ways of working with historical material, then GIS is worth consideration as a tool for the historian. As far as the discipline is concerned too, GIS lends itself to new currents and trends, such as the growth and interest in 'digital humanities', and the so-called 'spatial turn' that is occurring across historical subjects.[48] To those sceptics unconvinced of the value of GIS, it might be viewed as faddish, but really interesting and innovative historical research where spatial technologies are playing a role – either behind the scenes or in a more upfront way – is certainly changing the way that some historians are approaching their subject matter and their sources. There are still some issues that need to be more fully addressed however, such as how to deal with temporal data within GIS, as well as conceptual and theoretical questions about the risks of presentism in using twenty-first century technologies to understand the past: accusations of anachronism, the historian's worst enemy, are rife. The answer though is to think creatively and also critically about how GIS can be deployed in historical research, just as is the case with any of the methods outlined in this book.

For those looking for further guidance and advice on how to make use of GIS, spatial technologies and digital mapping in their work, there are plenty of practical texts describing the sorts of procedures and techniques touched upon in this chapter (see Further Reading below). There is also a vibrant GIS-users community sharing data and techniques online to assist and guide the novice. For those thinking of incorporating GIS into their research, one obvious approach is to attend a conference such as Digital Humanities (DH), or Computer Applications in Archaeology (CAA), and simply talk to those there who are giving papers on their own research.[49] There is much potential for cross-fertilisation across historical disciplines, and in an increasingly competitive research funding environment that stresses collaboration, impact and multidisciplinarity, team-based research that includes GIS specialists is an obvious way forward, bringing together those with different yet complementary expertise. Indeed, it may well be that for those of us who see the potential of using GIS in our research, but do not have the necessary computational or technical skills to use it, such collaborative work is the *only* way forward. As well as the analytical and empirical benefits that this may bring to a particular project or subject, the growing field of digital humanities and historical GIS itself provides an important context and audience for publishing and disseminating such research. But as with any technique or method, GIS is a means to an end and not an end in itself in historical study. It will not provide all the answers and will almost certainly raise only further questions, but this is true for all methods that historians use. One final virtue of GIS, especially when served online to distribute spatial and historical data, is its transparency, allowing users to track back from outputs through to inputs, and therefore question the way that sources are being used. Whatever the future for GIS-based historical research, this ability to be able to unpick digital resources and trace their data, as well as potentially limitlessly linking together various data sets via the Internet, promises to be one of the most exciting prospects for historians over the coming decades.

NOTES

1. J. Conolly and M. Lake, *Geographical Information Systems in Archaeology* (Cambridge: Cambridge University Press, 2006); I. N. Gregory and P. S. Ell, *Historical GIS. Technologies, Methodologies and Scholarship* (Cambridge: Cambridge University Press, 2007); J.-L. Arnaud, *Analyse Spatiale, Cartographie et Histoire Urbaine* (Marseilles: Éditions Parenthèses, 2008). A. K. Knowles (ed.), *Placing History: How Maps, Spatial Data, and GIS are Changing Historical Scholarship* (Redlands, CA: ESRI Press, 2008).
2. See P. A. Longley, M. F. Goodchild, D. J. Maguire and D. W. Rhind, *Geographic Information Systems and Science*, 3rd edn (New York, NY: John Wiley, 2011).
3. Gregory and Ell, *Historical GIS*, pp. 21–40.
4. Ibid. pp. 54–7.
5. Longley *et al.*, *Geographic Information Systems*, pp. 238–40.
6. Conolly and Lake, *Geographical Information Systems*, pp. 80–1.
7. See C. D. Lloyd and K. D. Lilley, 'Cartographic veracity in medieval mapping: analysing geographical variation in the Gough Map of Great Britain', *Annals of the Association of American Geographers* 99:1 (2009), pp. 27–48.

8. I. N. Gregory, 'The Great Britain Historical GIS', *Historical Geography* 33 (2005), pp. 132–4; I. Heywood, S. Cornelius and S. Carver, *An Introduction to Geographical Information Systems*, 3rd edn (London: Pearson, 2006), pp. 144–50.

9. See http://edina.ac.uk [accessed 12 January 2016].

10. Such as the Archaeology Data Service at the University of York (http://archaeologydataservice.ac.uk [accessed 12 January 2016]), for example. For further suggestions, see Gregory and Ell, *Historical GIS*, pp. 186–7.

11. Conolly and Lake, *Geographical Information Systems*, pp. 61–4.

12. For a discussion of this, see Gregory and Ell, *Historical GIS*, pp. 94–100.

13. A. K. Knowles, 'Introducing historical GIS', in A. K. Knowles (ed.), *Past Time, Past Place. GIS for History* (Redlands, CA: ESRI Press, 2002), pp. xi–xx.

14. I. N. Gregory, C. Bennett, V. L. Gilham and H. R. Southall, 'The Great Britain historical GIS: from maps to changing human geography', *The Cartographic Journal* 39 (2002), pp. 37–49.

15. On historic maps as a source, see P. Hindle, *Maps for Historians* (Chichester: Phillimore, 1998).

16. See K. D. Lilley, 'Urban mappings: visualizing late medieval Chester in cartographic and textual form', in C. Clarke (ed.), *Mapping the Medieval City* (Cardiff: University of Wales Press, 2011), pp. 19–41.

17. P. Pinho and V. Oliveira, 'Cartographic analysis in urban morphology', *Environment and Planning B: Planning and Design* 36 (2009), pp. 107–27.

18. See J. B. Harley and D. Woodward (eds), *The History of Cartography Volume 1: Cartography in Prehistoric, Ancient, and Medieval Europe and the Mediterranean* (Chicago, IL: University of Chicago Press, 1987).

19. D. Wheatley and M. Gillings, *Spatial Technology and Archaeology. The Archaeological Applications of GIS* (London: Taylor and Francis, 2002), pp. 62–9.

20. K. Yano, T. Nakaya, Y. Isoda, Y. Takase, T. Kawasumi, K. Matsuoka, T. Seto, D. Kawahara, A. Tskusamoto, M. Inoue and T. Kirimura, 'Virtual Kyoto: 4DGIS comprising spatial and temporal dimensions', *Journal of Geography* 117 (2008), pp. 464–78; G. Guidi, B. Frischer, M. De Simone, A. Cioci, A. Spinetti, L. Carosso, L. Loredana Micoli, M. Russo and T. Grasso, 'Virtualizing Ancient Rome: 3D acquisition and modeling of a large plaster-of-Paris model of imperial Rome', in J.-Angelo Beraldin, S. F. El-Hakim, A. Gruen and J. S. Walton (eds), *Videometrics VIII*, 18–20 January 2005 (San Jose, CA: SPIE, 2005), pp. 119–33; K. D. Lilley, C. Lloyd and S. Trick, 'Mapping medieval townscapes: GIS applications in landscape history and settlement study', in M. Gardiner and S. Rippon (eds), *Medieval Landscapes* (Oxford: Oxbow, 2007), pp. 27–42. These projects have dedicated online resources; for example, see http:// www.geo.

lt.ritsumei.ac.jp and http://www.geo.lt.ritsumei.ac.jp/uv4w/frame_e.
jsp [accessed 12 January 2016], http://www.romereborn.virginia.edu/
and http://www.medievalchester.ac.uk [accessed 12 January 2016].
21. See V. Fronza, A. Nardini and M. Valenti (eds), *Informatica e Archeologia Medievale. L'esperienza senese* (Florence: Edizioni All'Insegna del Giglio, 2009); E. C. Robertson, J. D. Seibert, D. C. Fernandez and M. U. Zender (eds), *Space and Spatial Analysis in Archaeology* (Calgary: University of Calgary Press, 2006).
22. See Gregory and Ell, *Historical GIS*, pp. 89–118.
23. T. Bisschops, 'Ruimtelijke vermogensverhoudingen in Leiden (1438–1561). Een pleidooi voor een perceelsgewijze analyse van steden en stedelijke samenlevingen in de Lage Landen', *Stadsgeschiedenis* 2 (2007), pp. 121–38; A. A. Beveridge, 'Immigration, ethnicity, and race in metropolitan New York, 1900–2000', in Knowles (ed.), *Past Time, Past Place*, pp. 65–77.
24. Gregory and Ell, *Historical GIS*, pp. 124–9.
25. Ibid, pp. 129–36.
26. See E. Camacho-Hübner, *Traduction des opérations de l'analyse historique dans le langage conceptual des systèms d'information géographique pour une exploration des processus morphologiques de la ville et du territoire* (Lausanne: École Polytechnique Fédéral de Lausanne, 2009); B. Lefebvre, X. Rodier and L. Saligny, 'Understanding urban fabric with the OH_FET model based on social use, space and time', *Archeologia e Calcolatori* 19 (2008), pp. 195–214.
27. See D. J. Bodenhamer, J. Corrigan and T. M. Harris (eds), *The Spatial Humanities. GIS and the Future of Humanities Scholarship* (Bloomington, IN: Indiana University Press, 2010).
28. See W. G. Thomas II, 'Computing and the historical imagination', in S. Schreibman, R. Siemens and J. Unsworth (eds), *A Companion to Digital Humanities* (Oxford: Blackwell, 2004), pp. 56–68; P. Vetch, C. Clarke and K. D. Lilley, 'Between text and image: digital rendering of a late medieval city', in B. Nelson and M. Terras (eds), *Digitizing Medieval and Early Modern Material Culture* (Tempe, AZ: RSA/Medieval and Renaissance Texts and Studies, 2011), pp. 365–96. Projects exploring these themes: see http://www.lancaster.ac.uk/fass/projects/spatialhum.wordpress/ [accessed 19 January 2016] and http://web.stanford.edu/group/spatial-history/cgi-bin/site/index.php [accessed 19 January 2016].
29. I.N. Gregory and A. Geddes (eds), *Towards Spatial Humanities. Historical GIS and Spatial History.* (Bloomington: Indiana University Press, 2014). See the project, 'Spatial Humanities: Texts, GIS, Places'. This research project is funded by the European Research Council (ERC) under the European Union's Seventh Framework Programme (FP7/2007-2013)

ERC grant 'Spatial Humanities: Texts, GIS, places' (agreement number 283850).

30. C. Grover, R. Tobin, M. Woollard, J. Reid, S. Dunn, and J. Ball, 'Use of the Edinburgh geoparser for georeferencing digitized historical collections', *Philosophical Transactions of the Royal Society A*, 368 (2010), 3875–3889.

31. P. Murrieta-Flores, A. Baron, I. N. Gregory, A. Hardie and P. Rayson, 'Automatically analysing large texts in a GIS environment: The Registrar General's reports and cholera in the nineteenth century', *Transactions in GIS* 19:2 (2015), pp. 296–320. D. Cooper and I. N. Gregory 'Mapping the English Lake District: A literary GIS', *Transactions of the Institute of British Geographers* 36 (2011), pp. 89–108. I. N. Gregory and D. Cooper 'Thomas Gray, Samuel Taylor Coleridge and Geographical Information Systems: A literary GIS of two Lake District tours', *International Journal of Humanities and Arts Computing* 3 (2009), pp. 61–84. C. Porter, P. Atkinson and, I. N. Gregory 'Geographical text analysis: a new approach to understanding nineteenth-century mortality', *Health and Place* 36 (2015), pp. 25–34.

32. See http://www.visionofbritain.org.uk [accessed 12 January 2016].

33. See http://archaeologydataservice.ac.uk [accessed 12 January 2016] on 'distributed GIS' see Gregory and Ell, *Historical GIS*, pp. 147–9.

34. J. Pickles, *A History of Spaces. Cartographic Reason, Mapping and the Geo-Coded World* (London: Routledge, 2004), pp. 145–75.

35. See A. von Lunen and C. Travis (eds), *History and GIS. Epistemologies, Considerations and Reflections* (Heidelberg: Springer, 2013). I. N. Gregory, "A map is just a bad graph" Why spatial statistics are important in historical GIS in Anne K. Knowles (ed.), *Placing History: How Maps, Spatial Data, and GIS are Changing Historical Scholarship* (Redlands, CA: ESRI Press, 2008), pp. 123–49.

36. Gregory and Ell, *Historical GIS*, pp. 161–81.

37. K. Bartley and B. Campbell, '*Inquistiones Post Mortem*, GIS and the creation of a land-use map of medieval England', *Transactions in GIS* 2 (1997), pp. 333–46.

38. K. D. Lilley, 'The landscapes of Edward's new towns: their planning and design', in D. Williams and J. Kenyon (eds), *The Impact of the Edwardian Castles on Wales* (Oxford: Oxbow, 2010), pp. 99–113.

39. See Lilley *et al.*, 'Mapping medieval townscapes', pp. 33–41.

40. Further discussion of this method is given in Lilley, 'Urban mappings', pp. 21–33. See also, K. D. Lilley and G. Dean, 'A silent witness? Medieval urban landscapes and unfolding their mapping histories', *Journal of Medieval History*, 41:3 (2015), pp. 273–91.

41. For examples of such maps, see those included in the following two

online resources: K. D. Lilley, C. D. Lloyd and S. Trick, *Mapping Medieval Townscapes: a Digital Atlas of the New Towns of Edward I* (York: Archaeology Data Service, 2005), accessible http://archaeology-dataservice.ac.uk/archives/view/atlas_ahrb_2005/ [accessed 19 January 2016]; C. Clarke, H. Fulton, K. D. Lilley, P. Vetch and M. Faulkner, *Mapping Medieval Chester: Place and Identity in an English Borderland City c.1200–1500*, accessible at http://www. medievalchester.ac.uk [accessed 12 January 2016].

42. See Lilley, 'Urban mappings', pp. 26–9.
43. See entry under 'Winchelsea' in Lilley *et al.*, *Mapping Medieval Townscapes*.
44. K. D. Lilley, C. D. Lloyd, S. Trick and C. Graham, 'Analysing and mapping medieval urban forms using GPS and GIS', *Urban Morphology* 9 (2005), pp. 1–9.
45. K. D. Lilley, C. D. Lloyd and S. Trick, 'Designs and designers of medieval "new towns" in Wales', *Antiquity* 81 (2007), pp. 279–93.
46. An indication of this range of applications is given by Knowles, *Past Time, Past Place*.
47. For example, in uncovering and quantifying patterns of relative cartographic distortion evident in historic maps: see K. D. Lilley and C. Lloyd, 'Mapping the realm: a new look at the Gough Map of Britain (c. 1360)', *Imago Mundi* 61:1 (2009), pp. 1–28; K. D. Lilley and C. Porter, 'Mapping Worlds? Excavating cartographic encounters in Plantation Ireland through GIS', *Historical Geography* 41 (2013), pp. 35–58.
48. T. M. Harris, J. Corrigan and D. J. Bodenhamer, 'Challenges for the spatial humanities: toward a research agenda', in Bodenhamer *et al.* (eds), *Spatial Humanities*, pp. 167–76.
49. For more information on these conferences and links to associated organisations, see http//adho.org [accessed 19 January 2016] and http:// caa-international.org [accessed 1 February 2016].

FURTHER READING

Bodenhamer, D. J., J. Corrigan and T. M. Harris (eds), *The Spatial Humanities. GIS and the Future of Humanities Scholarship* (Bloomington, IN: Indiana University Press, 2010).

Gregory, I. N., and P. S. Ell, *Historical GIS. Technologies, Methodologies and Scholarship* (Cambridge: Cambridge University Press, 2007).

Gregory, I. N., and R. Healey, 'Historical GIS: structuring, mapping and analysing geographies of the past', *Progress in Human Geography* 31:5 (2007), pp. 638–53.

Hu, B., 'Application of Geographic Information Systems (GIS) in the history of Cartography', *World Academy of Science, Engineering and Technology* 42 (2010), pp. 1548–51.

Knowles, Anne K. (ed.), *Past Time, Past Place: GIS for History* (Redlands, CA: ESRI Press, 2002).

Knowles, Anne K. (ed.), *Placing History: How Maps, Spatial Data, and GIS are Changing Historical Scholarship* (Redlands, CA: ESRI Press, 2008).

Owens, J. B., 'Toward a geographically-integrated, connected world history: employing Geographic Information Systems (GIS)', *History Compass* 5:6 (2007), pp. 2014–40.

CHAPTER 9

Document to Database and Spreadsheet

R. J. Morris

Modern information technology is able to handle large quantities of information in a systematic manner. Such information can be explored and manipulated with considerable speed. Exploiting and controlling such possibilities imposes a variety of opportunities and needs on historians of all periods. Initial computer use tended to be restricted to limited areas of economic and demographic history, but by the end of the 1970s had extended to many areas of social and political history. From the start such computer-based work demonstrated an ability to challenge many features of accepted historical narrative. The contribution of railways to US and British history, the shape of the 'industrial revolution', the mechanisms of demographic change, the structures of family history, the meanings of political and constitutional change and the nature of convict flows to Australia were early examples.[1] The advance of information technology in the last twenty years has presented historians with enormous opportunities but also considerable issues, intellectual as well as practical.[2]

By the 2000s, there were few areas of historical discourse that had not been fundamentally influenced by information technology. Any historian engaged in project design needs to consider the powerful pattern-seeking abilities of the machine. Those who reject the strategies outlined in this chapter need to be aware of the practical and intellectual issues involved. Whatever their period or sub-discipline of history, they will enter a literature deeply, sometimes covertly, influenced by information technology and hence will need a critical understanding of what is involved.

Many of the skills required have long been familiar to historians, especially in matters of source criticism. Historians of the family have long dealt with sources that give information on households. Information on occupation always had to respond to the changing nature of work, whilst the text of court cases comes through the distorting mirror of an unequal authority structure.

Because the machine provides a means of dealing with large quantities of information, two areas of skill need emphasis. The first is a sense of number.[3] Numbers provide an initial and powerful way of summarising the particular instances recorded in the data. Perhaps more important is the need for a critical sense of social science concepts: social class, gender, the life cycle, occupational status are some of many concepts which enable the historian to make sense of the patterns and relationships involved in large universes of information. It is best that they influence judgement openly and critically.

Two historical examples are explored here to indicate many of the issues involved. Both seek to explore and impose pattern and regularity on information. There is an enormous range of database software available for this task. It is wise to start simple and at its most simple the database[4] takes a named entity: a person, an event, an area, even an object like a shard of pottery, and then attributes a variety of qualities and characteristics to that entity: a name, a date of birth, a price, a population count, a verdict or a chemical composition. There is a wide variety of historical records – often called particular instance papers – which are especially suited to such functionality. Court records, tax records, voting records, inscriptions on tombstones, the archaeological find are but a few. Database technologies have a number of characteristics. They were not invented for historians but for active situations in which the structure of data is stable but the content is changing, such as a business following customers as they place orders and pay bills, or a hospital recording patients' details as treatment progresses. Database technology has a number of advantages for historians. It is able to deal with complex data structures. The examples, such as the Poor Law Entry Book, are flat file, in other words all the information is related to one entity such as a person or an event. Other sources may be hierarchical or relational. Thus, in a census manuscript, an entry referring to the third child of a butler in a rural parish takes characteristics from the individual as well as from the household and the geographical unit. In other cases, say, information from customs records, the characteristics of an entry (nature, quantity and value of named cargo) might belong to individual owners (who had cargoes in many ships) or a ship (which has cargoes owned by many individuals).[5] The database can be an ideal way of presenting information for others to search for entries with specific characteristics. Most are able to handle large amounts of text such as entries from wills or court cases. However, they require reasonable initial certainty over the structure of data involved. The spreadsheet, of which EXCEL has become nearly universal, allows a much more open presentation of information. It also allows considerable and easy-to-understand manipulation of information. The spreadsheet has an openness and flexibility suited to many historical enquiries where the information is fixed but the structure is uncertain.

Whatever the software used, the historian is left with a dilemma. The machine is a powerful pattern seeker and pushes the historian towards a narrative dominated by groups and regularities and away from the particularity of person, place and event. This was evident in studies of British voting during the eighteenth and nineteenth centuries which used the parliamentary poll books. These were published documents characteristic of the period before 1872 when the British Ballot Act brought in secret voting.[6] Line after line contained the same sort of information:

Name:
Address:
Occupation or Type of Property:
Nature of vote:

Machine-based methodology in many studies pushed attention away from speeches, diaries, letters and newspaper reports, from the intricacies of personality, alliance, interest and ideology. Above all it directed attention to 'party' and 'occupation', characteristics embedded in the regularity of the document.[7]

THE BELFAST POOR HOUSE

Many historical judgements are based upon the distribution of key assets and characteristics across populations. Judgements of justice, fairness, responsibility and differences of experience require such observations. The spreadsheet provides simple ways of making such judgements. Paddy Devlin, a much respected labour political leader in Belfast during the 'troubles' and historian of the Northern Ireland Poor Law, claimed that the tensions of Belfast could be understood by recognising that, although the chances of an individual Catholic being poor were greater than that of an individual Protestant, the majority of those in poverty were Protestant.[8] In the example which follows the spreadsheet is used to test and extend his hypothesis through an examination of the 1886 Entry Book of the Belfast Poor House.

The ruled pages of the Entry Book (Appendix 9.1(a)) were filled out with the handwriting of the clerks admitting individual after individual to the shelter of the workhouse. Such pages stare out as if waiting for the spreadsheet and database to be invented. It is an example of what the archivists call a particular instance paper, in other words a document which records the details of a particular sort of event that was repeated many times – a death, the proving of a will, a court case, a vote, an application for poor relief. Such documents often took a standard form.

The initial exploration of Devlin's ideas was undertaken by extracting the first sixty cases from the Poor Law Entry book. The information was entered as nearly as possible to mimic the structure of the original document, often called a source-orientated philosophy. The initial entry included evident 'mistakes' in the original such as the male gender attributed to Rachel Young. This probably tells us little about Rachel but a great deal about the care and attention of the clerk involved that day. An asterisk was included where handwriting made interpretation difficult. Sixty cases are not enough for a full analysis of the information in this source, but it is enough to explore the methodologies, opportunities and potential problems. It is always wise when entering a new source into a machine-readable form to work with a few cases and take them through to the end point of analysis, so as to deal with problems before investing time and effort in a major data entry.

This 1886 source provided several opportunities for understanding what happened in the poor house and how poverty impacted on different sections of the population. The most complex and fruitful item of information was that marked 'employment'.[9] Many documents include information of this kind, indicating occupation or employment. To be pedantic this should be called the 'occupational or employment title' and regarded as an indicator of what the individual actually did. The concept-indicator relationship is central to the critical use of documents of this kind. The 'concept' is the activity individuals undertook to earn income. The 'indicator' in this case was the title included in the document. Thinking about the presentation of information at these two levels helps a critical approach and awareness of the intellectual and practical processes involved. The leap of imagination involved in complex judgements, such as the attribution of social class on the basis of an occupational title, is usually easy to spot. Equally important are apparently simple leaps such as that from the age given in a document (the indicator) to the concept of age (time elapsed since birth). We know that people tend to round up their ages to the nearest decade as they grow older, whilst others exaggerate age to avoid restrictions on employment or to qualify for a pension. At the same time age-related concepts such as child and adult vary with legal and cultural context and deny consistency and universality to the apparent authority of the number. Initial interpretation, as with all historical documents, demands an understanding of the circumstances of the document. The occupational title entered into many historical documents was both a claim by the individual named and an attribution by the document maker. The balance of these two factors varied with the document. The Poor Law Entry Book was likely to be more attribution than claim, given the vulnerable position of the individual named. The unfortunate women labelled as prostitute or 'prot' were unlikely to be in a position to argue. In other documents, such as the poll book, the titles are likely to be claims made by individuals more in control of their situation. The presentation of self in everyday documents was a complex process and varied according to the document.[10] The 'gentleman' in the poll book might be a 'merchant' in the trade directory, just as the 'cabinet maker' became a 'second hand furniture dealer'. The information in the column marked 'Employment' should more accurately be called 'Occupational or employment title claimed and attributed in the circumstances of entering the poor house'. No doubt the prostitutes would have preferred to call themselves something else. There were after all no prostitutes in the printed census tables.

The 'employment title' required further manipulation before producing comprehensible information. Most documents of this type yield very large numbers of occupational titles. The first sixty entries into the poor house contained eighteen different titles, although some were very minor variations. The Leeds Trade Directory of 1834 yielded over 2,000 titles from just over 9,000 entries. A table with so many lines would be incomprehensible and of little value, especially as about half the titles occurred only once. The titles needed grouping into consistent categories as the basis of analysis. The set of categories should have a number of qualities:

- They must be comprehensive and include all the values attributed to the relevant variable, even if one category is that admission of defeat, 'others'.
- They must be mutually exclusive – the poor publican will be left in confusion faced with the choice between 'retailer' and 'drink trade'.
- Complex and information-rich variables require multidimensional categorisation. Occupations might be coded according to education, or type of output, or the relationship to capital. The publican can be placed as a retailer, distinct from merchants, manufacturers, professional men in one dimension based upon the relationship to capital. In terms of the services or output produced, the publican can be placed in the 'drink trade' separated from textiles, education, engineering.
- The code needs a theoretical basis. Thus a code based on the relationship to capital assumes that this relationship has a major influence on political and social behaviour, and that the nature of output has a different sort of impact.
- The process of attributing a particular title to a category should depend on the information in the title and only that information. Cross-referencing to other information in the document will invalidate later analysis. A title like 'baker' can indicate employer, employee, retailer, bread manufacturer or wholesaler. If the individual is allocated to one group or another through, say the address or the presence of servants in the household, then any claim that employers have servants and employees do not would be meaningless.
- The nature of the categories should be sensitive to the context. We know that in the nineteenth century many bakers would produce and sell. Thus it

makes sense to have a category for 'distribution and production' recognising the imperfect division of labour of the period.

- In an ideal world a system of categorisation will be compatible with that used by other historians and analysts. This is a counsel of perfection as systems of categorisation vary quite rightly with the purpose of the historian, the nature of the documents and the structure of work as it varied over time and place.
- Finally, a system should avoid categories with small numbers of cases, although if in doubt it is better to start with more rather than less and amalgamate categories as analysis proceeds. Thus the analysis of the Leeds Poll Books, Trade Directories and associated nominal information for the 1830s began with over twenty categories in the status-related dimension. In the end about six categories did all the work.[11]

The very simple information under 'employment' in the Poor Law Entry Book included eighteen titles. It was decided to code them according to status as implied by the relationship to capital (see Table 9.1). 'None' (i.e. lacking any title) and 'labourer' stood on their own, as did the prostitutes. There was then a group linked to the textile mill industry of Belfast. There were some craft occupations and a number of minor retailers, perhaps penny capitalists.[12] An extra column was added to the table of employment titles and a code attributed to each title. 'Chainy' seemed to be 'dairy' badly written. Many specialist words, such as 'hackler' for those who worked in the preparation of flax for spinning, can be checked in the *Oxford English Dictionary*, now available online in many libraries.

The information in the first three columns of Table 9.1 (title, frequency, code) forms a look-up table. This is simply an array of information which enables the user to instruct the spreadsheet, through a function, to examine the value of a variable, such as occupational title in the database, 'look it up' in the look-up table and attribute a value from that table to the individual case in the database (see Appendix 9.1(b)). Thus a plasterer would be allocated the value 5, placing this individual in the category 'craft'.

Like much of the literature on Irish history, Paddy Devlin's study invites us to look at religious identity as an important analytical category. Indeed, it was symptomatic of a sectarian society that the Poor Law, like many agencies, saw the need to record 'religion' (see Table 9.2).

Table 9.2 gives an initial summary showing the relative security of Presbyterians, the shared vulnerability of Episcopalian and Catholic males and the extreme vulnerability of Catholic women. A critical concept-indicator approach is relevant here and issues of claim and attribution arise. At the same time the document and the methodologies invited by spreadsheet and database tend to reify religious identity. The categories are presented as bounded and

Table 9.1 Occupational titles drawn from the Entry Book to the Belfast Poor House, 1886, together with the code for each title and the category names

Title	Frequency	Code	Category	Code
None	18	1	None	1
Lab	11	2	Labourer	2
Mill	6	3	Mills	3
Servant	5	6	Retail	4
Prost	4	7	Craft	5
Carpenter	2	5	Servant	6
Dealer	2	4	Prostitute	7
Weaver	2	3		
Barber	1	4		
Chainy*	1	4		
Hackler	1	3		
Labourer	1	2		
Plasterer	1	5		
Plougher	1	5		
Prot	1	7		
Servy*	1	6		
Smoother	1	3		
Winder	1	3		

* Handwriting made interpretation difficult.

Source: Indoor Relief Register of the Belfast Poor House, 1886. Public Record Office of Northern Ireland. BG 7/G/3.

Table 9.2 Religion and gender of the first sixty entrants to the Belfast Poor House, 1886

Religion	Gender		Total
	Female	Male	
Episcopalian	5	12	17
Presbyterian	4	4	8
Catholic	21	14	35
Total	30	30	60

Source: as for Table 9.1.

unproblematic and avoid issues of mixed marriage and those who 'turned' from one religion to another.[13]

We can go further and relate religious identity to the occupational groups we created earlier (see Table 9.3).

These are small numbers but they already show the importance of Episcopalian labourers and Catholic mill workers and prostitutes. As always these results need critical interpretation, the striking cell total suggesting a large Catholic share of prostitution may well be a result of chance distributions

Table 9.3 Religion and occupation of the first sixty entrants to the Belfast Poor House, 1886

Occupation	Religion			
	Church of Ireland	Presbyterian	Catholic	Total
None	5	1	12	18
Labourer	6	2	4	12
Mills	1	2	8	11
Retail			4	4
Craft	1	2	1	4
Servants	3	1	2	6
Prostitutes	1		4	5
Total	17	8	35	60

Source: as for Table 9.1.

within small numbers. Given the concept-indicator issue, it may also tell us that Catholics were more likely to be attributed the label 'prot' when they entered the poor house. Does this mean they were more likely to be prostitutes?

A final insight can be gained by exploiting the manner in which EXCEL stores dates. Thus John Cairns entered the poor house on 12 March 1886. In fact EXCEL stores this as a number, 30021, which it then formats and presents as 12 March. A complication we can ignore for the moment is that the earliest date which EXCEL recognises is 2 January 1904 which equals one, a reminder that the software was not made for historians, but for most purposes such as the calculations we are about to carry out this does not matter. A simple function, '= date of leaving minus date of entry' provides an output which can be formatted as a number giving the number of days spent in the poor house. Over half the entrants spent less than ten days in the poor house, eight of them one to two days. The longest stayer was eighty-three days.

Thus preliminary analysis gave support to Devlin's judgements, but the ability to handle larger amounts of information in a systematic manner provided a greater complexity of judgement. The vulnerability of Catholic women brings gender as well as religion into the analysis. The comparison of Episcopalian and Presbyterian points to differences of experience amongst Protestants, and the short stay of most of those in the poor house invites an examination of the meaning of entry into the poor house.

SEMI-STANDARDISED DOCUMENTS

Many particular instance papers, especially those from earlier centuries, fit uneasily into the spreadsheet. Documents such as wills and records of court cases are semi-standardised. The last will and testament of Joseph Rollinson comes from the records of the Ecclesiastical Courts in York in the early 1830s (see Appendix 9.2(a)). It was one of several hundred wills used in a study of the relationships of family, gender and property amongst the nineteenth-century English middle classes. The wills proved a rich source of information on property and social, especially family, relationships. The approach adopted in the study was a simple and direct one. It required a short learning curve (important when planning the time budget of a research project) and adopted the metaphor of the social science questionnaire.

Much of the information from the wills fitted easily into the 'face sheet' of a questionnaire – name, occupation, address and the sworn value of probate. After that the text of the will became the 'respondent' for a series of questions related to the research project:[14]

Do you have a wife who is alive?
What provisions are made for your widow?
Do you have children; how many sons and daughters?
Do you make provision for other relatives [sisters, cousins, nieces . . .]?
How do you describe your property?
What items of real estate do you mention?
What other specific items of property do you mention?

And so on. The answers were then coded and placed in a spreadsheet for further analysis. Again it is wise to process a small number of cases and carry them right through the analysis before conducting a full exploration of the source. Following the metaphor of the survey, this was the trialling of the questionnaire.

Rollinson's will was one of many in which men made provision for widows under a variety of conditions. The conditions were placed into four groups:

absolute transfer of property to the widow;
trust established to provide widow with income for her natural life;
trust established to provide widow with income until she remarried;
trust established to provide widow with a reduced income if she remarried.

Initially it appeared that this might represent major differences in the way men regarded their marriage, its powers and obligations. After a while, several examples emerged in which the 'widowhood only' and the 'reducing on remarriage' provisions were linked with evidence of minor children. Wills contained phrases such as 'when reaches age of majority'. At this point, the question: 'Do you have any children below age of 21' was added and the trial group re-read. Iterations of this kind often produce the most fruitful analysis.[15]

Table 9.4 Conditions on which property was left to widows and evidence of children in Leeds wills, 1830–4

(From variable 'condition')	No children	Children	Minors
Absolute	13	8	2
	(52.00)	(13.79)	(4.17)
Natural life	12	35	15
	(48.00)	(60.34)	(31.25)
Reducers	0	3	11
	–	(5.17)	(22.92)
Widowhood or natural life	0	12	19
	–	(20.69)	(39.58)

N.B. The figures in brackets give each condition as a percentage of each group of the variable children.

Source: Leeds Wills proved in the Ecclesiastical Courts of York, 1830–4, Borthwick Institute, University of York.

Other questions were suggested by contemporary advice on will making. For example, great emphasis at this period was put on treating children with equity rather than with any form of primogeniture. The data set was created by a careful reading of the text of the wills and the systematic asking of questions. There is an extract in Appendix 9.2. Each case was provided with an ID number, enabling easy reference to the notes and copies taken from the original wills. Some variables were simple binaries (0 or 1), such as the answer to the question, 'Do you have a wife?' Others coded qualitative information such as the manner in which equity was sought for children. The occupational titles were coded in terms of social status. The keeping and updating of a codebook was crucial, and included notes on the logic of coding decisions essential to the integrity of the process.

A cross-tabulation of the manner in which men left property to their widows and the evidence in the wills for the existence of children (adult and minors) showed strong evidence of a relationship. Table 9.4 was typical of the outcomes from the type of analysis outlined here.

This table highlighted a tension present in many historical studies. At one level it enabled useful generalisation. Some of the scores were very strong: sixty per cent of widows with grown-up children gained an income for the rest of their life, but the man retained control over the distribution of the capital to children. Where there was evidence of minor children, sixty-two per cent of women who remarried lost all or part of their income. At the same time, others deviated from the generalisations. Who were the two men who ignored the social convention that minor children should be protected? Extracting them from the data showed them both to be men with a low sworn value of probate. In cases like this, it may be that the two men displayed their individuality, or that the table examined the relationship of two key factors in situations of complexity, where other factors such as economic status were important. This led to other tables looking at the relationship between indicators of economic status and the conditions for widows. Examining the 'deviants' from the initial child to condition relationship provided a more subtle understanding of the choices made by individuals.

RECORD LINKAGE

Many of the most important advances in historical understanding over the past thirty years have depended on some form of nominal record linkage.[16] This may take place within a specific record, as in the case of parish register-based family reconstitution. It often takes place between records, as in the case of the inter-census mobility studies common in the United States.[17] The use of particular instance papers and other nominal listings, together with the resources of information technology, create the possibility of such linkages on a massive scale and demand careful rule-based procedures if the implications of this process for historical judgement are to be controlled.

Nominal record linkage is essentially the task of creating a new document which attributes information from two or more documents, or entries in the same document, to create 'new' individuals. An extract from the Leeds study used in this example is given in Appendix 9.3. The first column identified the document of origin. It was useful to choose document IDs which sorted entries into a required sequence. Thus the large directory was first with 99 and the poll books in sequence as 100 for 1832 and 400 for 1834. The requisitions were gathered together in the 100s and subscription lists in the 500s. The second column gave an ID to each newly created 'individual'. Several manipulations were required before this material was ready for statistical analysis.

This example, taken from a study of middle-class associational culture in the nineteenth century, was modelled on the community studies which dominated British sociology in the 1960s.[18] As always the first task was to define the research aims which, in this case, were to trace patterns of behaviour and structure in the middle classes of a north of England industrial town, and then to identify the sources which enabled these aims to be made operational. The town of Leeds was chosen because it was large enough to generate a variety of social and political actions, and to generate a wide range of the sources required. Many aspects of the study sought simple measurements of the middle class. How big was it, what was its economic and social structure? In some cases the sources provided varied operational definitions of the middle classes. The Parliamentary Poll Book was directly related to the £10 householder voting qualification which had been chosen by the reformers of 1832 because they believed it included the bulk of the middle class. Trade Directories selected entries in a different way. They included those with sufficient status to be sought by outsiders and by those sending letters as well as those who had some form of independent economic existence, a business or professional service. The poll books tended to include about fourteen per cent of the adult male population. The Trade Directory of 1834 listed around twenty-five per cent of adult males and three per cent of adult females. These figures alone were representative of the gendered presentation of class. The variation was a reminder of the fluidity of definition and boundary, which was part of the experience of class rather than a warning that one source was somehow wrong. Both sources contained large numbers of people. There were 4,062 entries in the 1832 Poll Book, 4,644 in the 1834 Poll Book and 9,101 in the Trade Directory of 1834. Given the considerable cost of data entry, consideration should be given to sampling. Letter cluster sampling has proved the most useful. Entries starting with the same group of letters are used, thus maximising the possibility of entries representing the same individual coming together. It is important to avoid or to balance clusters that favour regional or ethnic groups.[19]

In the case of the middle-class study, sampling was of little use because large lists were to be linked with shorter lists that allowed other forms of the presentation of self. Lists came from various religious congregations, subscriptions for the local hospital and voluntary poor relief funds, requisitions for holding public meetings and memberships of various associations. Linking, say, a 200-strong membership list to a ten per cent sample of a 5,000-entry poll book would at most produce twenty links. The numbers in the resulting analysis would be too small to be of value.

Most studies choose lists created close together in terms of time and space, as this produces a strong likelihood they contained the same people. However, proximity had the consequence that this choice favoured those who were stable in terms of residence. Research designs to overcome this require considerable resources. A study of French national social structure based upon the letters TRA – chosen because they have minimal regional and ethnic bias – revealed a population with much greater geographical and occupational mobility than could be anticipated from the locality studies of the *Annales* School.[20] Many Scandinavian population registers, like the Roteman archives of Stockholm, recorded all changes of residence, enabling links to be made within the document. Such reconstructions of personal histories have shown the importance of short-distance and short-term migration and return migration in the lives of many. This is no reason for avoiding the community study; it does show the need for the critical evaluation of results.

Table 9.5 Quality of linkage between the Leeds Parliamentary Poll Book of 1832 and that of 1834

Inference code	Inference type	N	%
0	No link at unique name level	1223	13.3
1	Link at unique name level	4444	48.2
3	Second and third entries linked or null	271	3.0
5	No link at address level	318	3.3
6	Link at address level	2242	24.3
9	No possible link or null link	728	7.9

Source: Morris, R. J., *Class, Sect and Party: the Making of the British Middle Class, Leeds, 1820–50* (Manchester: Manchester University Press, 1990).

Rule-based record linkage enables greater critical control over the results. Strategies vary but they all steer a path between two types of risk – making false links and failing to make true links. In some cases rules can be enhanced by the logic of the document. In family reconstitution it seems reasonable to decide that individuals cannot marry a few years after their death, even if name and occupation are the same. More controversially, few mistakes will be made by deciding that a woman cannot give birth to a child within sixteen years of her birth. Most documents do not have this logic. Most historians like to make maximum use of information. Such a strategy will reduce the chances of failed links but create hidden biases in favour of those who generate most information.

The alternative strategy proposed for the middle classes was to use unique names as a basis for linkage and add an inference code when other information had been used (see Table 9.5). The basic rules were:

- If individual entries had the same name and the name occurred once in each list then a true link was made. Minor spelling variations were allowed.
- If a name occurred in only one record it was held to be a null link. A confident negative link was as important as a positive one. The change in results between the 1832 and 1834 elections was caused by 1832 voters who were not in the 1834 list, and by new entries for 1834 rather than people who changed their mind between elections.
- A further group of links was made using information from the address. This was signalled by an inference code, so that the effect of using this additional information could be monitored. This information was a bias towards stability.
- The remaining entries were simply noted as having possible but undecided links.
- Information on occupation was not used as the occupational title played a central part in analysis.

Table 9.6 Distribution of votes in the Leeds Parliamentary Election, 1834

	1834 Poll Book	Linked population	Unique name links only
Beckett (Tory)	41.3	43.2	44.2
Baines (Whig)	41.5	45.1	42.5
Bower (Radical)	0.5	0.7	1.0
Did not vote	16.6	11.6	12.4

Source: as for Table 9.5.

Thus, in Table 9.5, over sixty per cent of the entries were linked or classified as null on unique names alone, over ninety per cent if address information was used. The influence of the method of linking can be seen by comparing the distribution of votes for all the voters in the 1834 Poll Book, for those who were in the linked population and for those who were linked by unique names (see Table 9.6).

Unique names reduced the number of non-voters and increased the Tory vote. Both of these suggested that unique name links were of higher social status than the overall population of the poll book. In general higher status people had more complicated and unusual names and hence were easier to link. When address level was used, the bias to stability reduced the non-voters even further, reflecting stability, but restored the share of Whig voters.

When the three big lists were linked with smaller lists, further depth was added to the understanding of middle-class behaviour and structure. Membership of religious congregations proved an excellent guide to political behaviour, and the leadership of commercial and professional males in the key voluntary associations was very evident. Record linkage drew attention to many patterns of behaviour within populations. These were often patterns hidden by the attention given to prominent individuals. In this example the leadership of professional and commercial males in an 'industrial' community was very clear as was the importance of religious identity as much as social status in political behaviour.

CONCLUSIONS

The methods entailed in these examples do involve some technical skills, albeit very simple ones, but the most important demand on the historian is intellectual. The ability of the machine to handle large bodies of information in a consistent rule-based manner will magnify the impact of decisions. Often this is hidden in the apparent authority of the table and its numbers. The decision to use 'address' in record linkage had an important impact on results. The use of 'occupational titles' required an analysis of text and discourse often forgotten in apparently quantitative studies. IT-based methods favour pattern seeking and generalisations, which can be countered by examining individual decisions.

Many of the techniques outlined here have received little attention from historians in the recent past. Methodologies have tended to focus on the text, the discourse and the narrative. Ironically, the advances in information technology in terms of learning curves, speed and capacity have made the use and creation of machine-readable data easier.[21] The growth of online sources has made the contextualisation of such source material easier and more extensive. Some of the barriers arise from current methodological preferences. Others arise from historians' reluctance to use datasets created by others (unlike social scientists who regularly employ household and election surveys and the like from earlier generations). Barriers also arise from the tendency to create many online datasets for the 'family history' industry, present them in forms suited to the search for individuals rather than total populations, and offer access in return for credit card details. There is much negotiation to be done to gain access to such information and exploit its potential for historical analysis.

Other barriers arise from several characteristics of a carefully created dataset. It is resource greedy. It takes time to construct. The time budget for data entry is still high. It requires an investment in technical skills, even the minimal ones outlined here. It requires disciplined techniques of data structuring and the creation of analytical tools such as occupational categories. Perhaps the most serious problem arises from the density and massive quantities of information in a high-quality dataset. Such datasets are evidence of the extraordinary complexity of human interaction and its change over time.[22] The comprehension and comprehensible presentation of such information is not an easy task. Each cross-tabulation is evidence of the tension between the need to generalise and the individuality of each 'case'. Each time an occupational title is grouped into a category, however theoretically sound and operationally appropriate, comprehensibility is increased and information is destroyed. The well-constructed table, and generalisations derived from it, needs to be balanced by the individuality of the example, both typical and deviant. This is one version of the tension between the specific and the general that dominates all good history. It is both an art and a social science.

APPENDIX 9.1 (A)

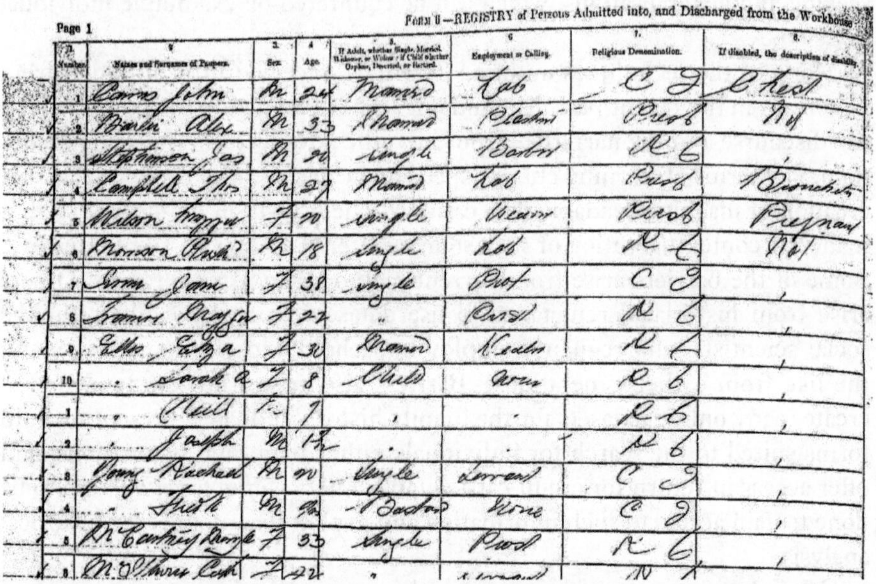

Page 1

FORM 8.—REGISTRY of Persons Admitted into, and Discharged from the Workhouse

1. Number	2. Names and Surnames of Paupers.	3. Sex.	4. Age.	5. If Adult, whether Single, Married, Widower, or Widow: if Child whether Orphan, Deserted, or Bastard.	6. Employment or Calling.	7. Religious Denomination.	8. If disabled, the description of disability.
1	Cairns John	M	24	Married	Lab	C I	Chest
2	Martin Alex	M	33	Married	Plaster	Presb	Nil
3	Stephenson Jas	M	20	Single	Barber	R C	"
4	Campbell Thos	M	27	Married	Lab	Presb	Bronchitis
5	Wilson Maggie	F	20	Single	Weaver	Presb	Pregnant
6	Morrison Richd	M	18	Single	Lab	R C	Nil
7	[illegible] Jane	F	38	Single	Prost	C I	"
8	Travers Maggie	F	22	"	Prost	R C	"
9	Ellis Eliza	F	30	Married	[illegible]	R C	"
10	" Sarah A	F	8	Child	None	R C	"
1	" [illegible]	F	7	"	"	R C	"
2	" Joseph	M	1½	"	"	R C	"
3	[illegible] Rachael	F	20	Single	Servant	C I	"
4	" Fredk	M	½	Bastard	None	C I	"
5	McCartney [illegible]	F	33	Single	Prost	R C	"
6	[illegible] Cath	F	22	"	Servant	R C	"

Source: Public Record Office Northern Ireland, BG7/G/3.

Figure 9.1 Indoor Relief Register from the Belfast Poor House, 1886. Reproduced with permission of the Deputy Keeper of the Records and the Public Record Office Northern Ireland.

APPENDIX 9.1(B)

Table 9.7 Data from page 1 of Entry Register of Belfast Poor House as entered into a spreadsheet

Number	Surname	Prenames	Sex	Age	Status	Employ-ment[a]	Relig[b]	Address	House	Obser-vations	Residence	Date entry/ birth	Date left/ died
1	Cairns	John	M	24	married	lab	CI	Edward St	3	ill clothed	Belfast	12/3/86	7/4/86
2	Bailin	Alex	M	33	married	plasterer	P	Lynas St	7	ill clothed	Belfast	12/3/86	3/4/86
3	Stephenson	Jas	M	20	single	barber	RC	Verner St	18	ill clothed	Belfast	12/3/86	18/3/86
4	Campbell	Thos	M	27	married	lab	P	Greenland St	32	ill clothed	Belfast	12/3/86	12/4/86
5	Wilson	Margaret	F	20	single	weaver	P	no address		ill clothed	Belfast	12/3/86	15/4/86
6	Morrison	Richd	M	18	single	lab	RC	no address		ill clothed	Belfast	12/3/86	22/3/86
7	Grey*	Jane	F	38	single	prot	CI	no address		ill clothed	Belfast	12/3/86	15/3/86
8	Travers	Maggie	F	22	single	prost	RC	no address		ill clothed	Belfast	12/3/86	15/3/86
9	Ellis	Eliza	F	30	married	dealer	RC	no address		ill clothed	Belfast	12/3/86	17/3/86
10	Ellis	Sarah A	F	8	child	none	RC	no address		ill clothed	Belfast	12/3/86	17/3/86
11	Ellis	Neill	M	7	child	none	RC	no address		ill clothed	Belfast	12/3/86	17/3/86
12	Ellis	Joseph	M	1.9	child	none	RC	no address		ill clothed	Belfast	12/3/86	17/3/86
13	Young	Rachael	M [sic]	20	single	servant	CI	no address		ill clothed	Belfast	12/3/86	19/3/86
14	Young	Fredk	M	0.9	bastard	none	CI	no address		ill clothed	Belfast	12/3/86	19/3/86
15	McCartney	Maryle*	F	33	single	prost	RC	North Queen St		ill clothed	Belfast	12/3/86	24/3/86
16	McIlhoren	Cath	F	22	single	servant	RC	no address		ill clothed	Belfast	12/3/86	24/3/86
17	O Connell	Ann	F	25	single	servant	RC	Hopeford Ave	16	ill clothed	Belfast	12/3/86	8/4/86
18	McBride	Mary	F	60	widow	mill	RC						

* Handwriting made interpretation difficult.

[a] See Table 9.1.

[b] RC, Roman Catholic; CI, Church of Ireland; P, Protestant

APPENDIX 9.2 (A)

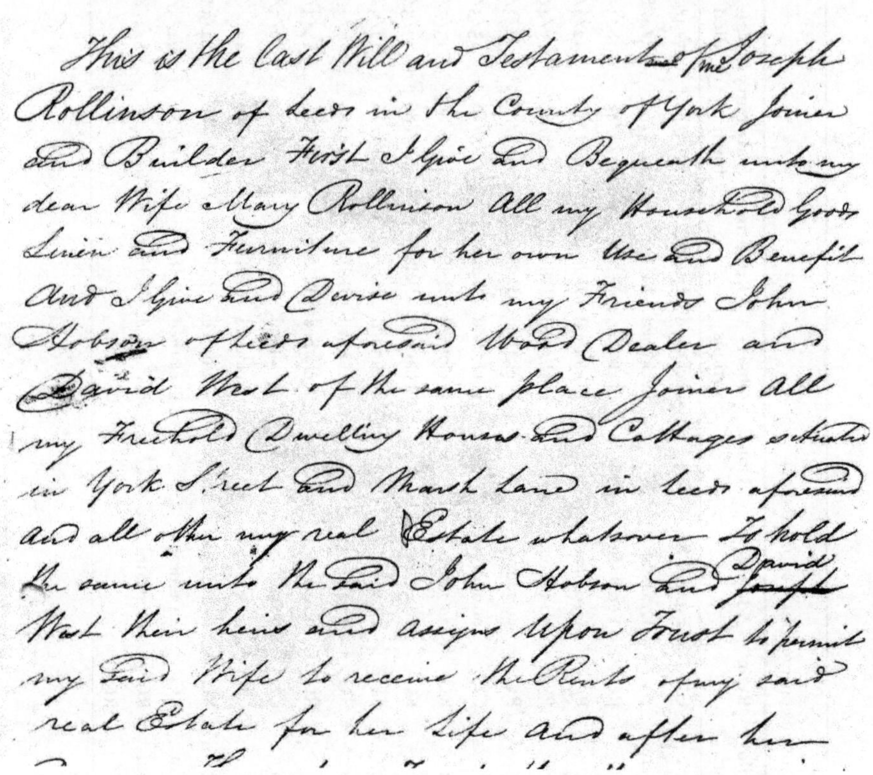

This is the last Will and Testament of me Joseph
Rollinson of Leeds in the County of York Joiner
and Builder First I Give and Bequeath unto my
dear Wife Mary Rollinson All my Household Goods
Linen and Furniture for her own Use and Benefit
And I Give and Devise unto my Friends John
Hobson of Leeds aforesaid Wood Dealer and
David West of the same place Joiner All
my Freehold Dwelling Houses and Cottages situate
in York Street and Marsh Lane in Leeds aforesaid
and all other my real Estate whatsoever To hold
the same unto the said John Hobson and ~~Joseph~~ David
West their heirs and assigns Upon Trust to permit
my said Wife to receive the Rents of my said
real Estate for her Life and after her

Source: Borthwick Institute, University of York.

Figure 9.2 Will of Joseph Rollinson, joiner, probate 8 June 1830. Reproduced with permission of the Borthwick Institute, University of York.

APPENDIX 9.2(B)

Table 9.8 Extract from a database of Leeds wills proved in the Ecclesiastical Courts of York, 1830–4

Id	Forename	Surname	Occupation	Civil status	Sworn value	Gender	Status	Sons	Daughters	Wives	Equity	Condition	Minors	Categories
1	Ann	Fowwether	no title	Widow	20	2	99	3	3	0	10	99	1	1
2	James	Dufton	carpenter	Male	100	1	55	0	4	1	1	2	1	3
3	Phillis	Phillips	no title	Spinster	100	2	99	0	0	0	10	99	0	2
4	Michael	Thackrey	Esq	Male	10000	1	90	2	1	1	2	2	1	2
5	Sarah	Padgit	no title	Spinster	20	2	99	0	0	0	10	99	0	2
7	John	Scott	woolstapler	Male	100	1	45	0	0	0	10	99	0	2
8	George	Baker	gentleman	Male	200	1	90	0	0	1	10	2	0	2
9	James	Mann	maltster	Male	1000	1	30	2	8	0	10	99	1	2
11	Edward	Armitage	Esq	Male	18000	1	90	4	0	1	3	2	1	3
13	Christopher	Slater	yeoman	Male	300	1	12	0	0	1	10	1	0	0
14	George	Hanson	potter	Male	100	1	55	0	0	1	10	1	0	2

APPENDIX 9.3

Table 9.9 Sample from the linked population, Leeds, 1830–40 (ID indicates the indentity number given to each individual case that was created from the original data. IND was the code given to the 'industrial activity' or type of economic output indicated by the occupational title.)

Doc	Id	Inference	Vote	Area	Sub	Status	Ind	Surname	Forename	Occupation/property	Address
99	348	6				48	805	Bailey	Thomas	bookkeeper	17 Portland Street
100	348	6	4	10		12	70	Bailey	Thomas	house	Portland Street
400	348	6	4	10		55	603	Bailey	Thomas	tailor	Wellington Lane
99	349	1				30	603	Bailey	William	tailor and draper	4 Meadow Lane
100	349	1	3	10		30	30	Bailey	William	house and shop	Meadow Lane
400	349	1	1	10		55	603	Bailey	William	tailor	Meadow Lane
99	357	0				30	151	Baines	William C	tea dealer and tobacconist	43 Meadow Lane
99	358	0				50	119	Baker	Ann	tobacco manufacturer	26 St Peters Square
99	359	0				55	630	Baker	Ann & Mary	dress	17 Broans Pl North St
99	360	0				50	504	Baker	Benjamin	cloth dresser	8 School Street
99	361	0				66	957	Baker	Elizabeth	ladies boarding seminary	Nassau Cottage Roundhay Road
99	363	1				10	100	Baker	John	farmer	Nassau
100	363	1	3	19		14	70	Baker	John	house and land	Potternewton
400	363	1	1	19		10	100	Baker	John	farmer	Nassau
99	364	0				50	534	Baker	Joseph	woolsorter	126 York Street
99	366	0				66	950	Baker	Maria & Louisa	preparatory school for young gentlemen	3 Spencer Place Roundhay Road
99	367	0				55	630	Baker	Mary & Emma	dress makers	Sandford Street S C
99	368	1				61	922	Baker	Robert	surgeon	27 Park Row
100	368	1	4	10		12	70	Baker	Robert	house	Kirkgate
201	368							Baker	Robert		
214	368							Baker	Robert		
225	368							Baker	Robert		
230	368							Baker	Robert		
400	368	1	2	10		61	922	Baker	Robert	surgeon	Kirkgate
510	368	1		0	105			Baker	Robert		

NOTES

1. Robert W. Fogel, *Railroads and American Economic Growth* (Baltimore, MD: Johns Hopkins Press, 1964); G. R. Hawke, *Railways and Economic Growth in England and Wales, 1840–1870* (Oxford: Oxford University Press, 1970); N. F. R. Crafts, *British Economic Growth during the Industrial Revolution* (Oxford: Oxford University Press, 1985); E. A. Wrigley and R. S. Scholfield, *The Population History of England, 1541–1871* (Cambridge: Cambridge University Press, 1981); Hartmut Kaelble, 'Social mobility in America and Europe: a comparison of nineteenth century cities', *Urban History Yearbook* (1981), pp. 24–31; Michael Anderson, *Family Structure in Nineteenth Century Lancashire* (Cambridge: Cambridge University Press, 1971); John Phillips, *Electoral Behaviour in Unreformed England, 1761–1802* (Princeton, NJ: Princeton University Press, 1981); Frank O'Gorman, *Voters, Parties and Patrons* (Oxford: Clarendon Press, 1989); S. Nicholas, *Convict Workers: Re-interpreting Australia's Past* (Cambridge: Cambridge University Press, 1988).

2. Sonja Cameron and Sarah Richardson, *Using Computers in History* (London: Macmillan, 2005); Daniel I. Greenstein, *A Historian's Guide to Computing* (Oxford: Oxford University Press, 1994); Pat Hudson, *History by Numbers: an Introduction to Quantitative Approaches* (London: Arnold, 2000).

3. For taking forward methods discussed here, see Catherine Marsh, *Exploring Data: an Introduction to Data Analysis for Social Scientists* (Cambridge: Polity Press, 1988).

4. A database is any discreet body of information organised in a manner suitable for electronic exploitation.

5. Charles Harvey and Jon Press, *Databases in Historical Research* (London: Macmillan, 1996).

6. John Foster, *Class Struggle and the Industrial Revolution: Three English Towns* (London: Weidenfeld and Nicholson, 1974); John A. Phillips, 'Computing parliamentary history', in John A. Phillips (ed.), *Parliamentary History* (Edinburgh: Edinburgh University Press, 1994), pp. 473–89; J. C. Mitchell and J. Cornforth, 'The political demography of Cambridge, 1832–1868', *Albion* 4 (1977), pp. 242–72.

7. R. J. Morris, 'Computers and the subversion of British history', *Journal of British Studies* 34:4 (1995), pp. 503–28.

8. Paddy Devlin, *Yes We Have no Bananas. Outdoor Relief in Belfast 1920–39* (Belfast: Blackstaff Press, 1981).

9. Penny Corfield and Derek Keene (eds), *Work in Towns, 850–1850* (Leicester: Leicester University Press, 1990), on changing structures of work over the long term.

10. Graeme Morton, 'Presenting the self: record linkage and referring to ordinary historical persons', *History and Computing* 6:1 (1994), pp. 12–20.

11. R. J. Morris, *Class, Sect and Party: the Making of the British Middle Class, Leeds, 1820–50* (Manchester: Manchester University Press, 1990); R. J. Morris, 'Occupational coding: principles and examples', *Historical Social Research/Historische Sozialforschung* 15:1 (1990), pp. 3–29.

12. John Benson, *The Penny Capitalists: a Study of 19th Century Working Class Entrepreneurs* (Dublin: Gill and Macmillan, 1983).

13. Similar issues arise with documents that invite 'ethnic' categories.

14. R. J. Morris, *Men, Women and Property in England, 1780–1870* (Cambridge: Cambridge University Press, 2005).

15. Ibid. pp. 101–9.

16. *History and Computing* 4:1 (1992) and 6:3 (1994). These two special issues surveyed a variety of approaches.

17. Hartmut Kaelble, 'Social mobility in America and Europe: a comparison of nineteenth century cities', *Urban History Yearbook* (1981), pp. 24–38 for an excellent survey.

18. Margaret Stacey, *Tradition and Change: a Study of Banbury* (London: Oxford University Press, 1960).

19. Sarah Richardson, 'Letter cluster sampling and nominal record linkage', *History and Computing* 6:3 (1994), pp. 168–77.

20. Jacques Dupâquier and Denis Kessler, *La société française au XIX siècle: tradition, transition, transformation* (Paris: Feyard, 1992).

21. Terry Coppock (ed.), *Information Technology and Scholarship: Applications in the Humanities and Social Sciences* (Oxford: Oxford University Press for the British Academy, 1999); Terry Coppock (ed.), *Making Information Available in Digital Format: Perspectives from Practitioners* (Edinburgh: Stationery Office, 1999); Edward Higgs (ed.), *History and Electronic Artefact* (Oxford: Clarendon Press, 1998).

22. Alan MacFarlane, with Sarah Harrison and Charles Jardin, *Reconstructing Historical Communities* (Cambridge: Cambridge University Press, 1977). In his study of Earls Colne, the control of this complexity was directed by the theory and practice of anthropology. For structured theory-related argument based on detailed tabulation from the population registers of Sweden, Göran Hoppe and John Langton, *Peasantry to Capitalism: Western Ostergötlands* (Cambridge: Cambridge University Press, 1994).

FURTHER READING

Cameron, Sonja, and Sarah Richardson, *Using Computers in History* (London: Macmillan, 2005).

Greenstein, Daniel I., *A Historian's Guide to Computing* (Oxford: Oxford University Press, 1994).

Harvey, Charles, and Jon Press, *Databases in Historical Research* (London: Macmillan, 1996).

Higgs, Edward (ed.), *History and Electronic Artefact* (Oxford: Clarendon Press, 1998).

History and Computing, 4:1 (1992) and 6:3 (1994).

Hudson, Pat, *History by Numbers: an Introduction to Quantitative Approaches* (London: Arnold, 2000).

Marsh, Catherine, *Exploring Data: an Introduction to Data Analysis for Social Scientists* (Cambridge: Polity Press, 1988).

Morris, R. J., *Class, Sect and Party: the Making of the British Middle Class, Leeds, 1820–50* (Manchester: Manchester University Press, 1990).

Morton, Graeme, 'Presenting the self: record linkage and referring to ordinary historical persons', *History and Computing* 6:1 (1994), pp. 2–20.

CHAPTER 10

Digital Research

Bob Nicholson

Have you ever typed the word 'historian' into Google's image search engine? If not, you can probably guess what the results will be: page after page of men (and the occasional woman) sitting in a library or archive, pouring over stacks of leather-bound books and crumbling old documents. According to the popular imagination, we exist in a dimly-lit world of dust, paper, and tweed. Of course, there is some truth to this stereotype; many historians *do* spend plenty of time handling old objects and working in archives. But not as much as we used to. Over the past fifteen years, historical research has undergone a 'digital turn'.[1] The digitisation of historical books, periodicals, government records, artworks, photographs, films, maps, and a range of other sources has made it possible to explore sections of the world's great archives without ever leaving home. As a result, many historians now spend more time exploring the past with their laptop than they do in the library. Crucially, this is more than just a revolution of convenience. Digital archives have also enabled new kinds of research. As later sections of this chapter explore, we can now use full-text search engines to instantly pick out specific words and phrases from millions of pages of books and newspapers. Within a matter of seconds, we can unearth sources that have been buried for centuries under a 'vast terra incognita of print', or track the transnational movements of individual words, texts, people, and ideas with unprecedented precision.[2] Using more advanced digital tools, we can 'distant read' an entire archive and identify patterns that would never have been visible via conventional reading. This is just the tip of the iceberg. Digitisation is continually encouraging us to imagine new kinds of history; to ask new questions, develop new methodologies, and recover aspects of past experience that were once considered unknowable.

Much of this new research is being spearheaded by scholars working within the Digital Humanities (generally abbreviated DH). This is a rapidly expanding and dynamic field. DH 'laboratories', journals, conferences, degree programmes, and research networks are appearing all over the world. The interdisciplinary nature of this community, and the speed at which it is evolving, makes DH notoriously difficult to define, at least with any kind of lasting precision.[3] Broadly speaking, it involves the application of tools and methodologies from computing (and other technical/quantitative disciplines) to traditional humanities subjects such as history, literature, and linguistics. In many cases, this requires humanists to work collaboratively with computer scientists and software developers in order to design new archives, unpack complex historical datasets, and build new analytical tools. An increasing number of historians are also teaching themselves how to program in order to play more active roles in these projects.[4] This is exciting work, but the technical skills and funding required to work at the cutting edge of DH makes it difficult for many historians to enter the field. Fortunately, there is a middle ground between the library and the lab. You do not need to be an expert coder in order to make innovative use of existing digital tools and archives. Many of these resources are simple to use and open to anybody with a computer. Navigating them effectively requires some basic technical knowledge, but largely relies on the same critical thinking and detective skills that historians have always relied on.

This chapter provides an introduction to the core skills required in order to conduct digital research. Before we begin, it is important to stress that digital tools and archives are expanding and evolving too quickly to provide an in-depth guide to specific resources. Every archive's interface is slightly different, and by the time you read this book many of them will have been updated or replaced by new collections. Instead, this chapter outlines the core methodological questions that all historians need to ask whenever they log in to a new digital archive. It will offer practical tips on:

How to find and access new digital archives.
How to critically 'read' a digital archive.
How to construct effective keyword searches.
How to manage and analyse your results.

Most of the examples used to demonstrate these tips come from my own research on nineteenth-century Britain and America. However, the basic principles will apply to digital archives based on other time periods and locations.

FINDING AND ACCESSING DIGITAL ARCHIVES

A comprehensive survey of the world's digital archives lies beyond the scope of this chapter. There are thousands of collections available online and new ones are being continually unveiled. We have now reached a point where even the most enthusiastic proponents of digital research cannot keep pace with the volume of material that is now available. While it is possible to find some subject-specific guides on the internet, there is currently no comprehensive directory of digital archives. As a result, it can be frustratingly difficult to find out if a particular source has been digitised or not. A couple of years ago, I travelled all the way from England to the New York Public Library to consult books that later turned out to be available online. Similarly, I have spoken to colleagues who have spent months spooling through rolls of microfilmed newspapers in search of articles on a specific topic, only to discover that they could have found the same information (and a good deal more) after a few hours of keyword searching. So, before booking a hotel room and decamping to a distant record office, it is worth making absolutely sure that the sources you need are not available somewhere online. Unfortunately, there is no easy way to do this – it is likely that even the most comprehensive searches will miss something. Nevertheless, there are a few key techniques that usually produce results: search engines, social media, and library catalogues.

SEARCH ENGINES AND SOCIAL MEDIA

The obvious place to start is with a standard internet search engine such as Google, Bing, or DuckDuckGo. Each of these platforms derive and organise their results in slightly different ways, so it is worth running your enquiries through a few of them. Combining your specific search terms with words like 'archive', 'online', and 'digitised' will often return useful results. It is usually best to start with a fairly narrow search. For example, if we wanted to locate digital copies of a specific historical newspaper we might start by searching for the phrase 'Derby Mercury digital archive'. If this did not work, we could move onto broader search terms such as 'Derby newspapers digital archive' and then 'British newspapers digital archive'. These broader searches are particularly useful for identifying subscription-based archives. While many open-access repositories are fully indexed and searchable via google, their commercial cousins are trapped behind paywalls that make their contents trickier to locate. For example, if we wanted to locate copies of the Victorian comic periodical *Funny Folks*, a search for 'Funny Folks digital archive' on google would not return any useful results. However, a search for 'nineteenth century periodicals archive' would lead us to a promising-looking subscription database named *19th Century UK Periodicals*. After more digging, we would eventually discover that this archive contains the source that we are looking for. This kind of searching can be a time-consuming process, particularly when dealing with subscription-based archives that do not provide a publically accessible list of their holdings. Nevertheless, it is worth battling with these obstacles and persevering beyond the first page of results. Your searches may not lead directly to the archive itself, but they might lead you to a website, blogpost, forum, or even a tweet that points you in the right direction.

Indeed, social media platforms like Twitter, Tumblr, Facebook, Pinterest and Instagram are surprisingly useful tools for discovering lesser-known digital collections. Plenty of academic researchers and history enthusiasts now share their latest discoveries on these platforms, and these posts often provide links that lead back to the archive itself. Some libraries even use social media hosting services such as Flickr and YouTube as the main platform for displaying their digital collections. Searching these networks may require you to wade through thousands of selfies and cat pictures, but it is worth a try if conventional search engines do not do the job. On a similar note, try using your search engine's 'images' tab – these tools offer a useful way to skim through results and sometimes unearth images that lead directly to open-access collections. Finally, auction websites such as eBay can also function as unlikely digital archives. You do not need to buy anything, just search for historical items and view the pictures included with the auction listings. In some cases, this can help you find versions of a source that are not contained in conventional digital archives. For example, newspaper archives – in both their print and digital forms – usually acquire their content from bound volumes of periodicals rather than individual issues. These volumes often omit the covers and advertising wrappers that enclosed the paper when it was originally sold. Auction websites are a great resource for finding pictures of these discarded elements of the source. If you do plan to use eBay in this way, make sure you configure your search to include auctions that have finished – this gives you a much wider range of content to explore.

LIBRARY CATALOGUES

Library catalogues offer another avenue for discovering new digital tools and archives. They are particularly useful for identifying large, commercially pro-duced databases that are only available via institutional subscriptions. These archives do not tend to market themselves to the general public, so they are often difficult to find using conventional search engines. If you are affiliated with a university, the obvious place to start is with your own library catalogue. You should be able to remotely access most of its subscription databases using your university ID and password, though some will require you to be located on campus. It is worth remembering that your institution will probably not subscribe to every commercial digital archive in your field. Licenses for these resources can be extremely expensive, and even the world's largest and most prestigious research libraries do not provide access to everything. Try looking for useful databases in other university's catalogues – if you find one, you might be able to persuade your own librarian to sign up (or ask an obliging friend at a subscribing library to look things up for you). Finally, when you are searching these catalogues it is important to remember that they rarely contain detailed information on an archive's individual holdings. So, as with our earlier search for the periodical *Funny Folks*, you may need to use search terms that are likely to appear in an archive's title. Better still, some libraries have a section on their website that lists all of the databases that they subscribe to in alphabetical order. I recommend finding this list for your library and reading through it from top to bottom – you might be surprised by what you find.

SUBJECT-SPECIFIC SEARCH TIPS

As we have seen, looking for digital archives involves a bit of guesswork and plenty of perseverance. Once you have identified the key databases for your subject area and got to grips with their contents, you will soon find ways to bypass Google and focus your searches more effectively. In the meantime, you will find some general tips for locating commonly used historical materials below.

Books

Millions of out-of-copyright books have been digitised and made freely available online. The largest collections of historical publications are currently held by Google Books, the Internet Archive, the HathiTrust, the European Library/Europeana and Project Gutenberg.[5] These are all open-access (or part-open access) collections, so it is worth starting here before going in search of more specialist subscription archives. You can often view books in their original formats and search them for specific words and phrases. Some allow you to download entire books as pdf files. They have an eclectic range of material. In the Internet Archive, for example, you will find facsimiles of Charles Dickens' 1st editions as well as the 1908 yearbook of Spokane High School, a hydraulic jack repair manual from 1956, and millions of other texts. While these archives generally privilege British and American books, the Hathi Trust platform allows users to filter results by language and country of publication.

Newspapers

Historic newspapers are spread across a range of open-access and subscription-based archives. Some of these archives are devoted to well-known individual papers such as *The Times*, while others contain hundreds of different titles. Major archives include:

- Britain: Welsh Newspapers Online (open access); *British Newspaper Archive* (individual subscription); *Ancestry.com* (individual subscription); Gale's *19th Century British Library Newspapers, 19th Century UK Periodicals* and *18th Century Burney Collection* (institutional subscription); ProQuest's *British Periodicals Online* (institutional sub).[6]
- United States: Chronicling America (open access); Google's semi-abandoned news archive (open access); *NewspaperArchive*.com (individual subscription); ProQuest's *Historic Newspapers* (institutional subscription); Gale Cengage's *19th Century US Newspapers* (institutional subscription). Use the *Elephind* search engine to explore a range of smaller, open access archives.[7]
- Europe: The *Europeana Newspapers* (open access) search engine includes thousands of periodicals from libraries in France, Spain, Germany, Austria, the Netherlands and several other countries. Alternatively, try visiting the website of a country's national library – many offer some form of newspapers archive.[8]
- Other countries: Australia's *Trove* (open access); New Zealand's *Papers Past* (open access); Brazil's *Hemeroteca Digital Brasileira* (open access).[9] Commercial archives such as *Newspapers.com* and *NewspaperArchive.com* mainly focus on Britain and North America, but also have an eclectic range of content from other countries. The Centre for Research Libraries also hosts a fairly comprehensive list of newspaper archives organised by country.[10]

These archives have good (but by no means comprehensive) coverage for the nineteenth and early twentieth centuries. Holdings for the eighteenth century and earlier are often rather patchy – they suffer from a greater number of missing issues and often have older typefaces that reduce the accuracy of keyword searches. At the other end of the spectrum, copyright restrictions mean that the the twentieth century, and particularly the post-war period, is very poorly served by existing newspaper archives. From the 1990s onwards, born-digital news coverage is widely available via some newspapers' own websites as well as research databases such as *NewsBank* (institutional subscription).[11]

Personal/government records

Genealogy websites are the best resource if you want to access digital copies of census records, electoral rolls, birth, marriage, and death certificates, military service records, wills, passenger lists, or any other documents that contain personal information. *Ancestry.com* is currently the most widely used service and holds records for Briain, North America, Australia, Germany, Italy, France, and Sweden. This should be your first port of call, but investigate its many competitors before paying for a subscription. If you would prefer not to pay, the popularity of family history means that many of these databases can be accessed for free at your local library. National record offices are also a good source of official documents, though the quality of their digital services vary from country to country. The UK's National Archives has a particularly good online catalogue and a website that offers in-depth guides on how to access a wide range of archival sources in both digital and material formats.[12]

KEEPING UP TO DATE

Dealing with digital archives is a bit like keeping up to date with academic literature. It is essential to do a comprehensive survey at the start of a new project, but you should also aim to keep abreast of new developments as they occur. If you started your current project more than two years ago, there is a good chance that new digital resources have been developed that were not available when you first set out. The *British Newspaper Archive*, for example, is currently growing by more than 100,000 new pages every month. While some digitisation projects make an effort to document these updates, researchers still need to visit archives on a regular basis if they want to keep up with new additions. Indeed, it would be wise to repeat an in-depth search for useful tools and archives on a yearly basis. Alternatively, I recommend setting up a series of automated alerts that monitor new developments on your behalf. For example, I have configured Google's free 'Alert' feature to e-mail me on a weekly basis with any news stories that mention phrases like 'newspaper archive' or 'digitised newspapers'.[13] Similarly, I use Twitter's TweetDeck tool to automatically capture any tweets that mention the words 'digital archive'.[14] Finally, I am currently 'following' a custom eBay search that alerts me to all new auctions featuring stereoscopic images of nineteenth-century New York. These alerts allow me to spot many new resources as they arrive, though I am sure that plenty still slip through the cracks.

Finally, it is worth considering whether you actually *want* to keep constantly up to date with new resources. Working this way can have complicated ramifications. Rather than operate within the boundaries of a fixed archive, digital researchers have to build their projects on constantly shifting sands. The pace of digitisation requires us to come to terms with the fact that vital new documents might (or might not) appear online in next month's updates or, far worse, that a newly digitised source might fatally undermine one of our articles the week after it gets published. Of course, this uncertainty is not entirely new; historians' arguments have always been vulnerable to the discovery of new evidence. However, the accessibility of digital archives makes these revision-ist discoveries much easier. In 2015, for example, a 14-year-old high school student named Rebecca A. Fried used evidence from digital archives to chal-lenge Prof Richard Jensen's argument about the presence of anti-Irish adver-tisements in nineteenth-century America.[15] Jensen conducted his research in 2002 without the aid of digital archives and argued that advertisements reading 'No Irish Need Apply' were largely a myth. Using a digital newspaper archive, Fried was able to find plenty of these adverts and abundant evidence to cast doubt on each aspect of Jensen's argument. On the positive side, Fried's story demonstrates the democratising effect of digitisation; it is now possible for history students and enthusiastic amateurs to explore archives that were once the preserve of professional researchers. What is more, digital search tools allow them to interrogate these collections with far greater precision than his-torians who were manually working with these sources a decade ago.

This is an exciting development – one that should inspire a new generation of 'scholar adventurers' to go out in search of new perspectives on the past.[16] But the dynamism of digitisation also requires us to make difficult decisions. If a wonderful new digital archive is launched six months before your book or doctoral thesis is due for submission, do you make use of it and face the pos-sibility of extensive re-writes? If you are working with an archive that keeps expanding, do you need to keep repeating your searches so that they include this new material? How can other scholars replicate and check these searches if the archive keeps evolving? On the other hand, what happens if a digital archive runs out of funding and disappears before you have finished using it? There is no single answer to these questions, but they are worth thinking about as you design a new research project. No matter how you decide to respond to these challenges, you will eventually need to draw a line in the sand and accept that your research is ready to publish. If a teenager subsequently comes along with a shiny new tool and proves you wrong, that's just the nature of the game.

CRITICALLY READING A DIGITAL ARCHIVE

So, you've found a digital archive – what next? It is tempting to jump in and start searching, but if we want to make the most of the archive it is worth taking a bit of time to scope out its capabilities. To do this effectively, we need to understand how digital archives work. All digital archives are made up of three main components:

- Data – the digitised versions of the documents/objects that from the core of an archive. If you turned your old family photo album into a digital archive, then digitised scans of each photo would make up the dataset.

- Metadata – descriptive information about items in the core dataset. In the case of our hypothetical family photo archive, each picture could have several pieces of metadata, including:

  The date when the photo was taken.
  The name of the photographer.
  The names of people who appear in the photograph.
  The type of camera used.
  The type of photograph (portrait, landscape, colour, black and white, etc.)
  The subject of the photograph (holiday snaps, graduation photos, family portraits, etc.)

- Interface – the platform that we use to access the archive (usually a website), and the tools we use to explore it. In the case of our photo archive, a standard interface might let us browse through photographs in a gallery and search for images with specific characteristics (e.g. all colour portraits from 1986). An alternative interface might allow us to explore the photos using a map that plots the locations in which they were taken.

An archive's dataset, metadata, and interface combine to determine its capabilities as a research tool. The technical and curatorial decisions made when designing a database subsequently shape the questions we can (and cannot) ask and, more importantly, influence the answers we receive. For that reason, it is vital for historians to understand the basics of how these components work. With this information in hand, we can tailor our research methods in response to each archive's strengths and weaknesses. In order to critically 'read' a digital archive, we need to consider each of the three in turn.

DATA

Whenever you access a new digital archive, your first step will probably be to try and figure out what it contains. Many archives have an 'About' page that gives a basic overview of the collection, but in other cases you will need to do more exploration. Most databases have some kind of 'browse' feature, which should allow you to get a sense of how the archive is organised. If you cannot find a useful way to browse, try performing a search without entering any search terms – some archives do not allow this, but when it works it should display all of the items in a database. At this point, you should be able to sort and filter the results using the available metadata (type of document, year of publication, language, etc.). These techniques are useful when dealing with small, focused archives. However, larger, multi-purpose repositories can be very difficult to get a handle on. The Internet Archive, for example, currently holds over 8 million texts, 1 million images, 2 million videos, 2.5 million audio files, and over 100,000 pieces of archived software. In these cases, you might need to probe the archive using a series of keyword searches rather than attempting to browse your way through everything.

Identifying an archive's contents is just the first step. Next, you should consider *why* these items appear in the archive and, just as importantly, why other items *do not*. Firstly, it is important to remember that only a small fraction of the historical record has been digitised – there are millions and millions of items that are not available online. In 2005, the Victorianist Patrick Leary warned of the dangers of what he terms the 'offline penumbra':

> The offline penumbra is that increasingly remote and unvisited
> shadowland into which even quite important texts fall if they cannot
> yet be explored, or perhaps even identified, by any electronic means . . .
> Inevitably, more and more scholarly work will be done on texts that
> can be found online, whilst more inconvenient, costly, and laborious
> kinds of research, particularly with unpublished manuscripts, is likely
> to be correspondingly avoided. At a time when even accomplished
> researchers rely heavily upon online searching, and when many
> students and interested members of the public rely on little or nothing
> else, the offline penumbra represents one side of a 'digital divide' that I
> suspect will subtly affect the ways in which we think, teach, and write
> about the [past] for years to come.[17]

Leary's warnings are worth heeding, not just because they remind us of the continued importance of conventional archives, but because they invite us to adopt a more critical attitude to the composition of digital collections. If a library has 1,000 books but can only afford to digitise 100 of them, how should these lucky 10% be selected? Who makes this decision, and why?

In an ideal world, all digital archives would be designed to act as a representative sample of their printed ancestors. Some digitisation projects have made an effort to do this by consulting historians, but even these experts must make subjective decisions about which items to include and which to omit. In other cases, digitisation is informed by more practical concerns. Most large-scale projects will follow the path of least resistance. It is quicker, easier, and cheaper to digitise content that has already been microfilmed, so new archives are often shaped by curatorial decisions that were made in the 1950s and 1960s. As a result, they will also inherit the gaps and errors present in the microfilm – this is why some newspaper archives have missing issues and text that is faded so much as to be illegible. It would be possible to plug these gaps by scanning replacement pages from other libraries, but most archives do not bother. In other cases, the selection of material for digitisation may depend on the holdings of a particular library, the condition of individual documents (some are too fragile to be scanned using normal methods), and even a source's size and shape. Where multiple editions/versions of a source exist, digitisation projects usually pick one of them to be scanned. For example, while multiple editions of *The Times* were published throughout each day, the *Times Digital Archive* only contains one. Why, we must ask, should this version be regarded as the edition of record? Copyright restrictions also play a part – this is why we have much more material for the eighteenth and nineteenth centuries than we do for the twentieth century. Finally, commercial archives are often aimed at genealogists rather than academic historians. As a result, they tend to focus on documents that are likely to contain the names of customers' ancestors. Services like the *British Newspaper Archive* contain a continually increasing number of local newspapers, while more popular and influential titles remain un-digitised. At present, for example, we can search nineteenth-century copies of the *Maidstone Telegraph* but not its bestselling, metropolitan namesake. On the plus side, this has had the happy effect of destabilising the established historical canon and encouraging researchers to examine previously under-used sources. Nevertheless, it is important to remember that the digitisation of any source is no indication of its historical significance.

Finally, researchers need to consider *how* the contents of an archive have been digitised. Digitisation is a transformative process. It does not simply copy a physical object; it remediates it into something new. During this process, some aspects of the original are inevitably lost. Most obviously, we lose the ability to explore a source's materiality; it's size, weight, texture and smell are all excised from the digital version. For example, the experience of reading broadsheet and tabloid newspapers on a computer screen is very similar. However, when you handle physical copies it soon becomes clear that they were designed to be consumed in different ways; their materiality reveals an aspect of their history that is necessarily obscured by digitisation. As we rush to embrace the new possibilities offered by digital archives, it is important therefore that we do not forget about the importance of materiality. On the other hand, digitisation is also a creative process – it generates new information about a source that allows us to explore it in new ways. The nature and quality of this new information depends on the way in which it is digitised.

For textual sources, there are two main approaches to digitisation:

- Scanning – this results in photographs of the document that cannot be searched for specific words and phrases. Instead, researchers simply browse through the digital archive in much the same way as a paper one. This approach is fairly rare now, but can still be seen in some early digitisation projects.

Table 10.1 Comparison of original text and an OCR reading

Original text	OCR version
Mrs Talbot: "I see by the paper, May, that Mrs. Folly is still dangerously ill, but insists upon having two wings added to her house before she dies." May Talbot: "Good idea, ma, judging from all reports, they are the only pair she will ever have."	.e–Mrs. Talbot: ".1I see by the paper, May, thatal ;r r.Folly is still dangerously ill, but insist~s no my upon having two wings added to her house before' Fr she dies." May Talbov: "Good idea, ma, judging from, haI ilug all reports, they are the only pair sile will ever pu uns, have."'

Anon., 'Laugh and Grow Fat: The Freshest Yankee Jokes', *Hampshire Telegraph and Sussex Chronicle*, 20 April 1889, p. 11.

- Scan + OCR – once the documents have been scanned they are fed into Optical Character Recognition software. This attempts to convert the text into a digitally readable (and searchable) format. This is now used in the majority of text-based digital archives.

The accuracy of the OCR process varies from archive to archive. The software usually performs well with modern text on well-preserved documents. If you were to scan this book page on the day it was published and run it through OCR software, you would probably receive something close to 100% accuracy. However, the results would probably be much less impressive if we were to scan the pages of an eighteenth-century pamphlet. Even the best, purpose-built OCR software struggles to read older typefaces and interpret documents where the text is faded or the paper is discoloured by foxing and other age-related marks. For example, an evaluation of the British Library's digital newspaper archives determined that the 'word accuracy' of their nineteenth-century papers is 78%, but that this figure drops to 65% for the seventeenth and eighteenth centuries. Table 10.1 shows a typical example taken from a Victorian newspaper's joke column:

Many commercial archives do not allow users to see this error-strewn OCR, in fear that it will shake our confidence in their products. Nor are they too forthcoming about the specific decisions made during the digitisation process. This can make it difficult to critically assess the quality of an archive's dataset. Fortunately, most open-access projects take a more relaxed view and display the OCR text alongside images of the source, or in a separate downloadable file. Some 'crowd-sourcing' projects even encourage users to help correct errors in the OCR. For example, as of 2013, users of Australia's *Trove* newspaper archive had voluntarily corrected more than 100 million lines of text. While these transcriptions are not 100% accurate, they significantly improve the quality of OCR data and by extension the accuracy of our searches. It is usually fairly easy to tell when an archive has been improved by crowdsourcing. Some build their correction tools into the archive's main user interface, so if you have the ability to correct the OCR yourself, then you know it is a crowdsourcing project. In other cases, if transcriptions and corrections have been organised on a separate platform, you can still spot a crowdsourced archive if the OCR text is visible and contains no obvious errors. Many of these transcription projects are still ongoing, so it is important to bear in mind that some areas of the archive might have been improved more than others.

METADATA

Once an archive has been converted into a digital format, its contents are organised and enhanced by the addition of metadata. Metadata is defined by the *Oxford English Dictionary* as 'data that describes and gives information about other data'.[18] While the term has only entered wide circulation in the last few decades, it actually describes a much older phenomenon. Metadata is the kind of information that appears in an old-fashioned library card catalogue – it is the key bibliographical and descriptive notes that help researchers locate items in a large collection. Digital metadata works in a similar way. Some archives stick to the basics and include the bare minimum required when citing a document, such as its title, author, publisher and date of publication. Higher quality archives add additional descriptive metadata. For example, the most sophisticated newspaper archives classify individual articles according to their genre. This makes it possible to focus your search on articles devoted to 'sport', or to omit sections that have been identified as 'advertisements'. Whilst this is a useful feature, it is worth remembering that some archives generate this metadata using computational methods, such as natural language processing, rather than human judgement. In other words, a piece of software is trained to automatically detect whether a newspaper article is about 'sport', 'news', 'business', or 'entertainment' based on the language used within it. This is the only practical way to process tens of millions of pages, but it means that the classifications can sometimes be inaccurate. Of course, human classification can also be rather subjective. In both cases, it is wise to make use of metadata to focus and filter your searches, but not to rely on it too heavily.

Metadata is particularly important for image and video-based archives. OCR software is effective at interpreting textual sources, but photographs, artworks, and film clips cannot, for the time being, be machine-read in the same way. Instead, this metadata has to be added manually. Once again, some digitisation projects are attempting to do this via crowdsourcing. For example, in 2013 the British Library uploaded 1 million nineteenth-century images to the photo-sharing website Flickr.[19] They invited the public to classify them and, at the time of writing, more than 200,000 descriptive tags have been added. Other projects, such as the *Database of Mid-Victorian Illustration*, have created their own high-quality metadata.[20] This archive allows users to construct complex image searches. For example, we could search the database for all images published in the 1860s that depict interiors, feature working-class men, include specific objects such as footstools, and represent a particular emotion like 'surprise'. Unfortunately, few image archives have such rich metadata – most provide basic bibliographical information and, in some cases, a brief description of the image. If, for some reason, you wanted to find a photograph taken in the 1940s of a man in a cowboy hat holding an ice cream and expressing regret, you would probably need to find an archive that covers this period and then browse thousands of images until you find (or do not find) a suitable match. Image recognition software is rapidly improving, so we may reach a point soon where the generation of metadata for historical images can be effectively automated. For now, however, they remain much less discoverable than their textual cousins.

INTERFACE

The third and final component of a digital archive is its interface. If metadata is akin to a library's old card catalogue, then an interface is the library's building and furniture; it is the space in which we encounter and explore an archive's holdings. The design of an interface is vitally important. A badly designed interface can undermine even the richest datasets. Some take a long time to load, others display documents in extremely small viewing windows, and some make it very difficult for researchers to download and save material. By the same token, a well-designed interface with a suite of powerful search tools makes an archive far more useful. Moreover, by designing new interfaces we can transform a dataset's methodological possibilities. For example, the *Old Bailey Online*'s standard search interface allows users to search for words and phrases mentioned in court reports and then presents the results in a textual format.[21] However, the *Locating London's Past* website uses the same dataset and displays it on a map, and the *Datamining With Criminal Intent* project allows users to analyse court reports using advanced textual analysis software.[22] 'Remixing' existing archives in this fashion promises to be an increasingly important feature of future digitisation projects.[23] Rather than spend millions of pounds scanning new material from scratch, the design of new interfaces and data analysis tools allows us to squeeze new insights from existing digital collections. Unfortunately, many of these existing datasets are currently locked behind paywalls and cannot be exposed to experimental new tools without the permission of their publisher. As a result, the most innovative work in the Digital Humanities is currently centred on open-access archives.

SEARCHING AN ARCHIVE

Constructing digital searches is an increasingly important skill for historians. The specific techniques required will vary depending on both the archive you are using and your own research topic. Nevertheless, there are some key principles to adhere to:

Digital archives do not work like Google

Google is an intelligent search engine. If I search for the word 'laverpool', it automatically guesses that I meant 'Liverpool', then assumes I must be searching for the football club and orders my search results accordingly. If I ask it a question such as 'where is Liverpool?', it answers by showing me a map. In other words, it does a lot of thinking on my behalf and tries to present information that it thinks I am looking for. Digital archives are different. They require us to be much more careful when selecting our search terms and generally leave us to decide which results are most relevant for our research. This of course is to be welcomed; after all, tracking down evidence and weighing up its significance is a key part of a historian's job and should not be outsourced to an algorithm.

Searching is hard work

When digital archives first arrived some historians haughtily claimed that entering words into a search engine did not constitute 'proper' research. They complained that this kind of work is too 'easy' and that it does not require the effort and expertise of 'true' archival research. This of course is nonsense. The selection of good keywords takes time and requires us to become deeply familiar with the language and culture of our chosen period and place. As Julie-Marie Strange points out in her chapter of this book, the meanings of particular words change over time and are informed by the complex historical contexts in which they are expressed. One of the quickest ways to check whether a word or phrase was in circulation during a particular time period is to use Google's Ngram Viewer – a free tool that charts the frequency with which words appear, year-by-year, in Google's book archive.[24] This is not a perfect reflection of historical language usage, but it provides a useful indication of when a particular word or phrase entered wide circulation. However, some searches require even greater linguistic precision. For example, a search for the term 'Jack the Ripper' will only find newspaper articles published after he had already murdered four women – before this point, he was referred to by other monikers such as 'Leather Apron' and the 'Whitechapel Fiend'.

I teach my students a five-step process for identifying and refining keywords.

• Step one: Identify preliminary keywords
Before you start searching, compile a list of preliminary keywords that you would expect to be used in relation to your topic. In the case of the Ripper murders, we might list things such as: victims' names, streets, 'Whitechapel', and 'murder'. Once you have compiled this list, try to identify any variations. For example, if we search for 'murder' we might also want to search for 'murders' and 'murderer'. You might also consider including synonyms, such as 'killing', 'slaughter', or 'homicide'. If you want to do this with added precision, consider visiting the Internet Archive and looking for a dictionary or thesaurus published in your period.

• Step two: Test preliminary keywords
Start to enter your preliminary keywords into an archive's search engine. As with our earlier attempts to locate new databases, it is best to start with something very specific and then progress to more general search terms. If you find some viable results, proceed to step three – if not, return to step one and try to come up with new keywords.

• Step three: Find new keywords
The most effective keywords can be found by reading sources from the time. Once you have generated some preliminary results, read through these sources and jot down any recurring words and phrases that could be used in new searches.

• Step four: Evaluate keywords
By this point, you should have compiled a fairly extensive list of possible keywords. Take some time to test and evaluate their strengths and weaknesses. Are some keywords effective for finding particular kinds of information? Are some too specific? Do others find too many irrelevant articles? Could you discard some?

• Step five: Refine keywords
Finally, consider how your most useful keywords could be refined and made even more useful. Do some of them work better in combination? For example, searching for 'murder' on its own would probably find too many results. But what if we looked for articles featuring both 'murder' and 'Whitechapel'?

Keep it short

If you are using an archive whose contents have been painstakingly transcribed, then you can conduct some fairly complex searches. However, most archives of historical print culture require you to work around the kind of OCR errors we discussed earlier. As a result, searching for an entire sentence is unlikely to be very reliable – there is bound to be a minor OCR error in there somewhere. Instead, try to pick out the most distinctive elements. For example, a few years ago I was trying to find reprints of this nineteenth-century joke:

> In a mining village in America, there was once an epidemic of pneumonia, which killed many people. A local undertaker had on his window the following advertisement: 'You kick the bucket; we do the rest.'

The full joke is far too long to search for, so I focused on the punchline. The phrase 'Kick the Bucket' is used in a range of contexts, but 'You Kick the Bucket' is less common. This proved to be a well-balanced search term, although I also had some success looking for articles that featured 'kick the bucket' and 'undertaker'. By entering these searches into multiple newspaper and book archives, I was able to track the journey of the joke from its origins in a New York magazine, to its circulation throughout the newspapers of mid-west America, its arrival in London, and its eventual usage at a small political meeting in North Wales.[25] This is an example of the kind of work that can only be accomplished using digital archives.

Use the advanced search options

Many archives have 'Basic' and 'Advanced' search windows. Avoid using the basic search and head straight to the advanced options. These are usually a bit more complex to use, but they give you a lot more control over the parameters of your search. Whenever you encounter a new archive, it is therefore worth taking time to explore these options and test them out; getting to grips with them now might save you from wading through thousands of irrelevant results later. Well-designed archives should have a 'help' button or a section on their 'about' page that explains these tools in more detail. It is worth seeking out these guides because some archives support search techniques that are not immediately apparent in their interface. The most useful of these 'hidden' search tools include:

- Wildcards – these allow you to search for variations of a word. For example, a search for 'America*' would find results for 'America', 'American', and 'Americanisation'. Similarly, a search for 'c?t' will find, 'cat', 'cot', and 'cut'.
- Fuzzy searching – this looks for variations of a word or phrase, but is primarily designed to spot OCR errors. A fuzzy search for 'America' will also find words that have been incorrectly transcribed as 'Anerica' or 'Americu'.

- Proximity operators – these allow you to specify the distance between two search terms. For example, a standard search for 'America AND press' will return all articles featuring these words, no matter how far apart they appear on the page – this results in a lot of irrelevant content. Conversely, a search for the precise phrase "American press" will not return articles with phrases like "The press has been very agitated of late in America". Proximity operators can be used to find some middle ground. A search for 'press n10 America*' will find all articles in which the two terms appear within 10 words of one another. This number can be tweaked in order to strike a good balance between precision and flexibility.
- 'Not' searches – using the 'Not' field is also an excellent way to purge irrelevant results. For example, searching for the word 'America' will also locate all references to 'South America'. If we want to focus exclusively on the United States, then a search for 'America NOT South America' will cut out some of the irrelevant hits. Excluding results in this fashion requires careful consideration. In this case, our search might eliminate useful articles about the United States that only mention the phrase 'South America' in passing.
- Image searches – some text-focused archives include an option to search for articles featuring images. As I explained above, the metadata for these is usually very basic and will probably include their caption and the surrounding text. Nevertheless, this can still be a useful way to locate visual sources.

These advanced tools are not available in every archive. Moreover, their name and usage techniques differ between databases. Experimentation will be required before you can evaluate and then use them to their full potential.

CONCLUSIONS

This is an interesting time to be a historian. Advances in technology have transformed the tools that we use to conduct our research, and over the coming years they will continue to push the discipline in new and unexpected directions. This chapter provides a short introduction to some of the basic skills and techniques that historians need in order to make the most of these developments. But this is just the tip of the iceberg – the digital turn has much more to offer historians. Once you've got the basics under your belt, consider experimenting with some of the more advanced tools and techniques that are currently being developed by scholars working in the Digital Humanities. The texts listed below are a good place to start.

NOTES

1. Bob Nicholson, 'The digital Turn: Exploring the methodological possibilities of digital newspaper archives', *Media History* 19:1 (2013), pp. 59–73.
2. Patrick Leary, 'Victorian Studies in the digital age', in *The Victorians since 1901: Histories, representations and revisions,* ed. by Miles Taylor and Michael Wolff (Manchester: Manchester University Press, 2004), pp. 201–14 (p. 206).
3. For a discussion of how DH has been defined, see: Patrik Svensson, 'The landscape of digital humanities', *Digital Humanities Quarterly* 4:1 (2010), http//www.digitalhumanities.org [accessed 12 October 2015]. For a more playful attempt to define DH, visit: http//www.whatisdigitalhumanities.com [accessed 12 October 2015].
4. If you want to make a start on learning to program, the *Programming Historian* website offers a free 'online, open-access, peer reviewed suite of tutorials that help humanists learn a wide range of digital tools, techniques, and workflows to facilitate their research.' See Adam Crymble, Fred Gibbs, Allison Hegel, Caleb McDaniel, Ian Milligan, Miriam Posner, and William J. Turkel (eds), *The Programming Historian,* 2nd ed. (2015) http://programminghistorian.org/ [accessed 12 October 2015].
5. *Google Books,* https://books.google.com [accessed 12 October 2015]; *The Internet Archive,* https://archive.org [accessed 12 October 2015]; *HathiTrust,* https://www.hathitrust.org [accessed 12 October 2015]; *Europeana,* http://www.europeana.eu [accessed 12 October 2015]; *Project Gutenberg,* https://www.gutenberg.org [accessed 12 October 2015].
6. *Welsh Newspapers Online,* http://newspapers.library.wales [accessed 12 October 2015]; *British Newspaper Archive,* http://www.britishnewspaperarchive.co.uk [accessed 12 October 2015]; *Ancestry.com,* http://www.ancestry.com [accessed 12 October 2015]; Gale and Proquest's archives can only be accessed via a subscribing library's catalogue.
7. *Chronicling America,* http://chroniclingamerica.loc.gov [accessed 12 October 2015]; *Google Newspaper Archive,* https://news.google.com/newspapers [accessed 12 October]; *Elephind,* https://www.elephind.com [accessed 12 October 2015].
8. *Europeana Newspapers,* http://www.theeuropeanlibrary.org/tel4/newspapers [accessed 12 October 2015]. The same collection of newspapers is also accessible via the *Europeana* portal, http://www.europeana.eu [accessed 12 October 2015]. For examples of European national newspaper archives, see: *Bibliothèque nationale de France,* http://gallica.bnf.fr [accessed 12 October 2015]; *Biblioteca Nacional De España,* [accessed 12 October 2015]; *Bibliothèque royale de Belgique,* http://belgica.kbr.

be/fr/coll/jour/jour_fr.html [accessed 12 October 2015]; *Koninklijke Bibliotheek*, http://www.delpher.nl/nl/kranten [accessed 12 October 2015]; *National Library of Greece*, http://www.nlg.gr [accessed 12 October 2015].

9. *Trove*, http://trove.nla.gov.au [accessed 12 October 2015]; *Papers Past*, http://paperspast.natlib.govt.nz [accessed 12 October 2015]; *Hemeroteca Digital Brasileira*, http://bndigital.bn.br [accessed 12 October 2015].

10. 'International coalition on newspapers', *Centre for Research Libraries*, http://icon.crl.edu [accessed 12 October 2015]. You can also find a similar list on Wikipedia: 'List of online newspaper archives', https://en.wikipedia.org/wiki/Wikipedia:List_of_online_newspaper_archives [accessed 12 October 2015].

11. *NewsBank*, http://www.newsbank.com [accessed 12 October 2015].

12. *The National Archives*, http://www.nationalarchives.gov.uk [accessed 12 October 2015].

13. *Google Alerts*, https://www.google.co.uk/alerts [accessed 12 October 2015].

14. *TweetDeck*, https://tweetdeck.twitter.com [accessed 12 October 2015].

15. Rebecca A. Fried, 'No Irish need deny: Evidence for the historicity of NINA restrictions in advertisements and signs', *Journal of Social History* (Advanced Access Online, 2015).

16. Bob Nicholson, 'Digital detectives: rediscovering the scholar adventurer', *Victorian Periodicals Review* 45:2 (2012), pp. 215–23.

17. Patrick Leary, 'Googling the Victorians', *Journal of Victorian Culture* 10:1 (2005), pp. 72–86 (pp. 82–3).

18. 'meta-, prefix'. *OED Online*, http://www.oed.com [accessed 12 October 2015].

19. 'The British Library', *Flickr*, https://www.flickr.com/photos/british library [accessed 12 October 2015].

20. *Database of Mid-Victorian Illiustration*, http://www.dmvi.org.uk [accessed 12 October 2015].

21. *Old Bailey Online*, http://www.oldbaileyonline.org [accessed 12 October 2015].

22. *Locating London's Past*, http://www.locatinglondon.org [accessed 12 October 2015]; *Datamining With Criminal Intent*, http://criminalintent.org [accessed 12 October 2015].

23. Bob Nicholson, 'The Victorian meme machine: remixing the nineteenth-century archive', *19: Interdisciplinary Studies in the Long Nineteenth Century* 21 (2015), http://www.19.bbk.ac.uk.

24. *Google Books Ngram Viewer*, https://books.google.com/ngrams [accessed 12 October 2015]. On the limits of this tool, see: Eitan Adam Pechenick, Christoper M. Danforth and Peter Sheridan Dodds, 'Characterizing the

Google books corpus: strong limits to inferences of socio-cultural and linguistic evolution', *PLoS One* (2015).
25. Bob Nicholson, '"You kick the bucket; we do the rest!": jokes and the
culture of reprinting in the transatlantic press', *Journal of Victorian
Culture* 17:3 (2012), pp. 273–86.

FURTHER READING

Berry, David M. (ed.), *Understanding Digital Humanities* (Basingstoke:
Palgrave, 2012).

Cohen, Daniel J., and Tom Scheinfeldt (eds), *Hacking the Academy: New
Approaches to Scholarship and Teaching from Digital Humanities* (Ann Arbor,
MI: University of Michigan Press, 2013).

Cohen, Daniel J., and Roy Rosenzweig, *Digital History: A Guide to Gathering,
Preserving, and Presenting the Past on the Web* (Philadelphia, PA: University
of Pennsylvania Press, 2006)

Gardiner, Eileen, and Ronald G. Musto, *The Digital Humanities: A Primer for
Students and Scholars* (Cambridge: Cambridge University Press, 2015).

Gold, Matthew K. (ed.), *Debates in the Digital Humanities* (Minneapolis:, MN
University of Minnesota Press, 2012).

Kelly, T. Mills, *Teaching History in the Digital Age* (Ann Arbor, MI: University
of Michigan Press, 2013).

Nawrotzki, Kristen, and Jack Dougherty (eds), *Writing History in the Digital
Age* (Ann Arbor, MI: University of Michigan Press, 2013).

Rosenzwieg, Roy, *Clio Wired: The Future of the Past in the Digital Age*
(New York, NY: Columbia University Press, 2010).

Terras, Melissa, Julianne Nyhan, Edward Vanhoutte (eds), *Defining Digital
Humanities: A Reader* (Farnham: Ashgate, 2013).

Weller, Toni (ed.), *History in the Digital Age* (London: Routledge, 2013).

PART 4

Deciphering Meanings

CHAPTER 11

Reading Language as a Historical Source

Julie-Marie Strange

Reading language within historical sources is fundamental to historical practice. We scrutinise textual sources for what they can tell us about the past but we also read texts for bias and to identify intended audiences, the author's value-judgements and rhetorical devices. Yet the bald articulation in the historical record is not always interpreted, or intended to be interpreted, literally. This is taken for granted when we evaluate fiction, poetry or drama, where examining choice of words, grammar and sentence construction are routine matters for investigation. Engaging with language in a historical source goes beyond analysis of what is explicitly said and the privileging of articulate narrators. Drawing on a case study of working-class language in the late Victorian and Edwardian period, this chapter outlines ways in which historians can read language as a dynamic process between different groups of people using specific varieties of language particular to their context. Utilising examples drawn from a group typically silent in historical sources, especially on intimate matters, the chapter also suggests that apparent silences in sources need not indicate absence but, rather, necessitate readings of absences as significant in their own right. Notably, the chapter will demonstrate how verbal presence and absence must be understood in a context, first, that recognises that language is always situational and, secondly, that language is extra-verbal, embedded as much in gesture, deed, touch and tone as in what is said. The chapter will argue that readings of language as a fluid and extra-verbal medium are necessary for approaching the histories of groups whose voices are under-represented in the archives and for accessing the voices of those on the margins of society.

READING LANGUAGE: THE HISTORY AND POLITICS OF A METHOD

The study of classical languages has a long history but the 'scientific' investigation of language is rooted in the late-nineteenth century with the study of language evolution and the relationship between language, nationality, place and politics. In 1916, Ferdinand de Saussure called for a science of language that sought to understand how meaning, or 'signification', was produced. For Saussure, language was a closed system of signs; the science of language investigated society's structural knowledge of language.[1] Saussure is often identified as the founder of modern linguistics and, while his contribution to the study of language was monumental, it is important to recognise that Saussure's emphasis on the production of meaning has been subject to heated contestation since. For many scholars, including historians, Saussure's primary focus on the study of language as the production of meaning is inseparable from broader consideration of the particular context in which that language is spoken or written. One of the earliest exponents of the view of language as social interaction was the Russian linguist Vološinov who argued in 1929 that the study of language was inextricable from consideration of space, time and socio-economic conditions.[2]

The question of whether language is a structure that orders and defines our social reality is politically charged. Since the 1920s, scholars have wrestled with this question and its implications: 'does thought precede language or can we only think within the boundaries of languages available to us?' Early anthropologists, for example, argued that cultures with little or no terminology for space or time would have little or no spatial and temporal conception.[3] Other anthropologists, however, argue that individuals have more agency (that is, the ability to take action) over language. Lucy Burke *et al.* suggest that the question of language, structure and agency can be thought of as a relationship between rules and freedom. That is, language has rules to enable communicators to understand and be understood. However, individuals also have the freedom to subvert rules, take shortcuts or develop alternative rules of speech.[4] Esperanto, a language invented in the nineteenth century as a neutral global language to promote international understanding, suggests both the freedom to create entirely new linguistic codes and the extent to which national languages are embedded with political meaning.

Given the importance of such debates for thinking about power and agency, it is not surprising that many of the seminal studies on language sought to examine the way speech (written and spoken) relates to power. In particular, anthropologists and sociologists from the 1960s onwards were interested in how different varieties of speech (often called 'codes') spoken by different groups of people ('speech communities') could endorse, uphold or subvert power. The idea of a 'standard', that is, dominant language has application to questions of political, personal and cultural identity. What these studies illuminate is that words alone do not wield power, but, rather, are inextricable from the social conditions in which language is produced and reproduced. Studying the power of language in relation to the church in France, Pierre Bourdieu suggested that it was the external signs of authority, such as the presence of an ordained priest, religious paraphernalia such as crucifixes or the sacrament, or the built environment of the church that vested power in religious language, not the words themselves. For Bourdieu, language used and endorsed by the power-holding elite was a form of domination but one which had to be examined in relation to other rites and signs of power.[5]

Scholars in anthropology and sociology were among the first to highlight the ways in which language and, indeed, theories of language could be used to oppress and liberate people. One example of this was the debate centred on research by Basil Bernstein and William Labov in the late 1960s and early 1970s over language, education and thought. Bernstein argued that children's success or failure at school bore direct correlation to the extent and sophistication of their vocabularies. Children who succeeded educationally had an 'elaborate' code of speech, that is, they possessed an extensive vocabulary and sophisticated grasp of grammar that enabled the construction and manipulation of abstract concepts. Elaborate codes of language mirrored 'standard' English as defined by educational, governmental and cultural elites. Children with 'restricted' codes of speech had limited vocabulary and rudimentary conceptions of grammar that curtailed their ability to engage meaningfully with the official language of education and hindered their capacity to formulate abstract and complex thoughts. Bernstein's study argued for recognition of the importance of speech in socio-economic and cultural life: a restricted code of speech had a direct connection with educational failure and low-income households whilst elaborate codes of speech were associated with high-achieving, affluent individuals.[6]

Bernstein sought to account for the lower rates of educational achievement among poorer schoolchildren but his theory was interpreted and applied in ways that had real consequences for members of the 'restricted code' community. Crucially, Bernstein's theory was developed and adopted in the formation of educational policy in Britain and America, demonstrating, first, the way that a non-standard speech community's linguistic form can be conflated with other types of socio-economic failure and, second, how dominant social groups attach value judgements to the language of marginal groups. The politicisation of language in this case was underlined by the research of William Labov who railed against Bernstein's theory and the uses to which it was put to justify educational policies that sought to eradicate the black-American children's speech community in Harlem. For Labov, the appropriation of Bernstein's so-called 'restricted' code of speech by policymakers placed the blame for educational failure on families, the place where vocabularies were nurtured, thereby detracting criticism from the failings of schools and policymakers. Far from inhibiting the capacity for abstract, logical or complex thought, Labov sought to engage the restricted-speech community on their own terms to illustrate how non-standard English users could express sharp, quick-witted arguments. In contrast, he argued that the elaborate code of speech was largely verbosity. Once the linguistic and grammatical flourishes were stripped bare, elaborate code users were no more sophisticated in thought (and in some cases, considerably slower witted) than restricted-code speakers.[7] Working within a context of tense race relations in America, Labov's contribution to the debate over speech, race and class indicates the extent to which language and the study of language is politically charged.

Within a historical context, the imposition of a colonising power's language on a colonised people is one of the classic examples of language as a tool and emblem of oppression. This is evident in the use of the colonisers' language in the bureaucratic, economic and legal administration of the colonised but, also, as Patrick Harries shows in his study of Swiss missionaries among the Tsonga people of Mozambique, the use of European language in creating new forms of knowledge in colonial contexts, such as taxonomy and cartography.[8] The flip-side of domination, however, is in the resistance to standardised or imported language and the association between indigenous identity and language. Anindita Ghosh has demonstrated how language, especially in print form, was subject to intense surveillance and debate in nineteenth-century colonial Bengal. Against the educated middle classes attempt to create a standardised Bengali language and culture, Ghosh has demonstrated how 'vulgar' Bengali speech communities used commercial 'low life' print culture to ensure the survival of non-standard languages and resist the imposition of standardisation and its political-colonial connotations.[9]

Examining language evidently necessitates a study of grammar, construction and vocabulary but, as many linguists are keen to highlight, language is not just about the written or spoken word. Language is made up of 'signs' that include word patterns but which extend beyond them to include things like gesture, intonation, touch and facial expression. We take this for granted when we participate in conversation. In fiction, a novelist takes care to note the expressions, contortions, actions and non-verbal sounds that accompany speech but these usually remain implicit in the historical document. Crucially, language can function without any words at all. Tears, laughter and touch are obvious examples of non-lexical 'signs' of communication. Within anthropology in particular, language is often inseparable from 'rites' (religious or profane) or customs that enable individuals and communities to make sense of, and give meaning to, the world. Scholars also locate language as a system of signs in relation to other signs, such as the built environment. Things, structures and spaces can function as languages (or patterns of meaning called 'discourses') in their own right. Hence, we 'read' the 'discourse' (language) of space, technology, bodies, images and, increasingly in history, material culture (see Chapter 4). For instance, Maria Haywood has examined dress at the court of Henry VIII to argue that clothes in Tudor Britain functioned as a language of power, status and wealth whilst Deborah Cohen, Dena Goodman and Kathryn Norberg read furniture and home decoration as languages of selfhood, consumerism and domesticity.[10]

READING LANGUAGE: THE PRACTICE OF A METHOD

Until the mid-twentieth century, historical methods tended to privilege the written standard language of elites because history focused on high politics, law, economics and the lives of leaders. The majority of archives preserved the formal or articulate documents of the literate classes. Increasingly from the 1960s, however, historians interested in the experiences and politics of ordinary people sought to access the 'voices' of the historically marginalised: working people, children, women, refugees and migrants. Related to this was the emergence of oral history, which, quite literally, asked people to tell their story about the past in their own words. Oral history and personal testimony more generally hold a range of methodological issues for historians (see Chapter 7) but the point here is that with the emergence of what was called 'history from below', historians sought to develop methodologies that redressed the under-representation of non-standard speech communities in official archives.

In 1987, noting the importance accorded to language and 'voices from below' within new histories underpinned by feminism, socialism or regionalism, Peter Burke called for a social history of language. His essay continues to offer an excellent introduction into linguistics for historians. In it, he draws attention to four rudimentary points about the relationship between society and language which historians need to consider: different social groups use different varieties of language; one individual can use different varieties of language in different contexts; language reflects the culture in which it is spoken; and language shapes the society in which it is spoken. Thus, language is not a fixed or static thing and any notion of 'standard' language as homogenous is misleading. As Burke noted, historians were habitually sensitive to the social and political contexts of the documents they worked with but they also needed to be alert to the rules of language in different contexts. One of the principal features of ethnographic studies of language was to understand the specific rules for language in particular cultures, that is, 'the medium, code, variety or register employed is a crucial part of the message'. That many of these rules could be implicit meant that, unless historians availed themselves of *how* language was used by different groups in particular contexts as well as what words were spoken, they risked misinterpreting documents.[11]

Roy Porter pursued these themes in a subsequent volume, noting that historians often dealt with 'a tangled skein of histories': many of the sources historians used were written versions of spoken language. Few historians attempted to unravel the discrepancies between what Porter called the 'discrete technologies of speaking and writing'. For Porter, historians were so habituated to 'translating' the written and spoken word that they rarely considered the differences between the two forms of language, not simply in terms of what was modified or omitted but also in the differing values of spoken and written word in different contexts. As Porter pointed out, many modern historians use archived committee minutes without acknowledging that minutes do not record verbal exchanges verbatim but make value judgements as to what is worth recording and, secondly, that the recorded language of minutes intimates a series of power relations, administrative routines, formalised language and obligations.[12] Even particular styles of written and spoken languages have shifting rules of communication and interpretation. David Randall, for example, has traced the transition from spoken to transcribed rhetoric from antiquity to the early-modern newspaper alongside corresponding shifts and continuities in rhetorical theory and form. Randall draws particular attention to the ways in which epistolary styles (the formality of letters, conventions of salutation and the delineation of a social relationship between the writer and recipient and so on) were adapted to suit context (public or private, bureaucratic or intimate) and subject matter over time.[13]

Other studies have analysed the values and codes of language utilised by different social groups or speech communities. One fine example is Melanie Tebbutt's research on gossip – historically associated with (especially working-class) women's talk and denigrated as 'tittle tattle' (mindless talk) – in Britain in the late nineteenth and twentieth century. Tebbutt demonstrated how masculine and elite conceptions of gossip were politically charged and intrinsic to maintaining women's subordinate role within society. Unpicking the rules of gossip, that is the content, geographical and temporal spaces for gossip and who could legitimately partake in gossip, Tebbutt argued that gossip not only had complex rules of engagement but was intrinsic to maintaining social status, order and hierarchies within the community of the home, street or neighbourhood. Far from being mindless, gossip had an internal logic and was a form of regulation (few women wished to be the subject of gossip), mutuality (friendship but also a conduit for information on welfare, for example) and resistance (taking time out from domestic tasks to ridicule errant men or exchange information about school inspectors, for instance). Gossip demonstrated how language codes are gendered, it mirrored the concerns and tasks of female life and indicated the geographical and temporal spaces women created for speech, for example, talking whilst washing at the laundry or when cleaning the doorstep.[14]

In line with a desire to recover and understand voices from the past, historians increasingly turned towards the earlier work of linguists to question how those voices had been constituted. The implications of this turn to language precipitated a temporary crisis in social history as scholars grappled with the idea that the socio-economic (objective) realm did not produce a reality that shaped individual consciousness and action (subjectivity) but, rather, that individuals were active participants in creating social meanings and social relations. This had ramifications for historical categories such as class and class consciousness.[15] In the social history model, class consciousness was a reflection or a cause of an individual's position within socio-economic structure; in the new model, class consciousness was an individual's exposition of the meanings of identity categories within a particular conceptual model and the historian's task was to understand and account for how those conceptual codes were composed and historically produced. The American scholar, Joan Wallach Scott, for instance, queried how historians used 'experience' as evidence without unpicking how the categories that made up 'experience' (notably gender and sexuality) were produced in particular historical and cultural moments.[16]

This approach to language and history did not kill social history but led to new avenues of inquiry whereby language as constitutive of experience and the 'social' might shape research questions but, equally, it generated a keen awareness among historians of the importance of language as a tool that people use to represent subjective states to an outside world and/or as an instrument for navigating social relations. Claire Langhamer, for instance, has analysed personal testimonies in the mid-twentieth century to track how different people defined the term 'love' in relation to courtship and, also, how the same person's conception of love changed over time. The testimonies rarely state explicit definitions of love, assuming rather that everyone shares knowledge of what the word love means. Langhamer deciphers shifting conceptions of love, however, from assessing how words associated with love were used in relation to other priorities: stability, friendship, romance, parenthood.[17] Linda Pollock has examined anger in early modern elite society. This was a period when, according to some scholars, the suppression of strong emotions such as anger was increasingly interpreted in elite culture as a sign of civilisation and 'polite' people learned circumspection in their expression of temper. By reading the personal correspondence of elite groups, however, Pollock demonstrated that although no correspondent ever wrote the words 'I am angry', letters were frequently suffused with rage. Rather, letter-writers expressed complaints and accusations in strongly worded language to communicate their anger. By locating such language within particular contexts (after being spurned romantically, for instance, or following disputes over money), Pollock argued that it was possible to discern how the choice of words was intended to be read by recipients. Far from early modern elite culture being characterised by the suppression of anger, Pollock concluded, violent passions thrived in particular styles of communication and coded rhetorical forms that rendered explicit proclamations of rage unnecessary. As Pollock asserts, 'sentiments could be conveyed without being named'.[18] In this approach, deciphering meaning in written language was located within particular contexts to enable an interpretation of the inference *behind* chosen words and sentence structure. As Pollock's illuminating study suggests, the meaning in language is not always self-evident but dependent upon probing the contextual rules of communication within a given speech community. To a point, we read language for what its content tells us about the author's perception of a social world.

CASE STUDY: LANGUAGE, GRIEF AND CHILD DEATH

David Vincent's pioneering study of working-class autobiography in the late nineteenth and early twentieth centuries noted two key trends in authors' use of language: first, they tended to stick to factual information in relating stories of social mobility, political and educational achievement. Secondly, where authors did write about personal lives, they tended to fall back on cliché.[19] Limited vocabularies and a sense of propriety thus made it difficult for Vincent to decipher the emotional life of working classes. Vincent noted that although working-class life stories were riddled with bereavement, especially of infants and children, very few authors wrote about their feelings in response to these losses. This taciturnity was repeated in everyday life too. Numerous contemporary social investigators drew special attention to the lack of emotive vocabularies among the working classes: they said very little about feelings and what they did say was often abrupt, seemingly irrelevant or fatalistic. For Vincent and his readers, such reticence is disquieting because, in the twenty-first century in the Western world, we commonly view child death to be the most harrowing form of bereavement. As Vincent highlighted, for historians working in a context where bereavement is immediately associated with emotional loss, we have an expectation of grief that appears to be confounded by working-class testimony. Does this mean we are more emotionally sophisticated than the late Victorian poor or just that we communicate our loss differently? If we seek 'emotional intelligence' in the past are we being essentialist (that is, assuming all humans experience the same emotions) or ahistorical (assuming that emotional responses will be the same across time). This is not a problem of history alone; consider all the competing interpretations of a single Shakespeare poem in literary criticism.

We could get hung up on this but, deciphering the meanings in the oblique language of a historical social group is not so very different from Roy Porter's example of decoding the bureaucratic language of minutes taken from committee meetings: we bring our contextual knowledge to bear and make a series of informed assumptions about what was spoken, how it was translated into written form and the discrepancies between. The nature of scholarly endeavour is to formulate arguments based on a logical process of interpretation (hence, Bernstein and Labov's famously differing interpretations of similar speech communities).

Vincent was reluctant to impose his empathy with child bereavement now onto the past but equally hedged an assumed equation between linguistic economy and a limited capacity to feel or think emotionally. As he noted, apparently brusque statements could intimate emotional resilience, social etiquette or the gendering of language and emotion. Nevertheless, set against the 'elaborate code' of grief expressed in elite culture, it was difficult to ignore the possibility that the limited language of loss for working-class people, with so much financial struggle and high rates of mortality (especially of infants), was a reflection of the influence of socio-economic conditions on the capacity for profound emotional ties. In Vincent's words, poorer people lacked the 'luxury' of grief. One way of developing Vincent's unease with this conclusion, however, is to revisit the limited verbal economy of the working classes and expand our understanding of 'language' from the written form to incorporate the context in which language is expressed, the actions that accompany words and non-verbal speech, that is, intonation, gesture and physical expression. Using the guidelines Blakemore (below) outlines for interpretation based on reading contextual knowledge and rules of communication around utterances, it is possible to offer alternative meanings of the verbal reticence surrounding child death.

First, let us consider context and our assumptions about verbal exchange. Histories of the working classes often rely on written transcriptions of verbal exchanges between people in differing social positions. Even autobiographies were written, as Vincent outlined, to relate a journey of social and educational mobility. On one level, the social relationship between speakers/listeners or writers/readers mediated the selection of language in terms of content and form. Many historians assume that the 'power' in linguistic exchange is held by the person with social status, professional influence and a sophisticated vocabulary, not least because they are usually charged with directing the verbal exchange (asking the questions) and transcription. Yet it is also possible to view the limited language of working-class participants as indicative of a speech community whereby verbal formulations of thought and feeling may be less abstract or complex but carry significance in their own terms. Spoken language involves a series of choices: both in terms of what words to select and how to say them. In this sense, the power relationship we assume in an exchange between a mission worker, say, and someone seeking assistance can be subverted. Offering minimal information in as few words as possible can be tactical (the less you say, the less likely you are to generate more questions) or indicative of pride or resentment. Furthermore, in a context whereby privacy as we know it had little meaning to people accustomed to sharing space, offering little in the way of verbal exchange could facilitate a form of discretion. By examining the context in which historical 'voices' are produced, we shift attention from interpreting purely what is said to questioning why and how people negotiate verbal encounters.

The infant mortality rate in Britain until World War I was disproportionately high and the first twelve months of life were particularly fragile. For some observers, parents who said little when babies died demonstrated that they were reconciled to the deaths. For instance, the social investigator Maud Pember Reeves in her study of working-class domestic life, *Round About a Pound a Week* (1913), noted that a woman whose baby had died told the doctor certifying the death that it was 'better' that the child was dead. Reeves noted that, at face value, the composed, apparently unfeeling statement intimated fatalism in the face of death. Nevertheless, the woman had nursed the sick babe with unstinting devotion and, prior to the doctor's arrival, had been utterly distraught with weeping.[20] The economical statement, therefore, was a conscious display of composure in the face of a professional. This is important. Many social history sources are taken from the findings of social investigators, philanthropists and professionals who observed or questioned members of a social class lower than themselves about their habits, economies and living arrangements and made value judgements about them. In the context of child death, we know that medical and legal professionals, aware that some child deaths brought financial relief to families through life insurance, were watchful for signs of parental neglect. For the professional, abrupt statements might rouse suspicion of emotional apathy but for parents, composure could be a line of defence against such suspicion. Thus a short statement, located in different contextual knowledge of the world, could carry different meanings.

Reading language is shaped by expectation and assumption. This is evident in Florence Bell's study (1907) of families of men employed in her husband's iron works in Middlesbrough. Bell noted the cruel frequency with which children died and expressed horror that bereaved mothers tended to talk about their loss in terms of financial relief. This was a language of materialism and apathy that ran counter to Bell's elite expectations of a language of loss. Bell cited one example of a mother who expressed bitter regret that her child had died one week prior to the validation of its burial insurance policy.

Another mother stated that it was 'better' her children died because their lives were insured.[21] Bell interpreted these statements as a literal reflection of the financial realism of the working classes. It may well be the case that, as Bell suggested, these women were 'immune' to the deaths of their children. Nevertheless, if we consider the context in which these statements are made, a degree of circumspection seems advisable. To begin, Lady Bell or any lady volunteers collecting data on her behalf were from a different social group to the women being interviewed. At a very basic level, why would working-class women speak of anything other than finance to someone so implicated in their livelihoods? Moreover, the pragmatic world of finance was a useful point of reference because it was impersonal information in the context of a formalised encounter with a stranger. Finance also represented a subject about which Bell was ostensibly investigating: how domestic economies were managed. To some degree, then, both parties to the verbal exchange assumed that financial concerns were a shared point of interest.

If verbal language is an unreliable indicator of feeling, it is worth examining the extra or non-verbal signs of communication surrounding grief. Ellen Ross's study of poverty and motherhood in late Victorian London emphasised that verbal language was unnecessary as a form of expression in the face of child death: parents wept, refused food, stumbled or crumpled. Further, hospital nurses who sought to communicate linguistically with the parents of sick or dead children marvelled at their reticence. But, as Ross asks, what was there to say? The same parents had, as nurses acknowledged, sat by their offspring's bedside for the duration. For Ross, the physical presence and watchful vigilance of parents 'spoke' volumes and words were superfluous.[22] As Ross's analysis demonstrates, participants in ostensibly the same encounter can belong to different speech communities (the professional/the personal) and attach entirely different meanings to the same utterances or, indeed, silences. Part of the historians' project, as Ross indicates, is to identify how speech operates between different groups of people in those contexts.

In this light, it is possible to read abstract or dismissive language as profound statements of loss. Deciphering the meaning in language is not the sole privilege of the historian; it is how ordinary people communicate in everyday contexts. The Labour MP Jack Lawson recounted his mother breaking news of his youngest brother's death in World War I: handing an old toy to her granddaughter she stated that her own 'babby' was 'gone'. According to Lawson, this was the most his mother ever said about her son's death; she was 'dry-eyed' and 'apparently stone hard' in the face of grief. At no point did Lawson suspect that her verbal reserve suggested a limited capacity to feel loss. Rather, his mother's linguistic economy needed to be read in the context of lifelong poverty: all the woman's affection for her children had been invested in feeding and clothing them. By reconfiguring her grown son as her 'babby', Lawson's mother not only intimated his status as the young-est son but drew to mind his former dependency and physical intimacy with her. Furthermore, what she said carried extra meaning because of how it was said: the simple phrase 'My babby's gone' was expressed whilst his mother looked sideways and her mouth tensed as she spoke the word 'gone'. Lawson notes that after the war, his mother preserved her silence on Willie's death yet kept some of his clothes and would tell stories about Willie's childhood whilst holding his clothing.[23] Again, for Lawson, the anecdote's content was not the point. Rather, his mother's reminiscence was an impersonal and affirmative path for talking about her grief. Writing in the 1930s, Lawson would have been aware that his mother's silence at the loss of her youngest son in the war was echoed nationally on an annual basis during armistice rituals. Silence, in the context of Remembrance Day, was a non-verbal language that multiple speech communities in Britain understood signified sincere and acute loss.

READING LANGUAGE: POINTERS AND PITFALLS OF A METHOD

Is it valid to read meaning into language?

Reading language as a layered mode of communication can, of course, be misleading. As Vincent warned in his study of late Victorian and Edwardian autobiography, we must be wary of imposing meanings on language, especially when the written record omits what we want to know or renders language's meaning oblique.[24] We must acknowledge the possibility that a bald statement at odds with what we expect to hear or read may have no alternative mean-ings beyond the words strung together. Interpreting the meaning, plain or obscure, in language can be a reliable and appropriate method, however, if the historian is willing to engage with the contexts, historical, personal and politi-cal, in which language is produced. It would be disingenuous to suggest that historians do not make assumptions about the dynamics behind the creation of archival records. What differs is the degree to which historians acknowledge and engage with inferred meaning. Of course, it is difficult to test inference. For interpretations of language to carry weight, scholars must make explicit their position of translation, their understanding of the context and their process of deduction.

Understanding the rules of language

We read around language to make interpretive decisions about what is com-municated. This includes making intuitive evaluations based on what is said, how what is said operates within known rules of communication and the context in which the utterance is made. To draw upon the word intuition might make us recoil but it is important to recognise that communication often assumes a degree of intuition. As the linguist Diane Blakemore notes, intuitive translation is not irrational but relies upon understanding rules of communication: we use logic to uncover meanings in utterances, we make inferences based on our understanding of the world and both the reader/listener and writer/speaker make assumptions about each other's knowledge of the rules of communication. As Blakemore observes, jokes often depend on listeners' perception that alternative inferences could be drawn from what is said. Although assumptions about the reader/listener can be explicit, they are often implicit. Again, Blakemore suggests that this level of apparently intuitive communication is often reliable because utterances are made in confidence that others will successfully interpret their meaning, they rest upon a mutual knowledge of the world and they depend equally on non-linguistic properties. In other words, successful communication depends on knowing the rules of specific languages. Highlighting examples of how much communication in everyday life is made in disjointed, fragmented speech or through statements which, out of context, appear oblique Blakemore demonstrates how listeners usually draw the right conclusion from what is being said. One example is the exchange: 'Is there anything on TV?'; 'Nothing'. Using logic and knowledge of the multiplicity of television channels, we deduce that what the respondent to the question means is 'There is nothing worth watching on television in my opinion' rather than, literally, there are no television programmes available today. Sometimes, Blakemore continues, we make intuitive interpretations that flatly contradict what is explicitly said: if someone is sobbing but declaring they are 'okay', the contradiction between the statement and the sight/sound is likely to advance intuitive interpretations that what is said is not a literal translation of feeling but indicative of the broader context (where, when, who with and for what reason) in which the person is crying.[25] The historian that is sensitive to how people navigate communication (the rhetorical devices, sentence structures, caveats and qualifications, omissions, euphemisms, degrees of formality, sequential ordering and levels of rationality) in particular contexts is less likely to make misleading value judgements about what is communicated.

Seeing language in context

Understanding the rules of communication is directly related to bringing contextual knowledge to bear on language. 'Intuitive' interpretations of language work best when we have access to reliable contextual information in order to make reasoned evaluations of the strength of implicit and explicit assumptions. Meanings of particular words shift over time but so do the dynamics in which words are expressed. Historians must use contextual information about the medium of expression, the time and place in which it was communicated and by whom to guide analysis of language and inform the evaluation of assumptions. Some meanings are intentionally veiled in the first place. For example, pornographic language or jokes about body parts in the past often relied on knowledge of euphemistic references to acts, objects or orifices deemed obscene. When a nineteenth-century gynaecologist told male colleagues in a lecture that he possessed a cabinet of different sized speculums for examining patients and some colleagues guffawed, it helps us to comprehend the 'joke' if we know that the word 'cabinet' had older connotations with erotic places and pleasures.[26] Michel Foucault famously challenged the notion that sex was hidden in Victorian culture by drawing attention to the ways in which the Victorians talked at length about sex albeit through coded languages of decency, virtue and chastity.[27]

Understanding non-linguistic components of language

When we read language in historical documents, the non-linguistic component of what is said is not always explicit. Again, however, we can conjecture through logical reasoning the manner in which language was expressed. Pollock's study of anger, for example, suggests that apparently rational and calm statements made on paper could contrast with handwriting (rushed, untidy, pressure points of a pen) and timing (following confrontation, for instance) to suggest barely suppressed rage. Often, however, we do have indications of gesture, intonation and expression to enable a layered interpretation of meaning. Questions to consider include: does what is being said contradict or complicate the form expression takes ('I am sincerely sorry for breaking your windows' but I am laughing; 'I immediately regretted breaking your windows' but I have taken two months to tell you)? Does the verbal expression support physical evidence ('I am happy' but I look sad; 'I am calm' but I am shaking)? Are there sufficient non-linguistic signs to render verbal language unnecessary (for example, weeping, fainting, laughing, caressing and so on)? Likewise, it helps to ask what is missing from expression. The women who responded to Lady Bell's survey gave coherent verbal answers to interviewers' questions but were hardly animated in expressing their apparent indifference to children's deaths. Did then, their appearance of resignation and the clipped manner in which they spoke, suggest another story?

NOTES

1. Ferdinand Saussure, *Course in General Linguistics*, ed. C. Bally and A. Sechehaye, trans. R. Harris (London: Duckworth Press, 1983).
2. V. N. Vološinov, *Marxism and the Philosophy of Language*, trans. L. Matejka and I. R. Titunik (Cambridge, MA: Harvard University Press, 1983).
3. See especially Benjamin Whorf, *Language, Thought and Reality* (Cambridge, MA: MIT Press, 1956).
4. Lucy Burke, Tony Crowley and Alan Girvin, *The Routledge Language and Cultural Theory Reader* (London: Routledge, 2000).
5. Pierre Bourdieu, *Language and Symbolic Power*, ed. John Thompson (Oxford: Polity Press, 1991).
6. Basil Bernstein, 'Elaborated and restricted codes: their social origin and some consequences', *American Anthropologist* 66:6 (2) (1964), pp. 55–69. See also P. Atkinson, *Language, Structure and Reproduction: an Introduction to the Sociology of Basil Bernstein* (Bristol: Falling Wall Press, 1985).
7. William Labov, *Language in the Inner City: Studies in the Black English Vernacular* (Oxford: Blackwell, 1972).
8. Patrick Harries, *Butterflies and Barbarians: Swiss Missionaries and Systems of Knowledge in South-East Africa* (Oxford: James Currey, 2007).
9. Anindita Ghosh, *Power in Print: Popular Publishing and the Politics of Language and Culture in a Colonial Society, 1778–1905* (Oxford: Oxford University Press, 2007).
10. Maria Haywood, *Dress at the Court of Henry VIII* (Leeds: Maney Press, 2007); Deborah Cohen, *Household Gods: the British and their Possessions* (London: Yale University Press, 2006); Dena Goodman and Kathryn Norberg, *Furnishing the Eighteenth Century: What Furniture Can Tell us About the European and American Past* (London: Routledge, 2006).
11. Peter Burke, 'Introduction', in Peter Burke and Roy Porter, *The Social History of Language* (Cambridge: Cambridge University Press, 1987), pp. 1–20.
12. Roy Porter, 'Introduction', in Roy Porter and Peter Burke, *Language, Self and Society: a Social History of Language* (Cambridge: Polity Press, 1991), pp. 1–16.
13. David Randall, 'Epistolary rhetoric, the newspaper and the public sphere', *Past and Present* 198:1 (2008), pp. 3–32.
14. Melanie Tebbutt, *Women's Talk? A Social History of Gossip in Working-Class Neighbourhoods, 1880–1960* (Aldershot: Scholar Press, 1995).
15. The literature on this issue is vast but one of the key texts at the heart of the debate was Gareth Stedman Jones, *Languages of Class: Studies*

in English Working-Class History, 1832–1982 (Cambridge: Cambridge University Press, 1983).

16. Joan Wallach Scott, 'The evidence of experience', *Critical Inquiry* 17:4 (1991), pp. 773–97.

17. Claire Langhamer, 'Love and courtship in mid-twentieth century England', *Historical Journal* 50:1 (2007), pp. 173–96.

18. Linda Pollock, 'Anger and the negotiation of relationships in Early-Modern England', *Historical Journal* 47:3 (2004), pp. 567–90.

19. David Vincent, *Bread, Knowledge and Freedom: a Study of Working-Class Autobiography* (London: Europa, 1981).

20. Maud Pember Reeves, *Round About a Pound a Week* (London: Virago, [1913] 1979), pp. 90–1.

21. Florence Bell, *At the Works: a Study of a Manufacturing Town* (London: Virago, [1907] 1985), pp. 191–200.

22. Ellen Ross, *Love and Toil: Motherhood in Outcast London, 1870–1918* (Oxford: Oxford University Press, 1993), pp. 168–9.

23. Jack Lawson, *A Man's Life* (London: Hodder and Stoughton, 1932).

24. Vincent, *Bread, Knowledge and Freedom.*

25. Diane Blakemore, *Understanding Utterances: Introduction to Pragmatics* (Oxford: Blackwell, 1992).

26. Sarah Toulalan, *Imagining Sex: Pornography and Bodies in Seventeenth-Century England* (Oxford: Oxford University Press, 2007).

27. Michel Foucault, *The History of Sexuality* (London: Allen Lane, 1979).

FURTHER READING

Bernstein, Basil, 'Elaborated and restricted codes: their social origin and some consequences', *American Anthropologist* 66:6 (2) (1964), pp. 55–69.

Bourdieu, Pierre, *Language and Symbolic Power*, ed. John Thompson (Oxford: Polity Press, 1991).

Burke, Peter, and Roy Porter (eds), *The Social History of Language* (Cambridge: Cambridge University Press, 1987).

Burke, Lucy, Tony Crowley and Alan Girvin, *The Routledge Language and Cultural Theory Reader* (London: Routledge, 2000).

Labov, William, *Language in the Inner City: Studies in the Black English Vernacular* (Oxford: Blackwell, 1972).

Porter, Roy, and Peter Burke (eds), *Language, Self and Society: a Social History of Language* (Cambridge: Polity Press, 1991).

Saussure, Ferdinand, *Course in General Linguistics*, eds C. Bally and A. Sechehaye, trans. R. Harris (London: Duckworth Press, 1983).

Strange, J.-M., *Death, Grief and Poverty, 1870–1914* (Cambridge: Cambridge University Press, 2005).

Vincent, David, *Bread, Knowledge and Freedom: a Study of Working-Class Autobiography* (London: Europa, 1981).

Vološinov, V. N., *Marxism and the Philosophy of Language*, trans. L. Matejka and I. R. Titunik (Cambridge, MA: Harvard University Press, 1983).

CHAPTER 12

Analysing Behaviour as Performance

Simon Gunn

A woman dons her mask in readiness for appearing at a society ball; a group of villagers bang pots and pans outside the house of a husband reputed to beat his wife; factory workers down tools and occupy a factory in support of a claim for higher wages. Such instances of social behaviour are the stuff of historical research. As historians we want to know why masks were so widely used by fashionable society in eighteenth-century Europe, what purpose the custom of charivari or 'rough music' had, and how the weapons of workers, such as the strike, came into use under the conditions of early industrial capitalism. Our task is both to re-describe and, more importantly, to explain such behaviour, its significance in relation to the time, place and social circumstances in which it occurred.

One way in which historians have come to interpret human behaviour historically is through the concept of performance, the idea that behaviour works in ways akin to drama and can be effectively understood within a dramaturgical framework. Even when the concept is not introduced explicitly we often see it reflected in the terminology used to describe situations: people are defined as 'social actors', the setting is a 'stage' and events may be seen as following a pre-existing 'script'. Historians are not alone in the turn to performance: this mode of interpreting human behaviour has strong roots in anthropology, sociology and social psychology as we shall see, and has become pervasive across the human sciences. It is also far from the only way of tackling this basic subject. Historians have more conventionally viewed behaviour as the product of fundamental drives (e.g. economic self-interest, the will to power) or of determining structures, such as class or *mentalité*, the consequence being that what shapes the actions of human subjects is understood to be the product of certain invisible, deep-lying societal or psychological formations. In the last twenty years or so, however, the concept of performance has increasingly been deployed in historical studies as a way of making sense of collective conduct, given impetus especially by the rise of cultural history.[1] As we shall see, in recent research the concept of performance has in part given way to the related but more complex model of 'performativity', understood as a means of ordering conduct through language and technology.

The object of this chapter is to analyse 'performance' as a method for interpreting social behaviour. We shall find it to be a slippery concept but one which has considerable utility for understanding subjects such as ritual, self-presentation and specific, recurrent forms of collective activity like carnival or strikes. There is no single authoritative way of utilising performance as a tool of analysis. By taking a number of examples from historical research, including my own on the Victorian middle class, I intend to draw up a minimum typology for how performance can be utilised as a historical method/ology, a means of organising and interpreting social behaviour, as well as identifying some of the attendant problems, conceptual or otherwise. To begin with, though, it is essential to know something about the history of performance as metaphor and method.

THE CONCEPT OF PERFORMANCE

One need think no further than Shakespeare's 'All the world's a stage' to recognise that the idea of human society as theatre – *theatrum mundi* – has a lengthy historical provenance. Such ideas seem to have been especially prevalent in eighteenth-century England where authors such as Tobias Smollett and artists such as William Hogarth revelled in presenting society, high and low, as a theatrical comedy, permeated by greed, pretension and dishonesty. Recent historians have gone further in suggesting a profound correspondence between the theatre and social life in perceptions of human personality during the long eighteenth century; the modern contrast between the actor and the person, between playing a role and possessing an authentic self, was, they argue, only emerging towards the end of the period. In general, the early modern man or woman possessed little sense of an interior self distinct from, and deeper than, outward appearances.[2]

It was in the late 1950s and early 1960s, though, that academic scholars began systematically applying the model of dramaturgy to human behaviour in the attempt to uncover the mainsprings of social and cultural action. Three works that helped establish the concept of performance in the human sciences were published in these years: Victor Turner's *Schism and Continuity in an African Society* (1957); J. L. Austin's *How to Do Things with Words* (1962); and Erving Goffman's *The Presentation of the Self in Everyday Life* (1959).[3] Turner, Austin and Goffman worked in different disciplines – anthropology, philosophy and sociology respectively – and while their ideas diverged from each other as well as from the orthodoxies of the fields in which they worked, we can also attribute to them the origins of the modern 'performative turn'. Here it is useful to investigate briefly the various approaches they advocated.

In *Schism and Continuity in an African Society* Victor Turner introduced the notion of 'social drama' as representing a moment of crisis in the life of a society or group. Turner was later to define 'social drama' as 'an eruption from the level surface of ongoing social life, with its interactions, transactions, reciprocities, its customs for making regular, orderly sequences of behaviour'.[4] A social drama could be identified by four phases: breach, when a public breaking of a fundamental group norm occurs; a phase of crisis, when the breach between the contending parties widens; a further phase of redressive action, marked by attempts to mediate between the parties and by collective action such as public rituals; and a final phase of reintegration, in which the conflict is either resolved or the original source of division is accepted and institutionalised.[5] The phases of the social drama, according to Turner, can be understood as theatrical or play-like: they follow scripts, involve certain stock characterisations and rely heavily on symbolism for the passage of events. The task of the anthropologist (or historian) is thus to identify, describe and analyse the phases of the social drama, including states such as 'liminality', denoting a transitional position between phases when a person is neither one thing nor the other (for example, teenagers caught between childhood and adulthood). Especially interested in the symbolic or ritual aspects of social interaction, Turner also provides a method or procedure for how to analyse them. First the historian should extract the meaning of the symbol or ritual for the persons involved (the 'exegetical' dimension). Next we should examine the operational uses of the symbol, what the group concerned actually does with it – how for example a ritual practice is performed. Finally, Turner suggests, there is the positional significance of the symbol, the place within a larger symbolic field which in turn shapes its larger meaning and effect.[6] Turner thus provides a number of guidelines for analysing group behaviour which can be usefully adapted by historians, as I will show.

Turner's concepts and methods can be profitably examined alongside those of his successor in the field of symbolic or cultural anthropology, Clifford Geertz. Unlike Turner, Geertz did not see ritual behaviour as pre-eminently dramatic in character but a combination of drama, game and text; events like royal coronations or football matches were 'an acted document' in which the anthropologist or historian had to understand the language or cultural script in order to decipher its meaning.[7] There was, though, a strongly dramaturgical dimension to Geertz's thought, evident in one of his most famous essays, 'Deep Play: Notes on the Balinese Cockfight' (1972) which has made an enduring impact on historical studies.[8] The subject of the essay – the cockfight as a cardinal, if illegal, pastime of Balinese men – is described in graphic, highly performative terms at the same time as it is scrutinised for its wider meanings within local society. Geertz's approach to this task is to peel off the layers of meaning that encompass an event and to decipher it through successive acts of re-description; this is what he meant when terming his method 'thick description'. For Geertz, the purpose of analysing social behaviour is to uncover its meaning; this meaning is always established relationally, so that, as with the classic 'hermeneutic circle', the interpreter moves continuously from the part to the whole, from the constitutive elements to the totality of the event, and ultimately to the event as part of a larger cultural system.[9] Geertz's method, we might note, is anti-functionalist. In Balinese culture, he concluded, the cockfight did not *do* anything: 'its function is neither to assuage social passions nor to heighten them . . . but to display them'. The cockfight is quite simply 'a story they tell about themselves' and as such its meanings are on the surface, embodied in the event and its relationship to other types of cultural performance, not an outcome of hidden or deeper structures.[10]

A different, linguistic model of performance was offered by the philosopher J. L. Austin in his classic 1962 study, *How To Do Things With Words*. In the book, Austin focused attention on 'speech acts' and specifically, what he termed 'performative utterances'. These are a category of statements like promises or declarations that constitute the reality they might be said to describe. As such they are neither true nor false but performative. Austin gave as examples wedding vows – 'I do' ('take this woman to be my lawful wedded wife') – and predictions 'I bet you sixpence it will rain tomorrow'. In each case, the statement also contains within itself an action; it constitutes the very deed of marrying or making a bet. Austin's theory of performativity is essentially linguistic but its significance for recent social scientists lies in the fact that it bridges words and actions. Here language is not seen as reflecting reality but making it. Judith Butler, for example, describes the constitution of gender identity as performative not because femininity and masculinity are acted in any simple theatrical sense, but because they are the product of the play of signs (behavioural and linguistic) on the body. In other words, gender is not the product of an essence, biological or otherwise, but a result of consistent ways of communicating and behaving that produce over time the effect of a durable, 'natural' identity of the biological body with a gender, masculine or feminine. That this identity is a fabrication – what Butler terms a 'regulatory fiction' – is revealed by the ability of groups such as drag artists and transvestites to pass as the opposite sex by operationalising the discursive codes that signify man and woman.[11] Taking the idea of performativity to explore gender identity in the manner proposed by Butler requires the application of techniques such as discourse analysis and textual deconstruction. It demands close attention to language and communication.

However, it was in the work of the sociologist Erving Goffman, especially his classic *The Presentation of the Self in Everyday Life*, that the dramaturgical model of behaviour was most fully elaborated in the mid-twentieth century. For Goffman the theatre was more than a metaphor for social life; it was the key to understanding both personal identity and social behaviour. Like Geertz he argued that human behaviour was not the product of deep structures or drives but produced relationally in the interaction between people – what he termed the 'interaction order'. Humans are actors who perform a wide variety of different roles. Their primary task is 'impression management', the consistent attempt to control how they appear to others through signs and expressions. Actors manage their self-presentation through what Goffman termed 'framing', by constructing interpretive schema in order to organise their appearance and behaviour in relation to others. The setting (or 'region') in which performances take place is also critically important. Goffman argued that people's behaviour was radically different when performing in front of others ('front stage') from their actions in relative or absolute privacy ('back stage'), which was also the site, as in the theatre, where self-presentation in public is planned and rehearsed. Human identity is therefore a highly wrought performance achieved through interaction with others; it is fundamentally a social production, not the product of an inner self or of attributes such as class, though these undoubtedly come into play. Nor does all this apply merely to individuals according to Goffman; 'teams' or groups can also collectively engage in 'impression management'.[12]

Like Turner and Geertz, Erving Goffman's methodology can be termed a form of ethnographic participant observation. It involved minute attention to people's behaviour in different places, from crofting communities in the Shetland Islands to the inmates of mental institutions in Washington DC, followed by detailed note-taking, reflection and analysis. The principle of such observation is to suspend normal judgements as far as is possible in order to apprehend and decipher the codes which govern people's behaviour in given situations, such as playing or eating.[13] Ethnographic observation of this order is obviously not an option for historians, but it is possible at least to use some of the concepts and techniques involved in the dramaturgical approach in organising and interpreting historical source materials. We now turn therefore to the question of how historians have begun to apply ideas of performance to their own historical subjects.

ANALYSING PERFORMANCE IN HISTORICAL SETTINGS

Since the 1980s historians have viewed all manner of historical events and behaviour as in some measure performative and have analysed them in a dramaturgical vein. Cases of insult and slander in the seventeenth century;

the drama of the public execution in the eighteenth; the performance of gentility in the Victorian middle-class household; the rise of striptease as an index of 'permissiveness' in the 1960s; each of these diverse phenomena have been examined by historians as forms of spectacle, speech act or ritual, and sometimes a mixture of them all.[14] These various accounts have very different methodological assumptions built into them. Some weave elements of performance theory explicitly into their analysis, following J. L. Austin in searching for speech acts and 'performative utterances' or the anthropology of ritual to depict ceremonial processions as performing historical memory.[15] Others, less satisfactorily, speak of social identity or power as 'performed' without specifying why, conceptually or methodologically, the phenomenon under review should be understood in this way. To comprehend more precisely how historians have deployed the notion, therefore, we need to look at some practical instances.

My first example is drawn from Peter Bailey, a pioneer of the study of popular leisure in Victorian Britain, whose work encompasses 'performance' in several senses of the term, including the acts played out in institutions such as the music hall, and the popular identities, such as Champagne Charlie, forged within them. Here we shall examine his classic 1979 article, '"Will the real Bill Banks please stand up?": towards a role analysis of mid-Victorian working class respectability'.[16] In the article Bailey takes issue with the view that the working class in Britain in the 1860s was marked by a social and cultural division between a 'respectable' section, identified with skilled, 'improving' workers and their families and the 'rough', predominantly unskilled or semi-skilled workers, more given to drink and improvidence. Mid-Victorian workers, it was claimed by middle-class contemporaries, were split by their adherence to different ways of life, one sober, temperate and 'respectable', the other hedonistic and profligate. This cultural or behavioural division has been seen as having a potentially larger significance by social historians. It appeared to map onto decline in popular support for radicalism post-Chartism, increasing trade-union 'consciousness', and the relative attractions of the existing political parties, Liberal and Conservative, to different elements of a popular audience. It was the existence of this apparent fault-line in working-class culture which Bailey sought to question.

How then does he go about this piece of historical investigation? In framing the problem (and its putative answer) Bailey borrowed the notion of 'role analysis' from the American sociologists Hans Gerth and C. Wright Mills, alert to the fact that 'role' here implied behaviour that was recurrent and regular as well as social in the sense of being responsive to others.[17] It corresponded, in short, to the idea of repeated performance. Further, he draws on Goffman's concept of 'role distance' in which 'the social actor can perform a role with sufficient conviction to meet the expectations of the role-other, while injecting some expression into the performance which conveys his psychic resistance to any fundamental attachment to the obligations of that role'.[18] Armed with these conceptual tools, Bailey investigates a series of primary sources, the most important of which is the story of 'Bill Banks' Day Out', written by Thomas Wright, the 'Journeyman Engineer', an often perceptive contemporary commentator on working-class life. The story is a piece of documentary fiction based on the day-out of Bill Banks, a London railwayman, and his family to Hampton Court, a historic house, which ends with an evening visit to the Alhambra Music Hall in Leicester Square. Bailey's point about the story is that it depicts Banks and his family in multiple guises: as a literate, self-improving artisan out with a wife who is a prudent manager of the household budget, at one point, but at others during the day, drunken, rowdy and spendthrift. Who, then, is the 'real' Bill Banks – rough or respectable? Other contemporary sources, such as newspapers and association records, are similarly read for indications that 'respectability' and 'roughness' were by no means hermetically sealed categories or tied to a particular social grouping. Following Goffman in his research strategy, Bailey particularly sought to identify signs of detachment or disassociation in his working-class subjects, evidence that the performance of respectability in front of those in authority might also disclose signs of resistance (such as sullenness or irony) to that role. Other indications of the breakdown of role categories were revealed by reports of occasions at 'improving' institutions, such as the Mechanics Institute, which might descend into a 'rollicking free and easy' to the dismay of bourgeois patrons.[19] In unpicking the easy distinction between the 'rough' and 'respectable', Peter Bailey represents working-class behaviour as a 'calculated performance of different roles that exploited the fragmented milieu of big city life', enabling a single worker to adopt multiple personae, at home, the workplace or 'out on the town'.[20]

Social behaviour can thus be analysed as a series of performances which an individual or group might improvise in different settings. There is in such an approach the implication that there is (and was) no essential self or core to social identity, that it is instead fluid, relational and situation-specific. These ideas informed my own research on the English middle class between 1840 and 1914, based on the major industrial centres of Manchester, Birmingham and Leeds, regarded both by contemporaries and subsequent historians as the classical birthplace of a modern middle class.[21] Such cities were large and sprawling, but with relatively compact and monumental central areas, dominated by warehouses, town halls, banks, department stores, theatres and music halls. Outside the close-packed slums and residential communities, the great industrial cities (no less than London) were fragmented and anonymous places, the forcing-ground of new types of behavioural modernity. Yet as Peter Bailey found, this modernity was not generally expressed as liberal individualism or the pursuit of self-interest. As it was described in contemporary sources, from association records to periodical journals, the behaviour of the middle classes – factory masters, shopping ladies, clerks, governesses, foreign merchants – was represented as predictable, even mechanical. Commuters to Manchester from the suburbs would take the same train and occupy the same seat each weekday morning; the promenade of the city's 'gilded youth' would occur invariably on Saturday mornings in the same fashionable shopping streets just as the multitudinous representatives of the cotton trade would gather in the Royal Exchange weekly for the practice of High 'Change. From chapel to concert hall and from warehouse to civic procession middle-class behaviour in Victorian cities seemed to exhibit similar formal, stylised traits.

In trying to comprehend this behaviour, I turned to the extensive anthropological literature on ritual. Within this literature the concept of ritual is contested. There is little agreement on what counts as a rite and still less on how rites work or what their larger purpose may be.[22] But certain aspects of ritual theory seemed to fit the pattern of middle-class behaviour I had observed: ritual behaviour was repeated, standardised and public. As the anthropologist Catherine Bell perceptively observed, it also sought to identify certain forms of conduct as 'strategically distinguished' in relation to other, more mundane or common ways of behaving.[23] In short, as with ritual the patterns of middle-class behaviour observable in Victorian cities were both performative and power-full. The research strategy therefore focused on the detailed analysis of a series of ritual performances: attendance at fashionable concert nights, participation in the civic ceremonial and processions that punctuated the urban calendar, and the spectacle of the 'centipedic' funerals of major employers. To begin with I examined who was present (and, equally important, who was not), what precise form the event took, how standardised and invariable it was, and how it was reported and represented in visual forms such as illustrations and photographs. Through this analysis it became clear that the regular appearance of the wealthy on the stage set of the monumental city centres worked to make authority visible in the otherwise anonymous spaces of the industrial city. Like the Balinese cock-fight described by Geertz, such ritual performances did not 'do' anything; their purpose was simply to provide an image of power by giving a striking visual form to the public appearance of the economic and political elite at repeated, stylised moments.

Nor was wealth and authority always displayed alone. The regular processions of urban inhabitants that wound their way around the symbolic sites of the city centre – town hall, exchange, main squares – incarnated the idea of an urban social order both to participants and the thousands who thronged the route. 'Social order' here had multiple meanings. It implied social hierarchy, displayed in the order in which groups marched, the trades of the city preceding (or sometimes following) the 'gentlemen' of the town, the mayor and the members of the city council. It also represented the orderliness and unity of the inhabitants, their capacity for self-control and peaceable mass occupation of public space, a factor that carried considerable significance when set against the memory of popular riot and repression in the first half of the nineteenth century. Finally, participation in civic parades and processions represented a claim to citizenship and to a public voice in the town or the city; those groups excluded from public display – women, ethnic minorities, youth – were precisely those groups in the later Victorian period who occupied a marginal position in an urban social order dominated, symbolically as well as literally, by male wealth and authority.[24] If the sources of industrial bourgeois power resided in the largely hidden operations of the capitalist economy, then the cultural expression of that power was to be found in the ritual drama of civic life, a drama enacted on the public stage of the newly created monumental city centres.

OUTLINING A METHOD

From these historical examples, then, we can begin to draw up a schema of how to analyse behaviour in performative terms. Only certain types of behaviour can be looked at in this way, as I shall indicate. Moreover, the methods of analysis will vary according to the precise theoretical model adopted: Turner's 'social drama' has different requirements, for instance, from those attaching to Goffman's dramaturgical model. Nevertheless, it is possible to draw up a rough guide as to how a historian might proceed by defining four stages.

1. *Identification*. We need to start by identifying behaviour as in some sense performative. It is in fact questionable if much if not most human behaviour can be defined in this way. Geertz famously distinguished between a blink and a wink; they represent the same bodily movement but one is involuntary and meaningless, the other purposive and meaningful.[25] Similarly, other forms of behaviour may be equally or better explained by models derived from linguistics, psychoanalysis or rational choice theory, for example, depending on the phenomenon and context. In other words, we need certain base criteria for construing one or more actions as constituting a performance. These might include its public nature (performances require an audience), its capacity for repetition and relative predictability (performances are scripted), and its degree of symbolism (performances carry meanings that require to be interpreted by others). Some events – carnival, trade processions, religious practices – are obviously performative; others, such as workplace customs or codes of politeness may be less so. It may therefore be useful, following the advice of Peter Burke, to distinguish

between 'strong' performances, like the rituals and festivals mentioned, and 'weak' ones associated with the behaviours of everyday life.[26] In the latter case, analysis is likely to be harder work, though potentially more rewarding in interpretative terms.

2. *Form and Content.* Once the performative occasions or events have been identified, their form and content requires precise analysis. As much detail as possible should be amassed on the performance. When did it occur and how regularly? Who organised it and why? What exactly took place and who were the actors or protagonists? The sequence of events may be especially important as is the question of their setting. Where did the performance take place? In what order did events unfurl and who (if anyone) devised the script? Similarly, you should try to establish the audience for the performance. Who or what was it aimed at? Who witnessed it? How firm was the line between audience and performer? Descriptions of major events or performances are subject to the usual methodological provisos. Accounts of a popular carnival retold through court proceedings or through the eyes of the authorities might be very different from those recounted by revellers or in the local press. Fortunately, there are often several accounts surviving of major events so there is the possibility of building a reasonably full picture from them.

3. *Interpretation.* Once you have assembled a picture of the performative occasion you can begin to interpret it. Some elements of interpretation will be largely documentary and factual, such as estimating the numbers and the occupational and social background of those involved. Performances, however, are symbolic as well as material events and the trickiest (though also the most exciting) part of interpretation is working out the meanings and significance of the performance. How did the process of symbolisation work, how was it communicated and how might it have been received by those watching? As the anthropologist Paul Connerton pointed out, ritual events might have different meanings for performers and spectators.[27] The interpretation of the symbolic import of the performance is likely to be the most contentious part of your analysis as well as the most interesting, so you need to take particular care in understanding how the performance operated and the multivalent meanings it might have generated at the time as well as those produced at a later date.

4. *Contextualisation.* Finally, it is necessary to relocate the performance within the wider set of events of which it was an instance or part. This might involve placing it in a larger context from which it derived its meaning, as in the case of a royal coronation whose precise significance derives from the constitution and political system in which it occurs. Or it might entail relating it to other similar events, as in my study of the Victorian middle class in which processions, promenades and funerals were seen to form part

of a larger public culture whose purpose was to create an image of power. In either case, the process involved is similar to that described earlier for the 'hermeneutic circle', in which meaning is adduced by relating the part to the whole or setting the event in a steadily widening cultural context. Contextualisation also enables your analysis of performance to be inserted into a larger historical interpretation. It allows you as a historian to relate the empirical instance to the bigger process of historical change you are describing.

DANGERS AND PITFALLS

By extrapolating from a larger literature on ritual and performance, therefore, it is possible to establish some minimum guidelines for analysing behaviour as performance. I do not claim that these guidelines are exhaustive, although an account that overlooks one or more of them is unlikely to be convincing. Historians no less than other scholars can be guilty of utilising concepts whose theoretical bearings they are unaware of and whose methodological requirements they have failed to appreciate: hence the often vague and airy use of 'performance' in cultural history to describe almost any form of public behaviour. However, even when following carefully these guidelines or the methodological prescriptions of Turner or Goffman, a number of problems may arise.

Firstly, assuming behaviour is symbolic and 'meaningful' raises difficulties. As we saw with Connerton's critique of ritual, a symbolic approach tends to privilege looking over doing, the view of the spectator over the experience of the performer. It simultaneously neglects the body, the fact that humans are physical beings engaged in a multiplicity of corporeal practices (breathing, sitting, sleeping) at the same time as or even before they are meaning-making machines.[28] This recognition has given rise to a number of new histories of the body and the senses as well as recasting traditional topics in the history of ideas such as the scientific revolution.[29] There is also the more obvious point that attributing meaning to events is inherently tricky. Any analysis of crowd behaviour, for instance, is likely to elicit a whole variety of motives and meanings. Which were the dominant sentiments of the crowds that gathered to watch the ritual hangings of criminals at London's Tyburn in the seventeenth and eighteenth centuries – horror, excitement, revenge, compassion or a mixture of these? If, as seems clear, a mix of emotions was at play in these highly theatricalised events, how should the historian evaluate the complex and shifting character of the execution crowd over time? What weight, in other words, should be given to the different emotions and behaviour on display and to the historical meanings we might attribute to them?[30]

Secondly, there is a danger that the historian confuses the object of analysis – human behaviour – with the categories of analysis or the method. It is very easy, in effect, to slip from dramaturgy as a model for understanding behaviour to thinking that human beings really do behave like actors or performers. The terminology encourages this: we speak of actor, role, drama, front stage, back stage, script, repertoire, as if performance was identical with behaviour rather than (at best) analogous to it. So it is essential to discriminate between object and method, to take the performative approach as a tool to understand what may seem alien or unintelligible forms of behaviour – especially the complex interaction between individuals and groups – not an end in itself.

Finally here, we should note that performance-centred analysis has been accused by its critics of being circular and functionalist. They claim that performance is always seen by its proponents as working to restore the status quo and a stable order of meaning. Thus despite its apparent rejection of structural functionalism, Victor Turner's model of social drama envisages the result of conflict over behavioural norms as being resolution between the parties concerned and reintegration of deviant modes of behaviour. Erving Goffman's dramaturgical model is likewise predicated on the ultimate resolution of the immediate social situation. As Randall Collins has commented: 'The situation itself has its requirements: it will not come off unless the actors do the work of properly enacting it'. Reflecting back on Bill Banks some twenty five years later, Peter Bailey was self-critical, seeing his earlier analysis as 'too tidy in its functionalist assumptions of an inherent equilibrium and a singular core self with which all role performances are reconcilable'.[31] Such strictures are sharp and pertinent but they do not imply that the performative approach as a whole can be dismissed as functionalist. There is, for example, no reason why analysing behaviour as performance should insist that divisions are necessarily reconciled and norms re-established. Conflict might equally be seen to persist, situations left open-ended and meanings defined as polyvalent and fluid. One of the strengths of the performative turn is its flexibility; just as it draws on diverse intellectual traditions, so it can be adapted for different ends and means.

CONCLUSION

In this chapter I have sought to provide an account of performance analysis as a resource for historical study. In attempting to present a workable methodology I have tried to convey something of the diversity of intellectual influences that have been brought to bear, from anthropology, sociology and social psychology among others. Performance as theory and method has indeed blossomed in recent years across the human sciences, including fields such as performance studies, a deliberate hybrid between ethnography and theatre.[32]

Within historical studies, the main usage of performance analysis up to the present has probably derived from ritual theory, an effect of the significance of anthropological thought within the wider cultural turn since the 1980s.[33] In certain areas, such as gender history, linguistic and psychoanalytic theories of performativity, mediated especially by the work of Judith Butler, have made an impress on scholarship, though they are rarely applied with the rigour and attention to argument of Butler herself.[34] Most recently, ideas of performativity emanating from the different direction of science and technology studies have begun to influence historical analysis, moving the understanding of performance from people to material things, or the relationship between the two. Performativity in this sense complicates matters by arguing that agency is not exclusively human: commodities like cookers and technologies like gas also have agency. They do not simply respond to human will but are 'scripted' to perform in pre-given ways, while also being prone to behaving unexpectedly, breaking down, leaking or even exploding.[35] Historical developments, such as the Victorian 'sanitary revolution', are therefore seen as co-produced – or co-performed – by material agents (water), technologies (drains, the water closet) and human agents (engineers, municipal inspectors).[36]

Clearly, such a concept of performativity requires a different set of methods – not to say a fresh theoretical understanding – from approaches based on ritual or role analysis. Above all, it poses the problem of tracing linkages through sources and establishing how networks of human, material and technological agents interacted and became durable. Put crudely, the emphasis in performativity is not on what things mean, but how they work.[37] As a result the interpretation of behaviour (human and non-human) in historical studies may be changing once again, moving towards performativity and actor networks. Yet as this suggests, the shifting perspective adds to rather than displaces earlier approaches. For all the changes, the concept of performance retains its central position in the human sciences as a metaphor and method for the study of how people and things behave.

NOTES

1. For a wider discussion see Peter Burke, 'Performing history: the importance of occasions', *Rethinking History* 9:1 (2005), pp. 35–52.
2. Dror Wahrman, *The Making of the Modern Self: Identity and Culture in Eighteenth-Century England* (New Haven, CT: Yale University Press, 2004); Lisa A. Freeman, *Character's Theatre: Genre and Identity on the Eighteenth-Century English Stage* (Philadelphia, PA: University of Pennsylvania Press, 2002); Richard Sennett, *The Fall of Public Man* (New York, NY: Knopf, 1976).

3. Victor Turner, *Schism and Continuity in an African Society: a Study of Ndembu Village Life* (Manchester: Manchester University Press, 1957); J. L. Austin, *How to Do Things with Words* (Oxford: Oxford University Press, 1962); Erving Goffman, *The Presentation of the Self in Everyday Life* (New York, NY: Doubleday, 1959).

4. Victor Turner, *On the Edge of the Bush. Anthropology as Experience*, ed. Edith L. B. Turner (Tucson, AZ: University of Arizona Press, 1985), p. 196.

5. Turner elaborated this schema in later work; see *Dramas, Fields and Metaphors: Symbolic Action in Human Society* (Ithaca, NY: Cornell University Press, 1974), pp. 33–9.

6. Victor Turner, *The Forest of Symbols: Aspects of Ndembu Ritual* (Ithaca, NY: Cornell University Press), pp. 50–1.

7. Clifford Geertz, *Local Knowledge: Further Studies in Interpretive Anthropology* (New York, NY: Basic Books, 1983), pp. 19–35; *The Interpretation of Cultures* (London: Fontana, [1973] 2000), pp. 20–1.

8. Clifford Geertz, 'Deep play: notes on the Balinese cockfight', *Daedalus* 101 (1972), pp. 1–37, reproduced in Geertz, *Interpretation of Cultures*, pp. 412–44.

9. Geertz, 'Thick description: towards an interpretive theory of culture', *Interpretation of Cultures*, pp. 3–32. For a helpful description of the hermeneutic circle see Brian Fay, *Contemporary Philosophy of Social Science: a Multicultural Approach* (Oxford: Blackwell, 2002), pp. 141–7.

10. Geertz, 'Balinese cockfight', pp. 444, 448.

11. Judith Butler, *Gender Trouble: Feminism and the Subversion of Identity* (London: Routledge, 1990), esp. pp. 136–41.

12. As well as *The Presentation of the Self in Everyday Life* a number of other works by Erving Goffman are important, often refining earlier ideas. They include *Stigma* (Upper Saddle River, NJ: Prentice Hall, 1963); *Interaction Ritual* (New York, NY: Pantheon Books, 1967); *Frame Analysis: an Essay on the Organization of Experience* (Boston, MA: Northeastern University Press, 1986).

13. On ethnographic methods see Paul Atkinson and Martyn Hammersley, *Ethnography: Principles and Practice* (London: Routledge, 2007).

14. Laura Gowing, *Domestic Dangers: Women, Words and Sex in Early Modern London* (Oxford: Oxford University Press, 1996); Thomas W. Laqueur, 'Crowds, carnival and the state in English executions, 1604–1868', in A. L. Beier, David Cannadine and James M. Roseheim (eds), *The First Modern Society* (Cambridge: Cambridge University Press, 1989); Linda Young, *Middle-Class Culture in the Nineteenth Century: America, Australia and Britain* (Basingstoke: Palgrave, 2003); Frank Mort, 'Striptease: the erotic female body and live sexual entertainment in mid-twentieth century London', *Social History* 32:1 (February 2007), pp. 27–53.

15. For example Gowing, *Domestic Dangers*; W. L. Reddy, *The Navigation of Feeling: a Framework for a History of Emotions* (Cambridge: Cambridge University Press, 2001); Gillian McIntosh, *The Force of Culture: Unionist Identities in Twentieth-Century Ireland* (Cork: Cork University Press, 1999).

16. The article was originally published in *Journal of Social History* 12:3 (Spring 1979), pp. 336–53. Here I refer to the version published in Peter Bailey, *Popular Culture and Performance in the Victorian City* (Cambridge: Cambridge University Press, 2003), pp. 30–46.

17. Bailey, '"Will the real Bill Banks"', fn. 14, 219.

18. Ibid. p. 39.

19. Ibid. p. 41.

20. Bailey, 'Introduction: social history, cultural studies and the cad', in Bailey, *Popular Culture*, p. 7.

21. Simon Gunn, *The Public Culture of the Victorian Middle Class: Ritual and Authority in the English Industrial City, 1840–1914* (Manchester: Manchester University Press, 2000).

22. For useful summaries see Catherine Bell, *Ritual Theory, Ritual Practice* (Oxford: Oxford University Press, 1992); Edwin Muir, *Ritual in Early Modern Europe* (Cambridge: Cambridge University Press, 1997).

23. Bell, *Ritual Theory*, p. 74.

24. For a fuller description of the analysis described here see Simon Gunn, 'Ritual and civic culture in the English industrial city, *c*.1835–1914', in R. J. Morris and R. H. Trainor (eds), *Urban Governance: Britain and Beyond since 1750* (Aldershot: Ashgate, 2000), pp. 233–4.

25. Geertz, *Interpretation of Cultures*, p. 7.

26. Burke, 'Performing history', p. 43.

27. Paul Connerton, *How Societies Remember* (Cambridge: Cambridge University Press, 1989).

28. The implications of this understanding are explored variously in Richard Biernacki, 'Method and metaphor after the new cultural history', in Victoria E. Bonnell and Lynn Hunt (eds), *Beyond the Cultural Turn* (Berkeley, CA: University of California Press, 1999), pp. 62–92; Pierre Bourdieu, *The Logic of Practice*, trans. R. Nice (Cambridge: Cambridge University Press, 1992).

29. David Howes (ed.), *Empire of the Senses: the Sensual Culture Reader* (Oxford: Berg, 2005); Catherine Gallagher and Thomas Laqueur (eds), *The Making of the Modern Body* (Berkeley, CA: University of California Press, 1987); Steven Shapin and Simon Schaffer, *Levitathan and the Air-Pump* (Princeton, NJ: Princeton University Press, 1985).

30. For a fine study that attempts to deal with these questions and the performative nature of public executions, see Thomas Laqueur, 'Crowds, carnival and the state in English executions, 1604–1868', in A. L. Beier,

David Cannadine and James M. Roseheim (eds), *The First Modern Society* (Cambridge: Cambridge University Press, 1989).

31. Steven Feierman, 'Colonizers, scholars and the creation of invisible histories', in Bonnell and Hunt, *Beyond the Cultural Turn*, pp. 193–6; Randall Collins, *Interaction Ritual Chains* (Princeton, NJ: Princeton University Press, 2004), p. 16; Bailey, *Popular Culture*, p. 9.

32. Richard Schechner, *Performance Studies: an Introduction* (Oxford: Routledge, 2002).

33. Historians influenced by anthropology are legion but examples might include the historian of ideas, Robert Darnton, the historian of *mentalités*, Natalie Zemon Davis, and the historian of labour, William Sewell.

34. Most apparent in the pioneering work of Joan Wallach Scott, who co-edited *Feminists Theorize the Political* (London: Routledge, 1992) with Butler as well as writing *Gender and the Politics of History* (New York, NY: Columbia University Press, 1988), heavily influenced by Butler and linguistics. For Butler's influence, see Judith Bennett, *History Matters: Patriarchy and the Challenge of Feminism* (Philadelphia, PA: University of Pennsylvania Press, 2006); Simon Gunn, *History and Cultural Theory* (Harlow: Longman, 2006), pp. 146–9.

35. For a discussion, see Frank Trentmann, 'Materiality in the future of history: things, practices, and politics', *Journal of British Studies* 48 (April 2009), pp. 283–307; Chris Otter, *The Victorian Eye: a Political History of Light and Vision in Britain, 1800–1910* (Chicago, IL: University of Chicago Press, 2008).

36. Patrick Joyce, *The Rule of Freedom: Liberalism and the Modern City* (London: Verso, 2003), esp. ch. 2. This line of thought owes much to Actor Network Theory and the work of Bruno Latour, e.g. *Science in Action* (Cambridge, MA: Harvard University Press, 1987).

37. A useful summary for historians is Thomas Bender, 'Reassembling the city: networks and urban imaginaries', in Ignacio Farías and Thomas Bender (eds), *Urban Assemblages: How Actor Network Theory Changes Urban Studies* (London: Routledge, 2010).

FURTHER READING

Austin, J. L., *How to Do Things with Words* (Oxford: Oxford University Press, 1962).

Bailey, Peter, *Popular Culture and Performance in the Victorian City* (Cambridge: Cambridge University Press, 2003).

Bell, Catherine, *Ritual Theory, Ritual Practice* (Oxford: Oxford University Press, 1992).

Burke, Peter, 'Performing history: the importance of occasions', *Rethinking History* 9:1 (2005), pp. 35–52.

Butler, Judith, *Gender Trouble: Feminism and the Subversion of Identity* (London: Routledge, 1990).

Geertz, Clifford, *The Interpretation of Cultures* (London: Fontana, [1973] 2000).

Goffman, Erving, *The Presentation of the Self in Everyday Life* (New York, NY: Doubleday, 1959).

Gunn, Simon, *The Public Culture of the Victorian Middle Class: Ritual and Authority in the English Industrial City, 1840–1914* (Manchester: Manchester University Press, 2000).

Laqueur, Thomas W., 'Crowds, carnival and the state in English executions, 1604–1868', in A. L. Beier, David Cannadine and James M. Roseheim (eds), *The First Modern Society* (Cambridge: Cambridge University Press, 1989).

Turner, Victor, *Schism and Continuity in an African Society: a Study of Ndembu Village Life* (Manchester: Manchester University Press, 1957).

PART 5

Rethinking Categories

CHAPTER 13

Ethics and Historical Research

William Gallois

How are history and ethics related to one another? While the development of ethics overlapped with that of history – given their ancient Greek origins and their formulation as disciplines or sub-disciplines in the nineteenth-century European academy – there has never really existed a field of 'ethical history', nor of 'historical ethics'. Within philosophy, the history of ethics constitutes a branch of the history of the discipline, while in history there has been some interest in the 'ethics of history', which has primarily been understood as the analysis of the moral consequences of particular forms of historical writing, such as those which served totalitarian or imperial regimes (in other words, with a concentration on malign rather than benign ethics). There exists a limited philosophical literature which critiques the ethical presuppositions of history, though since such work displays little interest in the practice of history, it has found scant audience amongst historians, who have remained untroubled by its debates as to whether Anglo-American pragmatism or Continental theory provides the more apt ground for a foundational critique of the discipline.[1]

The ideas of 'ethical history' and 'historical ethics' therefore seem misnomers in terms of the traditions of history and philosophy. Historians have tended not to assert that one of the values of their enterprise is a contribution to ethical understanding, whilst philosophers generally understand ethics to be situated in our present, often inflected by past debates but for and about the world today. While history concerns itself chiefly with paths which were taken, ethics is as interested in those which were not followed. Both history and ethics are founded on notions of judgement, but great differences lie between the historian's desire to narrate the truth of the past and the ethicist's hope to illuminate the moral value of human behaviour.

Nonetheless, a distinctive feature of the late-twentieth-century academy was the advent of an interdisciplinary 'ethical turn' and historians' engagements with this renewed interest in ethics revealed a slightly more tangled history of their own discipline than they had hitherto accepted. Empirical historians had long seen a central flaw in their nineteenth-century forebears' method as being their desire to promote certain moral and ideological causes in the course of the production of history. The classic example of this entanglement came in Whig histories of nineteenth-century Britain in which valorisations of parliamentary democracy and modern progress were also understood to be coded references to the moral superiority of the modern West and the place of Britain at the apex of this beneficent civilisation.

It was, however, only the retrospective judgement of subsequent genera- tions of historians which saw the Whigs cast in this light, for the Victorians themselves had viewed their practices as exemplifying the traditions of neu- trality which emerged with the empirical method. If the Whigs were thus blinded as to the moral values they smuggled into their histories, were later historians any more self-aware, especially given the charged political environ- ments of the twentieth century and the adoption of Marxist, conservative, feminist and other ideological positions and methods? The 'turn to ethics' introduced a slightly more sophisticated line of enquiry into these discus- sions for while it may have been relatively easy to identify a history which was overtly political or propagandistic – Nazi history, for instance – it was a tougher critical task to locate hidden assumptions about nation, place, gender, identity or selfhood which might feed into an ethical stance, no less complete than a politicised history, if rather less obvious.

Ultimately however, such debates have lain on the borderlines of history and historiography. The language of ethics – the good, the bad, justice, auton- omy, care and so on – has not been central to the language or the mindsets of historians. In many senses, then, what this chapter describes are disciplinary exceptions, though perhaps ones which are becoming more influential within history. It seems apt that such discussions about the language of ethics coin- cide with the prevalence of epistemic struggles over language, representation and truth in the discipline. This coincidence is no accident for the interroga- tive roots of these challenges to particular forms of history have their ancestry in the same forms of philosophical questioning, but I hope to show that an engagement with ethics may take many forms for history and need not simply draw on postmodern critique and other linguistically driven appraisals of the neutrality of empiricism.

The chapter is divided into four sections, each of which addresses a key question in relation to history and ethics using illustrative material from a dis- tinct field of historical study. It begins by unravelling the relationship between history and ethics, looking at the example of writing the history of medical ethics, before moving on to consider whether we can access ethical cultures in the past in a study of colonial history. It then examines the value of ethical categories through the study of medieval Islam and closes by asking how the discipline might change if ethics became central to its enterprise. Running across these discussions are a series of key questions – 'Should historical research be ethical?', 'How can we know the ethics of past cultures?', and 'Are there ethical principles which can help historians in their work?' – and an argument that the marriage of history and ethics can be a productive one. Drawing on my own experiences as a historian, I argue that the language of ethics has a descriptive power which enables historians to better explain past cultures, whilst enabling forms of narrative and judgement which acknowledge that moral categories such as freedom and justice change over time.

The chapter attempts to be as practical as it can be but it only briefly touches on the area of professional ethics, which considers areas such as honesty, the use of living sources, professional conduct and confidentiality. Such questions are increasingly well covered in professional codes of conduct and discussions of them, whilst the chief focus of this chapter is the question as to what ethics teaches us about the historian's duty to the peoples of the past.

DISENTANGLING HISTORY AND ETHICS

When we consider history and ethics today, I would suggest that one of our first tasks is to unscramble a whole series of different approaches and questions which lie embedded together and which can often deny us clarity when they are run alongside one another or intertwined. Four particular approaches are immediately apparent:

1. The study of codes, such as the Hippocratic Oath and the Geneva Convention, and the things they tell us about the morals of particular cultures and professions.
2. How practices in a culture might be determined by codified or non-codified ethical norms, for example 'Islamic medical ethics'.
3. The historian's retrospective identification of a particular ethical culture, which lay unnoticed at the time of its enactment, such as Tzvetan Todorov's typology of encounters with others in the New World, or Bertrand Taithe's description of the invention of a distinct form of nineteenth-century humanitarianism.[2]
4. Historians' moral judgements, as seen most obviously in accounts of empire or genocide.

While reflexivity as to method and theory can sometimes reach a disabling level, it does seem useful to try to distinguish between these different ethical approaches and approaches to ethics, most especially as they are often combined in rather unreflexive ways. Not that reflection provides easy answers or the satisfying neatness that can come from boldly choosing not to be reflexive, as I've found in my own work. My book *The Administration of Sickness: Medicine and Ethics in Colonial Algeria* aspired to address all four of the areas set out above, but there is no especially easy way of getting around the ways in which four seemingly distinct approaches merged with each other in the practice of writing.[3]

To take one example of this melding of approaches, the more texts I read from the 1830s and the 1840s, the more I became convinced that historians had not fully described the relationship between healing and killing in the Algerian colony. While writers such as Le Cour Grandmaison had written on the exterminatory politics of the French empire, and Turin, Lorcin and others had looked at the narrow, racially driven scope of French imperial medicine, I began to think that there might be more to say about the intimacy of drives to heal and kill to be found in the work of soldiers, travellers and administrators, as well as doctors.[4] Most particularly, I wanted to describe the existence of an *either/or* equation of a kind which seemed naturally suited to ethical analysis. In this case, a common French stance was to argue that *either* Algerians accepted the goodness of the offer of French civilisation *or* they faced annihilation. Where most studies of the French imperial stance towards colonial subjects are framed around opposed poles of assimilation and association, I wanted to contend that in some contexts this choice ought to be seen as having been between cooperation and annihilation.

Beginning with the first of my categories above, there was evidently ample scope for the consideration of the way in which codes such as the Hippocratic Oath determined the value systems of colonial doctors, most especially as the conquest of Algeria formed a key part of the revival of a neo-Hippocratic medicine. Using Hippocratic language, my thesis made sense if one conceived of a culture in which the beneficent drive came to utterly negate the doctor's apparent equal duty to ensure he did no harm. In a colonial setting it was not difficult to find examples of such ethical prioritisation in which the moral goodness of European civilisation was seen to trump all other ethical prerogatives.

Yet the second category of analysis was evidently also essential because much as the historian would love to find explicit reflections on the ethics of Hippocratic medicine, and the manner in which they influenced the creation of a new culture, it is more realistic to think that one will find indirect examples of such a phenomenon in the letters, diaries, tracts, memoirs and other writings of colonial doctors. Such works are plentiful in the Algerian context and it was already well known that leading medical theorists such as Eugène Bodichon advocated forms of exterminatory politics, while the field was well served by secondary works which detailed the manner in which racial hierarchies were organised within notionally universalist systems of humanitarian healthcare.

Of course, the description of such a culture merges imperceptibly into the third of my categories, for while there existed plenty of descriptions of 'European' and 'French' medicine, a certain reconstructive effort is needed on the part of the historian to find commonalties across texts and to plausibly describe a culture in the whole. There are of course also all sorts of medical preoccupations from that era which either struck me as irrelevant – in that they bore no relation to my own field of interest – or are more generally seen as redundant; as perhaps in the case of medical knowledge which was subsequently seen to be wrongheaded (though I am not suggesting that historians of medicine should ignore the understanding which can be gained from such misperceptions).

Lastly, there was my own form of moral judgement as a historian, which applied as much to other historical texts as it did to my nineteenth-century actors. Why, I began to wonder, had so many historians not acknowledged the degree to which descriptions of the virtues of exterminatory massacres were commonplace in French colonial writing? What had led my forebears to believe that such desires were mere rhetorical strategies, and why had so many historians implicitly focused on the goodness of individual encounters in which locals were healed by colonial doctors and then extrapolated from such points to describe a broader culture of benevolence? Did I as a scholar have a moral duty to expose those uncommented-upon killings which made up what Mike Davis called 'the secret history of the nineteenth century'?[5]

A certain circularity can be detected here for I came to conclude that the only way in which I could reach such a polemical position came through my decision to focus on ethics as a means of understanding the Algerian encounter. In taking colonial doctors at their word and focusing on their goodness and badness, I had concluded that deeply malign consequences flowed precisely from the particular kind of beneficence which they promoted in the colony. This was not a culture of indifference towards locals, as was perhaps seen in later *colon* culture, but one which was relentlessly focused on operating on the *indigènes* as individuals and as a collective. When Algerians rejected a French offer of healing and redemption, they had needed to understand that there would be dire consequences for having done so, which is where I think I will leave this discussion, for the relationship between the communication of that message and the practices of soldiers and doctors is a more complicated story.

ACCESSING ETHICAL CULTURES OF THE PAST

Having tried to unstitch the complex of questions which emerge when we start to consider history and ethics, let us now turn to perhaps the more fundamental question as to whether we can ever know the ethics of cultures in the past. A common objection to ethical historical investigations is that they fall down on the grounds of their 'presentism'; which is to say that they mistake the difference of the past in thinking that they can apply moral categories from the present and imagine that these can be mapped onto the ways people lived in the past and the understandings they had of such terms. To take a very simple example, does it not in some way seem deeply ahistorical to believe that contemporary notions of goodness should tally with ideas of the good in ancient Greece or Persia?

The logic of such objections is ultimately, however, wholly disabling, for if historians can really never escape the binds of the language and thought of their present, there can be no history. Second, it is not so hard to acknowledge that moral categories and understandings might change across time and one might even argue that one of the chief tasks of the historian is the tracing of how such changes take place. We are, after all, interested precisely in questions such as how ideas of justice changed over time. How was it the case that a National Health Service based on ideas of social justice in healthcare developed in Britain? Why did this take place in Britain and what shifts took place in British thought and society between the ethics which had informed benevolent paternalism in the Victorian era and the post-war socialist ethics of health in 1945? Were the moral notions which informed the creation of the NHS wholly grounded in Britain or did some come from elsewhere, and can we create an archaeology of the morals which informed the creation of different forms of healthcare systems? Moving from the meta- to the micro-, why was it the case that the broad stress on social justice in the British case traditionally excluded particular marginalised groups or fed into the rationale of, for example, age-based rationing which prioritised the survival of the young over the old?

An important variant of the presentist argument holds great sway in the history of medical ethics. This fragmented and relatively underdeveloped field long suffered from huge gaps in its knowledge, such that some remarked that we knew almost nothing of the subject between the time of Hippocrates and the ancient Greeks and the infamous medical experiments of the Nazi era. Underlying these gaps were serious and quite legitimate concerns that most historians and medical practitioners tended to operate with a particularly unreflexive form of presentism which allowed them to believe that the ethics of Hippocrates were broadly universal and as applicable and comparably understood in the late twentieth century as they had been in ancient or medieval times. Additionally, the modern bioethical movement, which grew up in the United States, was deeply ahistorical, most obviously in its claim that it in fact invented complementary ethics of justice and autonomy to add to Hippocratic concentrations on beneficence and non-maleficence.[6] This was a rather silly idea, for many historians knew of other cultures where ideas of justice and autonomy were much discussed by doctors and others involved in healthcare, but these debates structured a particular realm of discourse on the history of medical ethics which has culminated in the publication of a monumental new *World History of Medical Ethics*.[7]

The value of this work is hard to overstate for so many of the gaps which previously existed between the ancient and modern world are now beginning to be filled in, and have been collated in a rigorous, comparative perspective. Now if we wish to compare medieval medical ethics we know where to go to understand not only what Buddhist, Jewish or Christian texts said about such things, but also how the philosophical and medical cultures of India, China or the Arab-Islamic world informed and drew on such debates.

Funnily enough, one of the great conclusions of the editors of this collection is that they are uncertain that we can in fact speak of medical ethics having a history before 1803 (the year in which the Scottish writer Thomas Perceval first used the term). Drawing on presentist critiques of history they present a case that while the past may reveal all sorts of things which possess family resemblances to medical ethics, these ought to be treated as separate categories of thought. In doing so, they have pushed back the origin of medical ethics from 1945 to the start of the nineteenth century, but they also seem to be determined to disable the very field which they have so magisterially helped to construct. Why is this the case?

The doubts of Baker and McCullough may simply come from the differences between their own discipline of philosophy and the work of historians, for one might argue that the latter field simply does not have the luxuries of neatness and exactitude which characterises the abstraction and purported precision of philosophy. They argue for instance that:

> To construct a history around a problem or issue, one needs evidence
> that it was a problem or issue in some earlier era and not one that
> appears real to us from our perspective but that never actually vexed
> those who lived in earlier eras.[8]

Yet what do we do in terms of talking ethically about medical practices and cultures of health in which historical actors did not frame their own thoughts, or at least their recorded thoughts, in ethical terms? Do such histories not count as part of the history of medical ethics? It is as though we might never apply language from the present to describe the past, as though historians of gender might be disqualified from writing about Elizabeth I on the basis that neither she nor her contemporaries used gendered language in the way that Simone De Beauvoir imagined a sex/gender distinction. Baker and McCullough go on to say:

> To construct a history of medical ethics in terms of the continuity
> of issues or problems, one needs evidence that these problems were

thought to exist in earlier eras, that they continued to exist, and that they are, in some sense, the ancestors of the issues and problems that we face today.[9]

Here we again see what appear to be cultural differences between historians and philosophers when they tackle the common ground of the history of ethics. Philosophical demands for exactitude here demand limits on the field which seem wholly inappropriate to historians for whom the creative and imaginative task of reconstructing the past is central to their method. In fact, the authors' logic is shaky here on a number of levels, for even when we apply the relevant philosophical grammar – Beauchamp and Childress's 'Four Principles' of bioethics – we find that discussions of beneficence, non-maleficence and justice can be found in many past medical cultures. The principle of autonomy (which discusses the rights of patients to make choices as to their methods of care) is less common in the historical record, but it is not wholly unknown, which raises the important question as to what current literatures miss in their determination to believe that ethical principles are inventions of the modern world.

To take one example, let us briefly consider the question of the ethic of health justice from a historical perspective, first noting that, unlike philosophers, historians would be instinctively concerned to go 'beyond the text' (here, codes of ethics) to look at the ways in which ideas about justice played out in individual encounters between doctors and patients, as well as more broadly across cultures. Historians might also accept that discussions of justice might not necessarily make reference to the term as, for example, in medieval Islamic discussions of doctors' duties not to charge for their services. The question as to whom doctors should treat and whether they should necessarily be paid for the provision of care are, it transpires, central concerns in medical ethical literatures throughout the medieval and ancient worlds, and for the historian it seems wholly appropriate that attempts should be made both to codify/catalogue these positions and to track changes in attitudes across space and time, perhaps drawing on broader bodies of knowledge to explain such shifts in thought and practice. This version of the history of ethics is necessarily more contestable and provisional than the more limited, 'locked-down' narrative sought by Baker and McCullough, but its ambition to create comparative accounts of ethical ideas and their impact on medical practices is far more ambitious.

ETHICAL CATEGORIES AND THE CLARIFICATION OF THE PAST

Rejection of the presentist argument might in fact imply not only that one is able to access ethical cultures in the past but to clarify our knowledge of the past through the use of ethical categories. Let us now look at a very different kind of historical example as a means of exploring this claim.

An ethical concept central to late twentieth-century and early twenty-first century moral debate has been the notion of cosmopolitanism. In some fields, such as international relations, this idea or complex of ideas has become one of the central poles of the discipline, and across the social sciences and the humanities there has been a great interest in exploring cosmopolitan thought and ethics.

In this late twentieth-century revival of cosmopolitan thought, it quickly became apparent that the term could not be well understood unless its history was better comprehended and much of the best work on the idea has displayed a lively interest in the development of cosmopolitan ethics.[10] The term 'cosmopolitan' was originally coined by the Stoic philosopher Diogenes as a conjoining of the ancient Greek terms '*Kosmou*', meaning 'universe' or 'world' and '*politês*', meaning politics. As Heater and others have shown, the term had a specific resonance in Greek life for it referred to an ethics and a politics which rejected the particularism and the narrow self-interest of many forms of Greek political thought to argue that others, perhaps especially conquered others, ought not to be treated as lesser forms of human simply because of their origins. This fitted with the life stories of many Stoic and Cynic philosophers who came from North Africa, Spain, Sicily and the further reaches of the Greek world.

The term also, however, fitted neatly with the imperial politics of Diogenes' patron, Alexander the Great, for it seemed to legitimate the creation of global empires, so long as rulers treated all of their subjects in an equal fashion and did not privilege their own kinsmen. Such ideas were even more apparent in the development of Roman cosmopolitanism, for it was often emperors, such as Marcus Aurelius, who were the most enthusiastic advocates of the idea. Yet, simultaneous with cosmopolitanism being used to promote a form of universal politics, Roman thinkers stressed its power as a guide to one's most immediate behaviour towards one's fellow humans in daily life. It was not enough to imagine that distant others merited the same treatment as one's neighbours, for the good life actually consisted in treating others in ways which genuinely attended to their own views of the world and not simply the picture one might paint of them or want for them.

Historians of cosmopolitanism then tended to leap from the late classical world to its revival in Renaissance Europe, when the term 'cosmopolite' and its variants suddenly re-emerged in languages such as English, German and French. In these societies, cosmopolitanism became a form of thinking deployed to combat patriotism and what thinkers such as Hakluyt saw as the uncouthness and the barbarism which lay within its supposed civility. From such points, we can then see how Kant and the Enlightenment's re-theorisation of the world were able to try to draw new pictures of the globe which described how men of different nations might deal with each other and how cosmopolitanism might be imagined as a route towards peace and away from war between nations.

Yet it was arguable that this etymological investigation needed to be taken further if current discussions were to be able to explore the full resonances of cosmopolitan ethics and politics. Where had cosmopolitan ideas been in the period between the Romans and the Renaissance? Had they simply disappeared or, like so many ideas which were notionally rediscovered in late medieval Italy, had they migrated and lived on in some other form outside of Europe?

Cosmopolitanism thought had in fact thrived in the Arab-Islamic world in the medieval period and if it were not for the colossal translation projects of the courts of Baghdad and Toledo we would in fact know very little of the work of Diogenes, Socrates and many other key classical thinkers. What is of especial interest to intellectual historians of the development of cosmopolitanism was the way in which the idea developed new senses in the Islamic world. The term never acquired an exact form in Arabic but in al-Sijistani's translation of Diogenes the term was rendered as describing a 'house or home which covered all the homes in the world'.[11] In a Muslim culture, the anti-parochialism of cosmopolitanism also became a means of describing a collective politics which fitted neatly with a universal religion which saw no differences between colours and creeds. In some senses, this was similar to the Greek and Roman imperial ideas, but where Greek antecedents had been based in a polytheistic society, Arabs found a way in which cosmopolitanism could be a foundational idea in a monotheistic culture. This contrasted with developments in Europe where cosmopolitanism seemed to have waned in part because it did not mesh with the particular form of universalism espoused by medieval Christianity.

When the rich history of Muslim cosmopolitan ethics was added to our existing stock of knowledge, contemporary discussions were quickly made more complex and interesting, not least because they so often involved debates about the place of Islam within modern secular and Christian cultures. Historical studies revealed not just Muslim interest and development of cosmopolitan ideas but also their contribution to the development of later European culture (a part of the broader rethinking of a Renaissance which owed as much to Islam as it did to the classical world) and to societies such as that of medieval al-Andalus where Muslims created a society in which Christians, Jews and Muslims sometimes lived in a state of great tolerance and mutual borrowing.

Contemporary cosmopolitan theorists are centrally concerned with how one creates ethical cultures in which forms of respect trump fears of difference, so our more complex history of the idea of cosmopolitanism is critical in this regard. Unlike most ethical debates and systems, cosmopolitanism is emphatically not a form of Eurocentric imposition of fundamental ideas on the non-West, for arguably the most developed cosmopolitan ethics and societies came from the non-West.

BEYOND HISTORY? WHY DO WE STUDY THE ETHICS OF PEOPLES OF THE PAST?

It transpires that cosmopolitanism as an ideal form of ethical communication between peoples plays a central part in another historical text which would at first seem to have few connections to the story described above: Tzvetan Todorov's *The Conquest of America: the Question of the Other*. Like many key works of 'ethical history', this book is not written by a historian, yet it is ostensibly a history in that it uses the letters of Columbus and other European explorers to describe the arrival of Europeans in the New World. The role which the past plays in Todorov's work is, though, very different to the work of conventional historians, for history serves as a form of moral laboratory or sets of enacted ethics which might help us to think about human behaviour. Why, he asks, did Iberian travellers and priests behave in particular ways towards the indigenous peoples of the Americas and how were such modes of being dependent upon ideas about the alterity of the others they encountered?

These examples led Todorov to pose a set of basic questions about the behaviour of humans when they meet strangers, and more importantly cultures when they encounter unknown peoples, with the suggestion that such meetings fall into four broad categories: annihilation, domination, assimilation and co-existence, along with a fifth ideal type of dialogue or communication, which Todorov could scarcely locate in the historical record. The conquest of the Americas generally provided plentiful examples of the worst types of human behaviour, but it also revealed hints of what a dialogic relationship might look like, in which a self (as an individual or a culture) engaged with an other with an instinctive trust that the self might be enriched through dialogue with the other.

At first glance it might seem that there is something deeply ahistorical – or presentist – about Todorov's work, in that it appears to try to locate universal moral types from situations which historians would suggest are better viewed as being culturally and temporally specific. A closer reading of Todorov's argument, however, reveals it to be more nuanced, for like empirical historians one of his greatest concerns is to attend to the specificity of the events he describes, asking why Europeans at that particular moment in the fifteenth and sixteenth centuries felt able to behave in the way that they did towards the peoples of the Americas. What new kinds of knowledge and certainty were constitutive of an ethics of exploration and encounter which sanctioned, and indeed valorised, the mass slaughter of other human beings, or designed forms of neglect which led to similarly exterminatory outcomes?

Here Todorov's brand of ethical history, or perhaps we might call it an archaeology of morals, does deviate from some historians' work – in that he is suggesting that particular ways of being human were invented at that moment which still inform the behaviour of people today – but this extension across five hundred years of time is not especially aberrant, since many historians instinctively acknowledge a modern condition or a place called the modern West. Indeed, the basic framing structures of the Western discipline of history acknowledge a shift to an early modern world at precisely the moment Todorov focuses his interest.

In the Todorovian picture of world history, the year 1492 is of central importance because it marks the beginning of a new and primarily malign relationship between Western Europe and the world, but *The Conquest of America* is also a book about hope as well as the extinguishing of faith in man's goodness (as is also the case in Todorov's work on other places of moral extremes, such as the gulags and concentration camps).[12] While *some* Europeans massacred Native Americans, *others* expressed moral disgust at the actions of their peers. The moral reasoning which lay behind such approbation had various sources – such as Natural Law theory and particular branches of Christian theology – and a key part of Todorov's mission was the excavation of the ethical logic which induced some to resist the horrors perpetrated by the many. After all, if we accept that we live in a world where humans constantly find ways to justify killing others, should we, in our present, not know something of the ethical cases which men have made in the past to dissuade the killers?

A second form of excavation in this regard is a subtext which we find in Todorov's work: that the waning of European cosmopolitanism was a factor in the bleaker new moral world made in the Americas. The year 1492, after all, marked not only the arrival of Columbus in the Americas but also the culmination of the victory of parochial, national politics (sanctioned by a narrow Catholic theology) in the new Spanish nation, which saw the rapid expulsion of its 'Others' in the ethnic cleansing of Jews and Muslims from Spain and Portugal. My use of the term 'ethnic cleansing' is of course wholly Todorovian here, for the claim I make in using it is that our understandings of twentieth- and twenty-first century atrocities such as those perpetrated on Bosnian Muslims can be materially aided through moral comparison with events in the past, which serve not only as comparators but also as originary points of explanation.

This is a convoluted way of saying that in the work of Todorov ethics aids history, but history also helps ethics. Todorov began his career as an abstruse and brilliant structuralist literary theorist, developing an influential typology of 'the fantastic' in French fiction, yet almost uniquely amongst his Paris-based structuralist and post-structuralist peers, he translated the ideas of critical theory and Bakhtin to the study of subjects and situations which have resonance with both the broader academy and public audiences. History, it transpires, is the greatest resource for the moral theorist and without historical understanding – which, in the most traditional sense includes an acknowledge-ment of the specificity of past situations and a teleological desire to track their progression through time – we lack the resources to make better ethics for our presents and our future. As the title of one of Todorov's best moral histories has it, our duty as scholars is to try to describe *The Fragility of Goodness* (his book asks why so many Jews were saved in Second World War Bulgaria as compared with neighbouring states).

ETHICS AND THE ERASURE OF HISTORY

If Todorov's work provides new and exciting reasons for believing that the marriage between history and ethics can be deeply productive for both part-ners, much work from the 'ethical turn' is deeply critical of the academic discipline of history. This critique has been bolstered by the philosophical immaturity of history, for perhaps uniquely amongst the disciplines of the modern humanities and social sciences, history has not drawn extensively on shifts in philosophical thought to bolster the institutional places where it reflects upon its methods and epistemology: historiography and the philoso-phy of history. Indeed, such reflective pursuits have arguably lain rather at the margins of a discipline devoted much more to the virtue of practice rather than theory. Such a stance has left history open to attacks on a series of fronts, one of which is ethical.

The allegation which unites post-structural critiques of history is that it has chosen to remain blind to the manner in which it constitutes knowledge and deaf to those who criticise the consequences which emanate from histori-cal work and its logic. To alight upon a number of examples, Robert Young's *White Mythologies: History Writing and the West* argues that historians have failed to understand the way in which their project underpinned Western imperialism, Frantz Fanon and Aimé Césaire wondered how a globalised Western discipline might be decolonised, while Elizabeth Deeds Ermarth's powerful body of work has shown how ignorant many historians have been as to the history of the ideas which came together to make their discipline (and equally uninterested in the modern theoretical ideas which offer it the chance to rethink its project).

The moral dimension of each of these critiques draws on an ethic of justice, for in their different ways, these works contend that history's blindness leads it to commit and perpetuate injustices towards its subjects. Yet these are not injustices which cannot be rectified. Historians could take these criticisms seriously and they might reimagine their enterprise so that, for example, it might seek to do justice to the colonised, both in its descriptive content and in the methods it adopts to tell these stories, which is precisely what we find in subaltern histories or the work of a historian such as Mike Davis in *Late Victoria Holocausts: El Niño Famines and the Making of the Third World*. Davis's work is a classic in this new genre for it takes the task of restitutive history – a history that does justice to those whose suffering lay hidden – seriously in its account of the ways in which Western political, economic and intellectual power came together in the exploitation of 'natural disasters' such that they became coordinated new forms of modern genocide. Similar impulses can be found in the work of historians such as Dirk Moses and Olivier Le Cour Grandmaison who, in Australia and France, respectively have sought to find new ways of accounting for the horrors of the colonial past and their erasure in history.

There has, however, been another more nihilistic conclusion in one branch of critical theory's evaluation of history, which is the proposal that we abandon the rotting hulk of the discipline altogether. This was most vividly expressed in the title of Keith Jenkins work *Why History? Ethics and Postmodernity*, which in some senses marked the end point of a set of ideas which had been circulating amongst postmodern theorists, for the book contended that the only ethical path for history was its abandonment and that the work of thinking about the past could be subsumed within political theory, ethics and other more theoretically attuned fields.

While it is unsurprising that such arguments are seen as bunk by empirical historians, it seems of greater significance that such calls for the rejection of history are already being made to look obsolete by the work of writers such as Todorov and Davis, who have travelled on very similar theoretical trajectories to Jenkins to reach very different conclusions: ones associated with notions of hope and reinvention rather than despair. Of especial significance here is the growing body of historiographical literature on the possibility that history might learn and borrow from ethical traditions from the non-West, or that history might even *be* those things and look nothing like the historical genres of the modern West.[13]

While one might say that the impact of the 'ethical turn' has come rather late to history, it seems possible that its impact may be much greater than has been the case in fields for which an engagement with ethics was a mere fad. Historians increasingly see ethics as providing powerful analytical and descriptive tools, whilst the repertoire of genres of 'ethical history' is surely still in its infancy. How, for example, might we write histories about ethical clashes between peoples, or describe the manner in which different ethical priorities are ordered by people and institutions, revealing the ways in which ethics makes the world?

These are the kinds of questions which all historians, be they undergraduates, postgraduates or academics, ought to ask of themselves as they begin a new project. In practical terms, meshing ethics to history only works if the potential ethical dimensions of a project are explored at its inception and at key moments in its coming into being as a piece of published research (such as the first read-through of documentary evidence and the beginning of the writing process). We also ought to acknowledge that ethical approaches might suit some sorts of history and some types of historical enterprise more than others. Ethical history is one approach amongst many, though it might additionally be seen as a form of conceptual adjunct to more established historical methods, for the point of thinking about ethics as a historian is that it provides us with ways of deepening our understanding and our descriptions of the past.

In considering how historians might think through the ethical character of their work, we need not necessarily assume that there would be a disjuncture between the requirements of ethics committees (or 'ethics' sections of research grant applications) and the more intellectual forms of historical-ethical engagement this essay has described. Let us consider, for example, a PhD student who is beginning work on the history of a hospital which specialises in prosthetic medicine. An ethics committee vetting such a doctorate would almost certainly highlight a series of areas which the student would need to consider, including questions of patient confidentiality (and data protection), especially with regard to medical records and the collating of oral histories, the importance of respecting confidentiality in doctor-patient relations in any interviews with medical staff, sensitivity in the use of photographic images of mutilation and prosthesis, and the need for great care in addressing all areas of 'disability'.

These formal ethical requirements of the project need not, however, be divorced from the intellectual ethical historical drive of such work. The student's supervisor would doubtless impress upon them the ethical character of much work in the history of disability, given the importance the field has placed upon tracking the contours of the ways in which disability has been framed over time and the manner in which such framing has impacted on the lives of the disabled. As has been the case with the stories of other formerly marginalised and subaltern groups, histories of disability have often conceived of themselves as being narratives of empowerment and modes of combating injustice. For many activist and support groups, the history of fields such as prosthesis, war wounds or thalidomide, is not solely about and for the past, but an engagement in political and ethical battles in our present.

Much as they might like to, our doctoral student cannot stand outside the way in which this body of knowledge has been constituted. As well as satisfying the requirements of an ethics committee, they will also need to show their examiner that they are well versed in the genealogies of ethics embedded in discussions of the subject over a period of time. They might also choose to deploy ideas from either canonical work in ethics or contemporary bioethical writing in their methodology and in the manner in which they approach their object of study. In doing so, they acknowledge that the ethical dimension of such research lies not solely in the formal requirements imposed on studies of the contemporary world, but that considerations of ethics might be thought to be embedded in the work of history.

Such questions are even more live ones for historians studying countries or regions in military, political or social turmoil. Questions pertaining to the ethics of research are absolutely central, for instance, to historians and doctoral scholars working on the Middle East (and not solely the contemporary Arab and Islamic world, for some *historical* topics are as controversial as those which pertain to the present). Supervisory teams need to discuss at the outset the safety of researchers and that balance of free enquiry with the protection of the historian and her sources. They also need to consider the possibility that publication of work might lead to a researcher subsequently being banned from a state or a region, or the potential medium- and long-term consequences of engaging in such work for the researcher and his family or friends. Such things need to be thought through alongside a consideration of the degree to which careers in the western academy are often heavily dependent on the production of work which is critical or which 'speaks the truth to power'.

Alongside such issues lie more profound ethical questions relating to the purpose of scholarship and the question as to whether engaged researchers ought to use their work as a means of advancing political, theological or social programmes. These might vary from cases as different as the study of queer subcultures in Indonesia to sympathetic critiques of Salafi ideology in tape recordings of imams' 'sermons' in Jordan. Existing literatures concentrate on the ethical dilemmas facing western scholars and whether a tacit or open promotion of democratic ideals and the rights of man is an acceptable position to adopt in Middle East Studies, though a broader set of debates are taking place on the ground.

NOTES

1. David Carr, Thomas R. Flynn and Rudolf A. Makkreel, *The Ethics of History* (Evanston, IL: Northwestern University Press, 2004).
2. Tzvetan Todorov, *The Conquest of America: the Question of the Other* (Oklahoma, OK: Oklahoma University Press, 1993); Bertrand Taithe,

'The red cross flag in the Franco-Prussian war: civilians, humanitarians and war in the 'modern age', in Roger Cooter, Mark Harrison and Steve Sturdy (eds), *War, Medicine and Modernity* (Stroud: Sutton, 1998), pp. 22–47.

3. William Gallois, *The Administration of Sickness: French Medical Imperialism in Nineteenth-Century Algeria* (London: Palgrave, 2008).

4. Olivier Le Cour Grandmaison, *Coloniser, exterminer: sur la guerre et l'état colonial* (Paris: Fayard, 2005); Yvonne Turin, *Affrontements culturels dans l'Algérie coloniale: écoles, médecines, religion, 1830'1880* (Paris: François Maspéro, 1971); Patricia M. Lorcin, *Imperial Identities: Stereotyping, Prejudice and Race in Colonial Algeria* (London: I. B. Tauris, 1995).

5. Mike Davis, *Late Victorian Holocausts: El Niño Famines and the Making of the Third World* (London: Verso, 2001).

6. Alastair Campbell, '"My country tis of thee" – the myopia of American bioethics', *Medicine, Health Care and Philosophy* 3 (2000), pp. 195–8.

7. Robert B. Baker and Laurence B. McCullough (eds), *The Cambridge World History of Medical Ethics* (Cambridge: Cambridge University Press, 2009).

8. Ibid. p. 4.

9. Ibid. p. 4.

10. Martha Nussbaum, 'Patriotism and cosmopolitanism', *Boston Review* (October–November 1994), pp. 3–6.

11. Abû Sulaymân al-Sijistâni, *Muntakhab Siwân al-Hikma*, ed. 'Abdurrahmân Badawi (Tehran: Intishârât-i Bunyâd-i Farhang-i Iran, 1974), p. 170.

12. Tzvetan Todorov, *Facing the Extreme: Moral Life in the Concentration Camps* (London: Phoenix, 2000).

13. Peter Burke, 'Western historical thinking in a global perspective', in Jörn Rüsen, *Western Historical Thinking: an Intercultural Debate* (New York, NY: Berghahn, 2002), pp. 15–30; Donald J. Wilcox *The Measure of Times Past: Pre-Newtonian Chronologies and the Rhetoric of Relative Time* (Chicago, IL: University of Chicago Press, 2007); William Gallois, *Time, Religion and History* (Harlow: Longman, 2007).

FURTHER READING

Becker, Lawrence (ed.), *A History of Western Ethics* (New York, NY: Garland, 1992).

Bensaïd, Daniel, *Qui est le juge? Pour en finir avec le tribunal de l'histoire* (Paris: Fayard, 1999).

Carr, David, Thomas R. Flynn and Rudolf A. Makkreel, *The Ethics of History* (Evanston, IL: Northwestern University Press, 2004).

Clement, Cathie (ed.), Special issue on 'Ethics and the practice of history', *Studies in Western Australian History*, 26 (2010).

Gensler, Harry J., and Earl W. Spugin (eds), *Historical Dictionary of Ethics* (Lanham: Scarecrow Press, 2008).

Glover, Jonathan, *Humanity: a Moral History of the Twentieth Century* (London: Jonathan Cape, 1999).

Jenkins, Keith, *Why History? Ethics and Postmodernity* (London: Routledge, 1999).

Jonsen, Albert R., *A Short History of Medical Ethics* (Oxford: Oxford University Press, 2000).

Macintyre, Alasdair C., *A Short History of Ethics* (London: Routledge, 1998).

Young, Robert, *White Mythologies: Writing History and the West* (London: Routledge: 1990).

CHAPTER 14

Time, Temporality and History

Prashant Kidambi

'What, then, is Time? I know well enough what it is, provided that nobody asks me; but if I am asked what it is and try to explain, I am baffled.'

St Augustine, Confessions, 11.14

The idea of time is fundamental to the discipline of history. Yet outside the domain of the philosophy of history, the concept has led a fugitive existence in historical scholarship. Indeed, confronted by the question that prompted St Augustine's oft-quoted confession, many practitioners of the historian's craft would no doubt sympathise with his predicament. However, a proper appreciation of history as a mode of knowledge and understanding requires us to engage in a systematic fashion with the ideas of time and temporality.

This chapter has three principal aims. First, it seeks to clarify what is presupposed and entailed by the idea of historical time. Second, it delineates the different ways in which the temporal character of history has been conceived and represented by historians. Third, it considers the hermeneutic argument that history, as a form of understanding, is fundamental to the way in which humans reckon with, and make sense of, time. Cumulatively, the chapter suggests that a conceptual grasp of time and temporality is essential in order to write critically self-reflexive histories.

ON HISTORICAL TIME

It is widely acknowledged that the distinctive contribution of history to the human sciences lies in its reckoning with time. But what, exactly, is 'historical time'? Let us begin by noting that historical time is distinct from formal time conceived as an oriented succession of abstract instants that follow each other in a mathematical fashion, and different too from the temporal sequentiality to be found in nature. Historical time presupposes formal time and the events and the processes it deals with occur in naturally elapsed time, but it is not in itself reducible to these forms of temporality.

History is the 'knowledge of the actions of past human beings',[1] and its distinguishing feature is a concern with the fundamentally temporal character of human actions and preoccupations. The idea of historical time is, therefore, inseparable from the experiences, expectations and ends pursued by human beings in lived time. 'Historical time', as Reinhardt Koselleck pointed out, 'is bound up with social and political actions, with concretely acting and suffering human beings and their institutions and organizations.'[2] Integral to the notion of historical time is the idea that the past is fundamentally different from the present. But what distinguishes the past from the present within historical time? In one sense, the radical difference of the historical past stems from the fact that it has already occurred. 'In this sense', Paul Ricoeur has noted, 'the pastness of what has happened is taken as an absolute property, independent of our constructions and reconstructions.'[3] Moreover, as François Châtelet has observed, 'If it is true that the past event is gone forever and that this dimension constitutes its essence, it is also true that its "pastness" differentiates it from any other event that might resemble it.'[4]

A second sense in which the past is different from the present can be discerned in the frequent invocation of L. P. Hartley's suggestive remark in his novel, *The Go-Between*: 'The past is a foreign country; they do things differently there'.[5] This observation resonates with historians because it appears to capture the strangeness of the past, the utterly singular material conditions and mentalities of human lives and societies that no longer exist. The 'absolute otherness' of the past, Ricoeur has argued, poses a 'constitutive obstacle' in our ability to communicate freely across the barrier of time. And, as he suggests, we can understand human lives in the past 'only at the price of recognizing their irreducible otherness'.[6]

Significantly, the idea that the past is different from the present has not always been an essential feature of historical writing. For instance, it has been argued by some scholars that historians in the epoch of classical antiquity perceived historical time as a syncretic and seamless unity and therefore made no attempt to disentangle the present from the past. Moreover, it has been noted that in the ancient world the past was deeply implicated in the everyday conduct and practices of individuals and institutions: it was a source of political legitimacy, moral guidance, education and edification.[7]

When and where did the recognition of the irreducible difference of the past first become apparent? On this, there is no scholarly consensus. An influential strand in the historiography attributes this fundamental transformation in historical consciousness to the profound intellectual and social changes heralded by the onset of modernity from the mid-eighteenth century onwards. For instance, Koselleck has argued that the idea of historical time was dramatically transformed in Western Europe in the century between *c.* 1750 and *c.* 1850. Koselleck contends that prior to the eighteenth century, Europeans had taken for granted the 'always-already guaranteed futurity of the past'. However, as the human experience of social time altered in the eighteenth century there emerged a 'future that transcended the hitherto predictable'. This, in turn, made possible a new idea of historical time, one in which the past came to be conceived in its 'fundamental otherness'.[8] Other writers have highlighted the key role played in this regard by the so-called Romantic thinkers, whose writings strengthened belief in the radical alterity and strangeness of the past.

Yet others have argued that it was in early modern western Europe that a distinctive sense of anachronism in relation to the past truly became an integral part of an emergent *historical* consciousness of temporality. According to one historian,

> The Renaissance and the Reformation precipitated a historical revolution (and it is essentially a single revolution) so profound that it reversed the Western perception of the past within a single generation, from a perception of unity to one of division and difference, from a stillness to a dynamic motion.[9]

This view, in turn, has its scholarly critics. On the one hand, some historians have questioned the assumption that the Renaissance heralded a 'radical transformation in both consciousness of the past and how that consciousness was represented'.[10] In this view, there were a number of continuities between the historical approach to the past during the Renaissance and the centuries that preceded it, not least in terms of a tendency to collapse the 'present into past time, which made the development of a sense of anachronism virtually impossible'.[11] On the other hand, an emergent body of work, written from the perspective of global history, has highlighted how an awareness of the 'otherness' of the past was by no means a singularly European experience. Indeed, it has been suggested that as the early modern world began to be more closely bound together through the 'connected histories' of capital, commerce and conquest, a sense of anachronism in relation to the past can also be synchronously discerned in different regions of the globe.[12]

At another level, however, the idea of historical time also presupposes, somewhat paradoxically, an essential *likeness* between the past and the present. As Bernard Williams has noted, when we acquire an 'objective' historical consciousness we do not think only in terms of *the* past; we can also think of *our* past, not in the sense of our own life, but in the sense of what is past relative to us, or to now. We become conscious of our being, in temporal terms, some people among others, and with this comes the idea that some of our past was other people's present, that our present was other people's future, and so on: in particular, what for us, now, is the remote past, for past people was the recent past or the present.[13]

Thus understood, there are two ways in which the historical past could be said to stand in a relationship of similitude to the present. First, like the present, the past is real: 'what happened did formerly exist, in a specific time and place'. Thus, a historical approach to the past cannot 'treat what has happened as fictive, as unreal'; in other words, 'the non-presence of the past . . . cannot in any manner be identified with its nonreality'.[14] It is the 'reality' of the past, then, which distinguishes history as a mode of knowledge and understanding from other modes of reckoning with the past. In turn, the concern with what *really* occurred in the past also points to the integral link between *historical truth* and *historical time*. Indeed,

> to say that a statement about an event is historically true is to imply
> that it is determinately located in the temporal structure; if it is not,
> historical time leaves it nowhere to go, except out of history altogether,
> into myth or into mere error.[15]

One way in which historians seek to establish the historical truth about an event in the past is through the assignment and verification of the exact date when it occurred, and 'that places it in a certain relation to all the other real events that really happened'.[16] As Moses Finley has pointed out, 'Dates and a precise dating system are as essential to history as exact measurement is essential to physics.' Conversely, ancient myths are deemed 'unhistorical' because they are 'detached' from any such precise temporal location and are 'linked neither with what went before nor with what came after'.[17]

Second, within historical time, the past is also like the present in being subject to the same criteria of understanding and explanation as the present. In other words, underlying the similitude of the past and the present is the assumption that 'at some level the world is explanatorily homogenous'. As Bernard Williams has argued, 'If we are to place events in the framework of the past, on the strength of present evidence, then we must be able to relate them to each other and to ourselves in terms that make them intelligible'.[18] In the absence of such a presumption of intelligibility, the past would remain totally opaque to us.

The idea that events of the past ought to be subject to the same criteria of veracity and verifiability as the present has been, from the very outset, a distinctive feature of history as a mode of intellectual inquiry. Indeed, Bernard Williams has suggested that, construed in this sense, historical time was 'invented' some time during the fifth century BC when for the first time the historians of ancient Greece – in the transition from Herodotus (484–425 BC) to Thucydides (460–395 BC) – began to assess and account for the past through the lenses of truth and intelligibility.[19]

REPRESENTATIONS OF HISTORICAL TIME

The relationship between history and time can also be viewed from another perspective. From this standpoint, historical time has itself been seen to possess distinctive attributes and rhythms. This section pursues this theme through an analysis of the ways in which historical time has been represented in historiography.

A noteworthy feature of representations of historical temporality is that they have persistently tended to *spatialise* time and invest it with *qualitative* properties.[20] For instance, scholars have noted that in many ancient societies historical time was construed as 'cyclical'.[21] In these societies, they have suggested, time was generally represented as a wheel, whose inexorable revolutions symbolised the circularity of history. Historical problems and processes were thus seen to play themselves out in an endlessly recurrent pattern.

Furthermore, in such circular conceptions of historical time, the present was often deemed inferior and decadent in comparison with the past. Thus, in ancient Greece, the sense of time in the present 'was oriented toward either the myth of the Golden Age, or toward memories of the heroic era'.[22] Similarly, most Roman historians exalted the distant past and took as their leading theme 'the decline from past to present'. Likewise, it has been suggested that in ancient India human time (denoted by the *yuga*) was seen as a succession of four cycles, each inferior in quality to the preceding one, with the present age – the Kali *yuga* – being the most degraded of all. As Thomas Trautmann observes,

> the general shape of the historical process is decidedly one of long and
> inexorable decline from a golden age until, at the end of the Kali, there
> is a general dissolution followed by the restoration of the golden age,
> and the recommencement of the four ages.[23]

Cyclical notions of historical temporality were not, of course, specific to the ancient world. The circularity of history continued to be a structuring principle in some historical works in the medieval and early modern periods in different regions of the world. And even as late as the twentieth century, a variant of the cyclical conception of historical time – albeit one divested of the decisive role of fate in historical causation – continued to be espoused by some historians. In 1918, the German historian and philosopher Oswald Spengler published *The Decline of the West*, which sought to explain the rise and fall of civilisations in history.[24] Spengler saw history as the story of a succession of self-contained cultures, each possessing an 'identical life-cycle'. Starting from 'primitive' origins, each of these cultures underwent a process of growth that culminated in the full flowering of its social, political and cultural organisation, before an inevitable process of decline set in and it sank into its original state of 'barbarism'.[25] Arnold Toynbee's monumental multi-volume work, *Study of History*, published in three installments between the 1930s and the 1960s, also articulated a cyclical conception of historical temporality in seeking to explain how and why civilisations emerge, grow and disintegrate.[26] But unlike Spengler, with whom he is often compared, Toynbee's account eschewed cultural or biological determinism.

It is undeniable, however, that the dominant representation of historical time from the mid-eighteenth to the mid-twentieth century was one that regarded it as an 'immanent and continuous process in chronological, or secular, time'.[27] So deeply entrenched was the assumption that the notion of linear time was an essential requirement of a full-fledged historical conscious-ness, that non-linear modes of representing temporality were often deemed 'unhistorical'. Indeed, attempts to prove the existence of a historical con-sciousness in any given society frequently entailed claims about the presence of linear understandings of temporality.

Scholars have identified two critical moments in the development of linear conceptions of historical time. The first is the rise of Christian historiography which, drawing on the teleological representations of temporality in the Judaic tradition, construed history as a sequence of events, unfolding in a linear fashion. The first Christian historians saw mankind as passing through seven ages – an idea that they derived from the Old Testament – and believed that their own present represented the sixth (from the birth of Christ to his Second Coming) and penultimate stage, which would eventually culminate in the age of the Apocalypse. Moreover, historical time in this tradition was seen to be governed by a sacred logic, revealing as it did the workings of a divine provi-dence in an unfolding history of salvation.

The second major turning point in the transformation of linear concep-tions of historical time occurred during the Enlightenment, which gave rise to a new sequential understanding of universal historical development. Historical time was now seen as a marker of the unfolding story of human progress and the inexorable triumph of reason. The meaning of history, in other words, no longer lay outside of history in the works of a divine will; it was human beings themselves who were the makers of their own destiny.

The major works of 'philosophical' history produced in eighteenth-century Europe by Voltaire, David Hume and others, offered panoramic causal accounts of Europe's cultural emancipation from the thrall of religious belief. Simultaneously, in the 'conjectural' histories that were produced by Scottish and French scholars around the same time, the story of mankind was represented as undergoing a successive transformation from 'barbarism' to 'civilisation' in four stages leading from the earliest hunter-gatherers to the sophisticated commercial society of their own day.[28]

In one way or another, European historical thought in the nineteenth century developed many of the ideas regarding historical temporality expressed by the Enlightenment writers. We can see this most explicitly in the historical writings of philosophers such as G. W. F. Hegel and Karl Marx. Both these thinkers represented historical time as the inexorable unfolding of a rational logic that was immanent in human society. For Hegel, history was about the teleological self-realisation of what he called 'Spirit' (*Geist*), whereas for Marx, it was about the progressive development of human productive capacities.

The dominance of linear, teleological history was also crucially under-pinned by the rise of nationalism. The first half of the nineteenth century witnessed the rapid proliferation of national histories, especially in Germany, France, Britain and the United States. These accounts were deeply influenced by historicist ideas and were sceptical of the claims to universality advanced by philosophical history. Significantly, the historicist concern with the origins of phenomena lent their writings a distinctive teleological orientation 'that purported to uncover and revivify the heritage of what they called, by turns, *liberty*, the *people*, or the *nation*'.[29] In other words, history was seen as the record of the growing self-consciousness of a people of their identity as a national collectivity, and this in turn was an integral part of their inalienable claims to sovereignty in the territory that they claimed as their own. By the end of the nineteenth century, these ideas had begun to inform historical writing in the Asian societies that had been colonised by Europe, and which now began to deploy history in the service of their own claims to nationhood.[30]

Thus, the fundamental transformation in the conception and representation of historical temporality inaugurated by the Age of Enlightenment and its counter-currents had an enduring impact on the modern discipline of history. In particular, the idea of history as linear and teleological was to become the common sense of historical thought and practice. Within this framework there was a tendency 'to assume a harmony, or at least a co-incidence, between the single direction of formal time and the single direction of the material-meaningful process within time'.[31] Such views were especially predominant in imperial Britain prior to the First World War, a time when the facts of history 'were themselves a demonstration of the supreme fact of a beneficent and apparently infinite progress towards higher things'. Thus, writing towards the end of the nineteenth century, Lord Acton, holder of the chair in Modern History at Cambridge, argued that history was 'a progressive science' and that 'we are bound to assume, as the scientific hypothesis on which history is to be written, a progress in human affairs'.[32]

More than sixty years later, another Cambridge historian, E. H. Carr, still believed that 'history properly so-called can be written only by those who find and accept a sense of direction in history itself'.[33] But by this time the assumption that history was the ineluctable unfolding of human progress was no longer as self-evident as it had once seemed. The cataclysmic events of the first half of the twentieth century had rendered a blithe confidence in the future of humanity increasingly untenable. Within the historical profession, this took the form of a critique of the temporal assumptions that informed traditional historiography.

One line of attack centred on the notion of historical time as 'the slow, silent, unobserved, but continuous march of change'.[34] Some historians argued that the idea that there was an 'even flow' to historical time precluded an appreciation of its heterogeneous quality. For instance, there were some epochs in history that were revolutionary, when time became 'a swift sword, cleaving through old customs to a new world'. There were other eras, however, when 'time can be said to stand still'. And in yet others still, 'one may even properly have the sense of a reversal of time, as generations seek to revivify an earlier isolation or simpler ways; even when they are not successful, they often walk backward into the future'.[35] However, while this perspective highlighted the differential rhythms that characterised the content of history, it nonetheless preserved the notion that the structure of historical time mirrored the linearity of formal time.

A more substantive critique of the idea of historical time as chronological, homogenous and irreversible, was offered by the French historians of the *Annales* tradition. Fernand Braudel, the doyen of the *Annales* historians, argued that historical time was plural and characterised, at any given moment, by the simultaneous presence of the past, present and future. Moreover, historical time had different layers, each with its own specific temporal duration and rhythm. In his writings, most notably *The Mediterranean and the Mediterranean World in the Age of Philip the Second*, Braudel conceived and depicted a three-fold division of historical time spans that corresponded to three different levels of human activity. The most immediately perceptible, and the one that traditional narrative history was most transfixed by, he argued, was the short-time span, the time of days, months and years. Here, the focus was on the actions of individuals and the history of events: 'a surface disturbance, the waves stirred up by the powerful movement of tides'. A second type of historical time-span was one whose duration could be measured in decades and centuries, and which was concerned with the cyclical rise and fall of 'economies and states, societies and civilizations'. But underlying all these was yet another time span – what he termed the *longue duree* – 'which exists almost out of time and tells the story of man's contact with the inanimate'. This was a history that was 'almost changeless, the history of man in relation to his surroundings'.[36] Historical time for Braudel, then, was distinguished by the simultaneous presence and interaction of these three levels: geographical time, social time and individual time. But in the histories that he wrote, Braudel made clear his belief that it was the *longue duree* that constituted the most meaningful frame through which to examine and understand history.

Braudel's attempt to rethink historical temporality, especially his ideas regarding the synchronous presence in time of non-synchronous elements, ignited an animated debate in the 1960s and 1970s among historians and social scientists. One of the most important interventions in this context was by the Marxist philosopher Louis Althusser, who credited Braudel and his colleagues 'for breaking from the conception of history as the single and invariant stream of time by recognizing the multiplicity of rhythms and tempi'. However, Althusser also criticised the *Annales* historians 'for falling back on "ordinary time" as the scale upon which these different times are measured'. Althusser regarded the notion of 'ordinary, continuous, objective time' as an ideological construct. His critique of historical time queried 'not only the correspondence of the Now for diverse "levels" of the social formation, but the continuity of time as well'. According to Althusser, each level of history had 'its own time and history'; and each level was 'relatively autonomous', but not totally independent, of the other levels. What lent coherence to the different levels, he argued, was the totality of a given social formation.[37]

Unlike Braudel, then, Althusser sought to resist 'falling back upon a single reference of time as a way of connecting different levels and different social formations'.[38] This also had crucial implications for the relationship between one social formation and another. Given that the different levels of a given social formation acquired their identity only in relation to its overall structure, 'there would be no point to giving a simple chronological account of the *transition* from, say, feudalism to capitalism', and the two social formations could not therefore be synchronised. And despite the differential connection of some levels within a particular social formation to a preceding and emerging social formation, 'the two bear no overall temporal relation to one another'.[39]

Perhaps the most trenchant critique of history as a linear and sequential unfolding of events and processes is to be found in the writings of Michel Foucault, one of the most influential thinkers of the late twentieth century.[40] Foucault sought to undermine the idea that the present moment was the outcome of a series of inexorable, teleological developments originating in the past. Instead, his writings took up a radically different approach, focusing on retrieving the history of specific discourses and practices that were dominant in the present.

The point of departure for Foucault's histories is 'his perception that something is terribly wrong in the present'.[41] Foucault was drawn to the history of specific modern institutions (for example, the prison and the clinic) and discursive practices (those pertaining to punishment and insanity, for instance), which he regarded as 'intolerable'. His aim was to understand how such institutions or practices came to acquire their present form. To this end, he undertook a series of historical case studies that sought to retrace the long-forgotten paths by which they had come to acquire their status as the natural order of things. In doing so, however, Foucault's method avoided the twin pit-falls of viewing the past through the categories of the present and of regarding history as a seamless progression towards the present. Instead, he highlighted the alterity of past practices and discourses and their discontinuity with the present. Equally, his writings aimed 'to show the contingency – and hence surpassability – of what history has given us'.[42] In other words, dominant insti-tutions and discourses, he suggests, often mask the conflicts and suppressed alternatives that marked their emergence as the common sense of the present.

Significantly, Foucault's writings have had a major impact on the postcolo-nial critiques of history that have emerged in the last two decades. In particu-lar, a number of postcolonial theorists have taken up his ideas in rethinking the ways in which the discourse of history has played a critical role in producing the past as an object of knowledge in colonial and postcolonial contexts. There are three aspects to the postcolonial rejection of linear, progressive history that are salient in this regard. First, postcolonial theorists have highlighted the evolutionary and historicist assumptions of European writings about colo-nised societies, which were predicated on a denial of their contemporaneity in time.[43] Second, they have shown how nationalist writers in colonial societies internalised many of the assumptions of the European ruling elites and sought to deploy history as a signifier of their own modernity. In the process, history as a mode of knowledge became 'involved in fierce contests for domination over other modes of time and knowledge'.[44] Third, professional historians writing from a postcolonial standpoint have also sought to explore alternatives to chronological history by adopting a variety of innovative narrative strate-gies. These include moving back and forth between the past and the present in their accounts of specific historical events, and documenting the multiple narratives of the past that exist within a society at any given moment in time.[45] Cumulatively, then, these sustained critiques – from a variety of ideological standpoints – of chronological and teleological history, played a key role in undermining some of the most fundamental assumptions of historical thinking as it had evolved since the early nineteenth century. Yet, for all their radical undermining of 'traditional' chronological and sequential history, these critical perspectives have continued for the most part to conceive historical time itself in spatial terms.

Of late, however, some historians have queried the validity of spatialising historical time. In particular, they have retrieved the ideas of the French philosopher Henri-Louis Bergson (1859–1941) in making a case for a non-spatial understanding of historical time. Bergson was not only highly critical of the tendency to think of time in spatial terms, but also drew a critical distinction between the idea of 'succession' and 'sequence' in the human consciousness of temporality. This led him to articulate a conception of *duree* that was akin to the notes in a musical score.

In a recent essay, the historian Michael Bentley has argued that Bergson's critical insights 'into the nature of temporal succession in consciousness, and his warnings over reducing that succession to mere sequence through the spatializing of time, never reached the heart of historical theory'. Bentley believes that in order to complete the intellectual project initiated by Bergson, we need to take seriously the idea that temporal succession is a 'constitutive feature of the world' and that the past infuses the present with its presence in ways that are not captured by spatial conceptions of time.[46]

TIME AND NARRATIVE

Thus far, we have outlined some of the salient aspects of historical time and the different ways in which historians have conceived and represented it. But there is yet another angle from which the relationship between time, temporality and history might be viewed. From this perspective, history is a form of narrative discourse that is fundamentally concerned with the human experience of time. The most well-known advocate of this view was the French philosopher Paul Ricoeur (1913–2005), whose writings offer a highly distinctive account of historical time. Accordingly, this section considers Ricoeur's principal arguments regarding the relationship between time and history and points out some of the problems that critics have identified in his approach.

Ricoeur's reflections on historical time form part of a larger argument concerning the relationship between narrative and temporality. His point of departure is the assertion that 'time becomes human time to the extent that it is organized after the manner of a narrative; narrative, in turn, is meaningful to the extent that it portrays the features of temporal experience'.[47] Ricoeur argues that lived time in the practical world is intrinsically amorphous, discordant and fragmented. However, through narrative 'we re-configure our confused, unformed, and at the limit, mute, temporal experience'.[48]

Ricoeur's analysis highlights three ways in which narrative orders into a comprehensible form the diverse elements comprising the world of action. First, it 'draws a configuration out of a simple succession'. Second, it grasps together factors as diverse as 'agents, goals, means, interactions, circumstances, unexpected results'. And third, the act of 'emplotment' produces 'a synthesis of the heterogeneous'. In other words, it imposes the 'unity of one temporal whole' on 'multiple and scattered events'.[49]

His interest in the relationship between narrative and time led Ricoeur to the analysis of historiography. History, in his view, is a specific kind of narrative discourse that seeks to impose order and concordance on the disorder and discordance of lived time. Thus, like other forms of narrative, history is 'rooted in our pragmatic competence, with its handling of events that occur "in" time'; it too 'configures the world of praxis by means of temporal constructions of a higher rank'; and finally, it too 'reaches its meanings in the refiguring of the field of praxis'.[50]

In order to understand better his arguments about the relationship between time and history, we need to locate Ricoeur's work within a wider intellectual context. In particular, his ideas developed out of a sustained engagement with the debates that raged from the 1960s onwards between historians who embraced a structuralist, achronological approach to the study of the past and those who contended that it was a form of story-telling. For the structuralists, historical time bore no connection to the world of action and their aim was to sever history's long-standing association with the narrative mode in order to buttress its scientific credentials. The narrativists, for their part, saw history as a 'species of the genus Story' and emphasised what they perceived to be a 'directly readable continuity between the time of action and historical time'.[51]

Ricoeur's exploration of the relationship between time and history distances itself from both these mutually opposed positions. His principal thesis is that historical knowledge, for all its scientific ambition, arises out of an intrinsically narrative understanding of the world. To this end, Ricoeur highlights 'the intentionality of the historian's thought by which history continues obliquely to intend the field of human action and its basic temporality'.[52]

Ricoeur's analysis unfolds through a double movement. One part of his argument focuses on the 'epistemological break between historical knowledge and our ability to follow a story'. This break affects the process of narrative understanding at three levels: procedures, entities and temporalities. The procedural feature of history pertains to its claim to objectivity. While a historical inquiry offers an explanation of a set of occurrences by casting them in the form of a narrative, it also seeks to justify its intepretation by demonstrating its superiority vis-à-vis competing accounts of the same events. In other words, history is a self-critical exercise that is governed by the scientific protocols of research and inquiry. Second, history deals with 'entities that are anonymous': nations, states, societies and civilisations. It thus differs from the traditional narrative, which imputes action to persons. And following from this, the historical time of social entities had 'no direct connection to the time of memory, expectation, and circumspection of individual agents'. Since it did not refer to the 'living present of a subjective consciousness', historical time bore no 'apparent relation to the time of action' of individual agents.[53]

At the same time, Ricoeur argues that despite this 'triple epistemological break', history could not 'sever every connection with narrative without losing its historical character'.[54] For instance, notwithstanding its aim of objectivity, history is concerned with singular events that cannot be explained by reference to laws. Even in defending their account of a particular event vis-à-vis rival versions, historians are called upon to exercise their story-telling capabilities. Furthermore, their narratives are based on what Ricoeur calls 'singular causal imputation', by which he means a 'transitional structure between explanation by laws . . . and explanation by emplotment'.[55] Similarly, while the primary objects of historical inquiry – states, nations, classes and communities – are collectivities, these are treated in narratives as agents of action. Ricoeur uses the terms 'quasi-person' and 'quasi-plot' to designate, respectively, the agency attributed to such collective entities and the chain of 'singular causal relations' in which they are implicated.

Finally, at the level of historical time, Ricoeur argues that even structuralist histories that sought to eschew narrative were nonetheless 'bound to our narrative understanding by a line of derivation that we can reconstruct step by step and degree by degree with an appropriate method'.[56] Thus, through a painstaking analysis of *The Mediterranean*, he demonstrates how Braudel's magnum opus sets up a temporal configuration in which the individual parts of the tripartite division of time derive their signficance from the plot-like character of the whole. Indeed, as he points out, it is the structural unity of Braudel's account that enables us to distinguish between the three levels of time that comprise it. At the same time, Ricoeur is quick to acknowledge that Braudel had invented a 'new type of plot', which united 'structures, cycles, and events by joining together heterogeneous temporalities and contradictory chronicles'.[57]

However, while Ricoeur draws out the story-like qualities of even the most structuralist historical text, he differs significantly in his theoretical approach from other narrativists like W. B. Gallie, Louis Mink and Hayden White. As David Carr has pointed out, unlike these writers Ricoeur's interest in historical narrative is not cognitive in nature.[58] Instead, he is interested in exploring questions that are profoundly philosophical. Thus, Ricoeur interrogates the nature of the narrative function and asks what stories tell us about those who construct them. It also tries to relate the knowledge and understanding furnished by narrative to fundamental questions about the nature of human existence itself.

But Carr argues that while Ricoeur is to be commended for restoring the link between the world of text and the world of action, his work does not go far enough in this direction. Indeed, he suggests that in the final analysis Ricoeur is closer to those writers who have seen narrative as being 'descriptively discontinuous with the world it depicts'. Carr contends that even though Ricoeur recognises the 'prefigured' quality of life, he too sees human temporal experience as essentially shapeless. In other words, even though human action in Ricoeur's framework 'involves elements that can be taken up into the structure that narrative provides, action itself seems to lack that structure'. Thus, his 'basic scheme seems not to differ fundamentally from that which he subtly corrects'.[59]

In his own exploration of these questions Carr suggests that the world of action itself has an intrinsic temporal structure and that there is a direct continuity between 'life' and narrative. Hence, 'narrative is not in any way adventitious or external to the actions and experiences of real life but is part of its fabric'. Narrative, moreover, is constitutive not only of individual lives but also those of the communities to which they belong. One crucial implication of this, Carr points out, is that historians inhabit a world that is already saturated with multiple narratives about the past, which may well compete with each other for dominance. Hence, 'the material on which the historian works, to which he turns his attention, is anything but a mass of unrelated events waiting for a story to be told about them, as theorists like Ricoeur and Mink seem to suggest'.[60]

Carr also identifies another problematic aspect of Ricoeur's argument concerning the mutually constitutive relationship between time and narrative. As he notes, Ricoeur views the narrative conception of time as a 'transcultural necessity'. 'But', asks Carr, 'what if we find peoples who do not construe their temporality through the activity of narrating?' A disconcerting consequence of Ricoeur's analytical framework, it would seem, is that 'if there is a conflict between the "transcultural necessity" of narrative form and "peoples without history," this is to be resolved by saying that their time has somehow not yet become fully human'. Carr recognises that this is a conclusion that Ricoeur would have disavowed. However, as he rightly notes, Ricoeur's tacit assumptions are expressive of 'deeply embedded' evaluative notions about the link between history and humanity.[61]

CONCLUSION

'In truth', Fernand Braudel once wrote, 'the historian can never get away from the question of time in history: time sticks to his thinking like soil to a gardener's spade.'[62] Time matters because it is the lens through which historians construct their objects of inquiry, the context within which they frame their questions, and the measure by which they evaluate the actions of the agents whose stories they narrate. However, as Augustine's plaintive cry suggests, time is also a concept that is notoriously hard to pin down. This essay has tried to point out some of the conceptual and analytical distinctions that one needs to make in exploring the relationship between time and history. To this end, it delineated the salient features of historical time, identified the different ways in which historians have represented it, and finally, underscored its identity as the referent of a distinctive mode of discourse.

NOTES

1. Paul Ricoeur, *Time and Narrative*, vol. I, trans. Kathleen McLaughlin and David Pellauer (Chicago, IL: University of Chicago Press, 1990), p. 96.
2. Reinhardt Koselleck, *Futures Past: On the Semantics of Historical Time*, new edn (New York, NY: Columbia University Press, 2004), p. 2.
3. Ricoeur, *Time and Narrative*, I, p. 96.
4. François Châtelet, *La naissance de l'histoire: La formation de la pensee historienne en Grece* (Paris: Minuit, 1962), I, p. 12. Quoted in Jacques Le Goff, *History and Memory* (New York, NY: Columbia University Press, 1992), p. 10.
5. L. P. Hartley, *The Go-Between* (London: Hamish Hamilton, 1953), p. 9.
6. Ricoeur, *Time and Narrative*, I, p. 96.
7. J. H. Plumb, *The Death of the Past* (London: Palgrave Macmillan, 2004).
8. Koselleck, *Futures Past*.
9. Anthony Kemp, *The Estrangement of the Past: a Study in the Origins of Modern Historical Consciousness* (Oxford: Oxford University Press, 1991), pp. 96–104. See also, Peter Burke, *The Renaissance Sense of the Past* (London: Edward Arnold, 1969).
10. Thomas F. Mayer, 'Historiography during the Renaissance', in D. R. Woolf (ed.), *A Global Encyclopedia of Historical Writing* (London: Taylor and Francis, 1998), vol. II, p. 770.
11. Ibid. p. 770.
12. In this context, see Velcheru Narayana Rao, David Shulman and Sanjay Subrahmanyam, *Textures of Time: Writing History in South India, 1600–1800* (New York, NY: Other Press, 2003).
13. Bernard Williams, 'What was wrong with Minos? Thucydides and historical time', *Representations* 74 (Spring 2001), p. 10.
14. Châtelet, *La naissance de l'histoire*, p. 11. Quoted in Jacques Le Goff, *History and Memory*, p. 10.
15. Williams, 'What was wrong with Minos?', p. 9.

16. David Carr, 'Place and time: on the interplay of historical points of view', *History and Theory* 40: 4 (December 2001), p. 158.

17. M. I. Finley, 'Myth, memory, and history', *History and Theory* 4:3 (1965), p. 285.

18. Williams, 'What was wrong with Minos?', pp. 12–13.

19. Ibid. pp. 12–13.

20. In this context, see Michael Bentley, 'Past and "presence": revisiting historical ontology', *History and Theory* 45:3 (October 2006), pp. 349–61.

21. However, Arnaldo Momigliano has argued that the 'oft-repeated notion that the Greek historians had a cyclical idea of time is a modern invention'. See A. Momigliano, 'Time in ancient historiography', *History and Theory* 6:6 (1966), pp. 1–23. In this context, also see, Chester G. Starr, 'Historical and philosophical time', *History and Theory* 6:6 (1966), pp. 24–35.

22. Le Goff, *History and Memory*, p. 11.

23. Thomas R. Trautmann, 'Indian time, European time', in Diana Owen Hughes and Thomas R. Trautmann (eds), *Time: Histories and Ethnologies* (Michigan, University of Michigan Press: 1995), p. 171.

24. Oswald Spengler, *Der Untergang des Abendlandes, Gestalt und Wirklichkeit* (Munich: C. H. Beck'sche Verlagsbuchhandlung, 1926).

25. See, in this context, 'Oswald Spengler and the theory of historical cycles', in R. G. Collingwood, *Essays in the Philosophy of History* (Austin, TX: University of Texas Press, 1965), pp. 57–75.

26. Arnold Toynbee, *The Study of History*, 12 vols (Oxford: Oxford University Press, 1934–61).

27. Siegfried Kracauer, 'Time and history', *History and Theory* 6:6 (1966), p. 65.

28. Johnson Kent Wright, 'Historical thought in the era of the Enlightenment', in Lloyd Kramer and Sarah Maza (eds), *A Companion to Western Historical Thought* (Oxford: Blackwell, 2006), pp. 123–42.

29. Thomas N. Baker, 'National history in the age of Michelet, Macaulay, and Bancroft', in Kramer and Maza (eds), *Companion*, p. 188.

30. Prasenjit Duara, 'Postcolonial history', in Kramer and Maza (eds), *Companion*, pp. 417–31.

31. Nathan Rotenstreich, *Between Past and Present: an Essay on History* (Keele: Kennikat Press, 1973), pp. 65–6.

32. Quoted in E. H. Carr, *What is History?* (Harmondsworth: Penguin, 1961), p. 111.

33. Carr, *What is History?*, p. 132.

34. Lewis Einstein, *Historical Change* (Cambridge: Cambridge University Press, 1946), p. 107. Quoted in Starr, 'Historical and philosophical time', p. 33.

35. Starr, 'Historical and philosophical time', pp. 33–4.

36. Fernand Braudel, *The Mediterranean and the Mediterranean World in the Age of Philip II*, trans. Sian Reynolds, 2 vols (New York, NY: Harper and Row, 1972–4), 'Preface'.
37. John R. Hall, 'The time of history and the history of times', *History and Theory* 19:2 (February 1980), pp. 113–31.
38. Ibid. p. 121.
39. Ibid. p. 121.
40. Michel Foucault, *The Birth of the Clinic* (London: Vintage, 1994); Michel Foucault, *Discipline & Punish: The Birth of the Prison* (London: Vintage, 1995).
41. Gary Gutting, 'Introduction', *The Cambridge Companion to Foucault* (Cambridge: Cambridge University Press, 2005), pp. 6–16.
42. Ibid. pp. 6–16.
43. See, in this context, Edward Said, *Orientalism* (New York, NY: Pantheon Books, 1978); Johannes Fabian, *Time and the Other: How Anthropology Makes its Object* (New York, NY: Columbia University Press, 2002); Dipesh Chakarabarty, *Provincializing Europe: Postcolonial Thought and Historical Difference* (Princeton, NJ: Princeton University Press, 2000).
44. Prasenjit Duara, 'Why is history antitheoretical?', *Modern China*, 24: 2 (April 1998), p. 110.
45. See, for example, Shahid Amin, *Event, Metaphor and Memory: Chauri Chaura, 1922–1992* (Berkeley, CA: University of California Press, 1995); Ajay Skaria, *Hybrid Histories: Forests, Frontiers and Wildness in Western India* (Delhi: Oxford University Press, 1999).
46. Bentley, 'Past and "presence"', pp. 358–9.
47. Ricoeur, *Time and Narrative*, I, p. 3.
48. Ibid. p. 14.
49. Ibid. p. 65.
50. Ibid. p. 92.
51. Ibid. p. 92.
52. Ibid. pp. 91–2.
53. Ibid. pp. 175–7.
54. Ibid. p. 177.
55. Ibid. p. 181.
56. Ibid. p. 91.
57. Ibid. pp. 206–25.
58. David Carr, 'Review essay: Paul Ricoeur's Time and Narrative', *History and Theory* 23:3 (October 1984), pp. 357–70.
59. Ibid. p. 366.
60. David Carr, *Time, Narrative, and History* (Indianapolis, IN: First Midland Book Ltd., 1991); David Carr, 'Narrative and the real world: an argument for continuity', *History and Theory* 25:2 (May 1986), pp. 117–31.

61. Carr, *Time, Narrative, and History*, pp. 181–5.
62. Fernarnd Braudel, *On History* (Chicago, IL: University of Chicago Press, 1982), p. 47.

FURTHER READING

Carr, David, *Time, Narrative, and History* (Indianapolis, IN: First Midland Book Ltd., 1991).

Chakarabarty, Dipesh, *Provincializing Europe: Postcolonial Thought and Historical Difference* (Princeton, NJ: Princeton University Press, 2000).

Hall, John R., 'The time of history and the history of times', *History and Theory* 19:2 (February 1980), pp. 113–31. *History and Theory*, 6:6 Special Issue: *History and the Concept of Time* (1966).

Kemp, Anthony, *The Estrangement of the Past: a Study in the Origins of Modern Historical Consciousness* (Oxford: Oxford University Press, 1991).

Koselleck, Reinhardt, *Futures Past: on the Semantics of Historical Time* (Cambridge, MA: MIT Press, 1985).

Kramer, Lloyd, and Sarah Maza (eds), *A Companion to Western Historical Thought* (Oxford: Blackwell, 2006).

Le Goff, Jacques, *History and Memory* (New York, NY: Columbia University Press, 1992).

Ricoeur, Paul, *Time and Narrative*, vol. I, trans. Kathleen McLaughlin and David Pellauer (Chicago, IL: University of Chicago Press, 1990).

Williams, Bernard, 'What was wrong with Minos? Thucydides and historical time', *Representations* 74 (Spring 2001), pp. 1–18.

Notes on Contributors

Krista Cowman is Professor of History at the University of Lincoln. She has published widely on the history of women in political movements in Britain including *Women of the Right Spirit: Paid Organisers of the Women's Social and Political Union 1904–14* (2007) and *Women in British Politics, c. 1689–1979* (2010). Her more recent research looks at women in the post-war British city.

Lucy Faire is Honorary Visiting Fellow in the Centre for Urban History and also Lecturer in Humanities and Arts in the Vaughan Centre for Lifelong Learning, both at the University of Leicester. She researches the history of home, leisure and behaviour. Her publications include *The Place of the Audience: Cultural Geographies of Film Consumption* (2003) co-authored with Mark Jancovich, and 'The everyday usage of city-centre streets: urban behaviour in provincial Britain c. 1930–1970', *Urban History Review* 42:2 (2014), co-written with Denise McHugh.

William Gallois is Associate Professor of Middle Eastern and Mediterranean History in the Institute of Arab and Islamic Studies at the University of Exeter and specialises in the history of the Mediterranean, the history of medicine, and historical theory. His publications include *Time, Religion and History* (2007), *The Administration of Sickness: Medicine and Ethics in Colonial Algeria* (2008) and *A History of Violence in the Early Algerian Colony* (2013).

Jo Guldi is Assistant Professor at Southern Methodist University. Her book, *The Roads to Power* (2011), tells the story of how Britain invented infrastructure and strangers stopped speaking on the public street. She is currently working on her next monograph, *The Long Land War*, a history of capitalism and its relationship to land use that will focus upon the international land reform movement of the nineteenth century. She is co-author with David Armitage of *The History Manifesto* (2014).

Simon Gunn is Professor of Urban History in the Centre for Urban History at the University of Leicester. He has taught and studied research methods in Historical Studies for a number of years. His publications include *History and Cultural Theory* (2006) and *The Public Culture of the Victorian Middle Class* (2000). He is joint editor of the Cambridge University Press journal, *Urban History* and co-editor with James Vernon of *The Peculiarities of Liberal Modernity in Imperial Britain* (2011).

Ludmilla Jordanova is Professor of History and Visual Culture and Co-director of the Centre for Visual Arts and Culture at Durham University. She is the author of a number of books including *Defining Features: Scientific and Medical Portraits 1660–2000* (2000), *History in Practice* (2000, 2nd edition 2006) and *The Look of the Past: Visual and Material Evidence in Historical Practice* (2012). Portraiture continues to be one of her key research areas.

Prashant Kidambi is Senior Lecturer, Centre for Urban History, University of Leicester (UK). His research explores – through the prism of the city – the interface between British imperialism and the history of modern South Asia. In addition to a number of journal articles and book chapters, Dr Kidambi is the author of *The Making of an Indian Metropolis: Colonial Governance and Public Culture in Bombay, 1890–1920* (2007).

Michelle T. King is Associate Professor of History at the University of North Carolina at Chapel Hill, with a research focus on gender in late imperial Chinese history. Her book *Between Birth and Death: the Cultural Translation of Female Infanticide in Nineteenth Century China* (2014) explores the contrasting understandings of female infanticide among Western missionaries, diplomats, travellers and Chinese literati. She is also interested in forms of late nineteenth-century British imperialism, and is the author of 'Replicating the colonial expert: the problem of translation in the late nineteenth century Straits settlements', *Social History* 34:4 (2009).

Keith Lilley is Professor of Historical Geography at Queen's University Belfast. He has led significant GIS-based research projects for more than ten years as part of collaborative partnerships with historians, archaeologists, cartographers and geographers. He is particularly interested in developing spatial approaches and applying these to historical contexts, for example in mapping past landscapes and in analysing historic maps. His books include *Mapping Medieval Geographies* (2013).

Alan Mayne is Adjunct Professor at the University of South Australia and Honorary Professor in the Centre for Urban History at the University of Leicester. His many publications in modern urban and regional history include *Alternative Interventions: Aboriginal Homelands, Outback Australia* *and the Centre for Appropriate Technology* (2014), *Building the Village: a History of Australia's Bendigo Bank* (2008), *Hill End: An Historic Australian Goldfields Landscape* (2003), *The Archaeology of Urban Landscapes* (with Tim Murray, 2001), *The Imagined Slum: Newspaper Representation in Three Cities, 1870–1914* (1993), and *Fever, Squalor and Vice: Sanitation and Social Policy in Victorian Sydney* (1982).

R. J. Morris is Emeritus Professor of Economic and Social History at the University of Edinburgh and the author of numerous works on British, Irish and Canadian history, which include *Men, Women and Property in England, 1780–1870* (2007) and *Class and Class Consciousness in the Industrial Revolution* (1979). He was active in the founding of the Association for History and Computing and was President of the European Urban History Association, 2000–2. He has recently published *Scotland 1907* (2006) exploring the photographs of Valentine and sons, and an essay on 'Urban Ulster since 1600' in Liam Kennedy and Philip Ollerenshaw, *Ulster since 1600: Politics, Economy and Society* (2013).

Bob Nicholson is a Senior Lecturer in History at Edge Hill University. He works on the history of nineteenth-century Britain and America and is particularly interested in print culture, humour, transatlantic relations, and the digital humanities. He has published several articles on the subject of digital research, including: 'The Victorian meme machine: remixing the nineteenth-century archive', *Interdisciplinary Studies in the Nineteenth Century* 19 (2015); 'Sport history and digital archives in practice', with Martin Johnes, in Gary Osmond and Murray G. Phillips (eds), *Sport History in the Digital Era* (2015); 'The digital turn: exploring the methodological possibilities of digital newspaper archives', *Media History* 19:1 (2013); and 'Counting culture; or, how to read Victorian newspapers from a distance', *Journal of Victorian Culture* 17:2 (2012). He is currently working with the British Library to create a digital archive of a million Victorian jokes.

Catherine Porter holds a PhD in Geography and is a Research Associate on the European Research Council-funded project 'Spatial Humanities: Text, GIS, Places', Department of History, Lancaster University. Her research interests focus on the application of GIS and text analysis in the digital humanities, particularly the development of mixed method approaches as applied to historical geography and early cartography.

Julie-Marie Strange is Professor of British History in the School of Arts, Languages and Cultures at the University of Manchester. Her publications include 'The charity-mongers of modern Babylon: bureaucracy, scandal, and the transformation of the philanthropic marketplace, c.1870–1912', *Journal of British Studies* 54:1 (2015) with Sarah Roddy and Bertrand Taithe, and monographs *Fatherhood and the British Working Class 1865–1914* (2015) and *Death, Grief and Poverty in Britain, 1870–1914* (2005).

Alistair Thomson is Professor of History at Monash University and a Fellow of the Academy of Social Sciences of Australia. In 2007 he returned to Melbourne after 22 years in England at the University of Sussex, where he was Director of the Centre for Continuing Education, joint Director of the Centre for Life History Research, co-editor of the British journal *Oral History*, a Trustee of the Mass-Observation Archive and President of the International Oral History Association (2006–8). His oral history and life history publications include: *Anzac Memories: Living With the Legend* (1994; new edition 2013); with Rob Perks, *The Oral History Reader* (1998, 2006 and 2016); with Jim Hammerton, *Ten Pound Poms: Australia's Invisible Migrants* (2005); *Moving Stories: an Intimate History of Four Women Across Two Countries* (2011) and, with Alexander Freund, *Oral History and Photography* (2011).

Index

Page numbers in *italics* indicate illustrations.
The letter f following a page number indicates a figure, n an endnote and t a table.